Growing Up
in British India

GROWING UP IN BRITISH INDIA

*Indian Autobiographers
on Childhood and Education
under the Raj*

Judith E. Walsh

HOLMES & MEIER
Publishers, Inc.
New York **HM** London

First published in the United States of America 1983 by
Holmes & Meier Publishers, Inc.
30 Irving Place
New York, N.Y. 10003

Great Britain:
Holmes & Meier Publishers, Ltd.
131 Trafalgar Road
Greenwich, London SE 10 9TX

Book design by Rose Jacobowitz

Library of Congress Cataloging in Publication Data

Walsh, Judith.
    Growing Up in British India

    Based on the author's thesis (Ph.D.)—Columbia
University.
    Bibliography: p.
    Includes index.
    1. India—Civilization—1765-1947.   2. East Indians—
Psychology.   3. Personality and culture—India.
4. Acculturation—India.   5. Autobiography.   I. Title.
DS428.W34   1981   954   81-6865
ISBN 0-8419-0734-X   AACR2

Manufactured in the United States of America

To
Carmela, Antoinette and Mrs. Julay —
this book is lovingly and gratefully dedicated

Contents

Preface

WITH THE EXCEPTION of one autobiography written in Hindi (Rajendra Prasad's *Atmakatha)*, the works which comprise the major sources for this study are autobiographies written in English. The selection of these sources is by no means accidental. These books — as a group — are the sources most likely to answer the basic question of this study: what were the psychological consequences of growing up in British India for those who had to combine the heritage of their traditional world with the pressing realities of foreign power and Western education?

The genre of autobiography was a relatively late arrival on the Indian scene. It is virtually unknown in the rich literature of traditional culture and its appearance in the nineteenth century was clearly the result of Western influences. During the nineteenth and twentieth centuries, autobiographies written by Indian authors become a clearly definable literary genre. They share certain qualities of style, choice of subject matter, and world view that set them apart from comparable works of other countries and even from those written in indigenous languages in India itself.

An autobiographer is, by definition, someone who wishes to come to terms with his own life story. The marriage of Indian culture with this Western literary tradition produced some autobiographers reluctant to discuss personal matters and enthusiastic only when reciting the superficial chronologies of their lives. Nevertheless, the underlying purpose remained. Authors wrote about themselves in order to see their lives in new perspective, to weigh the significance of their experiences, to construct a written record of their pasts. We may reasonably use their books for the same purpose.

Autobiography, even in India, is the form of writing most suited to the study of personal psychological experience. Indian autobiographies written in English are, for similar reasons, the single best genre of sources for information about the psychological consequences of the exposure of

Indians to Western education and its values in the nineteenth and twentieth centuries. When an author of this period chose to write his life story in English he provided a priori evidence of that language's influence on his life. In most cases, he had learned English through the educational system of the British in India. In all cases, his English autobiography demonstrated an involvement with the foreign rule, values, and language of British India at least strong enough to have provoked the creation of his book. British rule in India touched the lives and fantasies of many Indians, not merely those educated in English. But a study interested in the psychological consequences of the contact between two cultures should focus on those most affected by that contact. The most obviously acculturated life histories of this period are those written in English. If we use the books, then, as sources for their authors' life experiences, we have a beginning point for the study of the psychological consequences of British rule in India.

In considering what the authors tell us about childhood and adult experiences, however, it is important to remember that one of the characteristics of Indian autobiography is the tendency of authors to obscure, rather than to emphasize, the regional and cultural backgrounds from which they came. As a rule, the autobiographers wished to be seen as modern, Western-educated (Westernized) people. They chose to obscure items of indigenous culture and tradition in order to emphasize things they felt more congruent with the Western image they wished to project For example, although many authors came from traditional villages and were the first in their families to receive an English education, their descriptions of family life most often center on memories of mothers and fathers. The larger joint families or caste groups in which we must assume they participated rarely appear.

Reticence on these matters limits our ability to probe too deeply into specific regional or caste traditions. Instead, autobiographies reveal only the broader outlines of the traditional cultures that shaped their authors' early lives. At the same time, however, autobiographical emphases on the "Western" aspects of life provide new insight into the degree to which English-educated Indians shared common experiences during the nineteenth and twentieth centuries. In these years Western-educated Indians existed in all parts of British India. They had been exposed to much the same educational system, shared many common problems and were, often, becoming conscious of themselves as "Indians" by contrast with their British rulers. English-language autobiographies remind us of the degree to which Indians from different regions, cultural traditions and even historical periods could be members of one group — the Westernized, English-educated elite. Authors from Bengal, Bombay, and South India, men who grew up in the 1850s and others born in the 1900s, writers from provincial villages with enormously varied customs, caste groups, and linguistic traditions — all shared commonalities of experience and perspective, first as a result of their exposure to the English-language schools and later through their relation to the Raj, and the institutions and occupations created by British power in India. Neither indigenous traditions nor historical period were unimportant in these authors' lives, but their reminiscences illustrate how the structures and new potentials of British rule cut across these differences. To read a cross-section of English-language autobiographies is to see the authors' lives in a context that does justice to their shared experiences and common elements of consciousness even as it blurs — as indeed the authors blur — the more distinct regional traditions from which they came. (For further discussion of these sources, their limitations, and their selection see Appendices I and II.)

Finally, one must note here that the words *indigenous, traditional, orthodox,* and occasionally *Hindu* have been used in this study in a particular way: they refer to life patterns and customs unaltered by Western influences. In part, this usage echoes that of the autobiographers. These writers, although raised within a wide variety of regions and castes, often portray themselves in sharp contrast to "orthodox" fellows, villagers, or family members. They emphasize qualities which mark their lives as those of Western-educated men. To adopt their terminology, however, is not to imply the existence throughout India of any *one* traditional, orthodox, or indigenous way of life. Although the presence in many areas of certain Sanskrit texts gives us the means of speaking loosely of *the* Hindu tradition, anthropological evidence has made equally clear the variety of forms such traditions may take in individual regions and localities. Our sources themselves occasionally indicate that even "indigenous" customs may be the result of cultural accretion and adaptation. Where autobiographical evidence has shown the more general presence of a custom or belief, these similarities have been noted and discussed. For the rest, however, terms such as *traditional* and *orthodox* have been used in a more restricted sense. They are meant only to distinguish in a general way (following the practice of our sources) the habits, values, and persons of Indians who were Western-educated from other countrymen who were not.

Research for this study was begun in London and New York in 1974 and completed during nineteen months in India in 1977 and 1978. I would like to thank the Fulbright-Hayes Faculty Research Abroad program and the American Institute of Indian Studies for the financial help that made two trips to India possible during work on this project. I am especially grateful to the staff members of these organizations in India; their respective directors, Mr. C.S. Ramakrishnan and Mr. P.R. Mehendiratta; and in addition to the staff and director of the Nehru Memorial Museum and Library in New Delhi for the advice, help, and encouragement that made research in India such a pleasure.

The manuscript on which this book is based was originally submitted in fulfillment of doctoral requirements at Columbia University. Since then, further research and substantial revisions have altered its contents and some of its concepts. Dennis Dalton and Leonard Gordon gave valuable comments and criticisms during the early stages of this project and equally helpful advice and criticisms since. As a working psychiatrist and psychoanalyst, Dr. Alan Roland helped immeasurably in thinking about the nature of Indian psychology and the application of psychological theories to India. His work and that of the Columbia University seminar on "The 'Self' in India" have provided an invaluable framework for thinking about these complex problems. Responsibility for the ideas, suggestions, and conclusions in this book, however, is fully my own. Ned Wilson and Carol Berkin provided the kind of constant support, advice, and critical suggestions given only by the best of friends. This manuscript and my own understanding of the craft of writing have benefited enormously from the help of Nancy Lanoue. Working both as a friend and an editor she pursued my fondness for literary aberrations through the many incarnations of this manuscript with a ruthlessness only equaled by her sensitivity and tact. I am most grateful for her help. Finally, to my dissertation adviser at Columbia University, Dr. Ainslie Embree — who was also my freshman history teacher — I offer my deepest thanks and appreciation for his advice, insight, criticism and almost endless patience — and for being the person who introduced me to the country in which this book is set, and whose peoples and culture have enriched my life beyond my ability to express.

Growing Up
in British India

Introduction

In MADRAS AN ELDERLY LADY took out her family album. Among the faded photographs was a picture of her grandfather. The patriarch, founder of the family's fortunes and architect of its cultural style, had been an early convert to Christianity from his South Indian Hindu community. He had studied religion, the English language, and British law in both missionary and government schools and had become, by his old age, a prosperous jurist, property holder, and acknowledged leader in his religious community. To his grandchildren he had been an awe-inspiring figure. Family legend held that when his eldest son, an athletic boy not much given to studies, failed a course in college, the old gentleman took from him the use of the family name. He did not lightly overlook failings or excuse intrusions on his time and comfort.

Yet he was a great lover of beauty. The pattern of his days bound together the contradictions of his temperament as closely as it held the mixed cultural traditions that had shaped his life. Every morning, his granddaughter remembered, he had had a drive, in a sort of carriage drawn by bullocks. "He had a cushion that was specially made for him," she recalled in her soft voice, "and he'd take a seat there and a servant had to pluck a rose from the garden and give it to him and he would smell it while he was taken for a drive right round the race course."[1]

* * *

A gentleman in his seventies, retired from the Department of Public Instruction in the old Bombay Presidency, now stays with his wife and granddaughter in a comfortable home in a modern suburb of Bangalore. There, one day early in the hot season, he pointed out that his present house was only a day's journey away from the small village where he had lived as a child. His family were Lingayats. In his childhood they had been proud of a tradition of literacy, but no longer prosperous. His father had worked his own lands as a farmer and he himself had made his way through school and college on scholarships and grants. When he was

1

eighteen, he had been offered money for travel and study at Cambridge University in England. But he found himself caught between his wish to go abroad and his family's conviction that he should be married. "You see the thing was," he told a visitor, "that the old people believed in child marriage. But. I was in Matriculation class and I was eighteen and they wanted me to marry. They forced me to marry."[2] Devoted to his father and his aunt, he found it impossible to refuse their wishes. "I was supporting myself," he recalled,

> but even then I couldn't cut altogether away from my family. I was not against marriage, only I felt I must complete my education. . . . [So] I told [my father] that on one condition I will marry, that you find a young girl. I particularly wanted a young girl because then there is no family life. So this was my condition. Because otherwise I would have been tied to one condition in life and I wanted to go abroad and I didn't like to begin married life so early.[3]

His family were strict vegetarians, but when he returned from Cambridge he was regularly eating fish and eggs. Did he tell his father that he had changed his habits while abroad? "Well, I didn't have occasion to tell him," he answered with a slight smile. "But . . . I tried to hide it as far as possible from him. Why should I hurt that old man you see?"

*   *   *

On the west coast of India, a young Chitpavin Brahmin, another Cambridge graduate, had returned home at the turn of the century. He had been given the principalship of a local college and, with the help of friends, his engagement to a young college student, a girl from his own community, had been arranged. Writing to her a few weeks before their marriage, he looked forward to a union in which both personal attraction and modern convictions would play their role. "We will show the world," he wrote, "that an educated couple can be happy — far happier than ordinary couples consisting of a boy & a girl brought together by their parents without their consent. . . ."[4] When a friend inquired what present the bride would like, her groom suggested a bicycle and wrote to her asking: "How do you like the idea of a cycle & of going out cycling with me?" "At this rate," he added in happy anticipation, "we are going to shock Poona completely."[5]

*   *   *

Through all of the nineteenth and half of the twentieth centuries, the British held power in India, and added, through the institutions of their power, a Western dimension to the cultures and traditions of the subcontinent. Numerous Indians who were children growing to maturity in that world felt the impact of its unique blend of cultures, values, and ideas. Their adult lives and actions reflected the dual heritage which had been their lot. This book is about that world and their experiences in it. It is a summation of accumulated memories and impressions garnered from over one hundred autobiographies written in English and published during the last century and a half. Interviews, private papers, and letters have complemented this material wherever possible, but its core is the reminiscences of Indian autobiographers, most of whom were men, born and growing to maturity between the years 1850 and 1920.

As early as the 1880s, there existed a group of Indians — small in relation to the total population but numbering perhaps as many as fifty thousand — who wrote and spoke English with relative skill and had at least a passing familiarity with the cultural assumptions and values of the West. By the turn of the century, these people were providing the organizational base of a burgeoning nationalist movement and made up the membership of a score of social and religious reform groups, caste associations, and literary societies.

The autobiographers on whose memories this book is based are good representatives of this group. Aside from the fact that almost all were born into families with traditions of literacy but none of manual labor, they share no single feature of culture or linguistic heritage. They undertook a variety of Western-oriented occupations — law, journalism, government service, education, and medicine — to which they had access because of their knowledge of English and their educational achievements. What they did share was an exposure to the British educational system in India and a strong desire to leave behind some testament to the influences that had shaped their lives. This wish found expression in a decision to describe their lives in a language, English, and in a genre, autobiography, that were both foreign to Indian tradition.

Some authors had been the first in their families to study in the English-language schools, while others had a father or perhaps an uncle who had already been exposed to the educational system of the Raj. Only a few could have traced their knowledge of English or familiarity with Western culture back through more than two generations. Western ideas were new to them and thus appear in these memories and stories clearly outlined against the background of older habits and customs. Watching a family over several generations, listening to sons talk about fathers or (more rarely) fathers talk about sons, one sees the contradictions — and also sees them visibly diminish as once foreign ideas blend slowly and imperceptibly into the unconscious assumptions of a family.

The formal entrance of Western ideas into Indian society was simple and straightforward. The British had been a dominant power in India from the end of the eighteenth century and had taken over most of the functions of government by the 1830s. But it was not until the middle years of the nineteenth century that an educational system in English was officially instituted on the subcontinent. Thomas Macaulay, the historian and parliamentarian, had argued in a Minute written in 1835 for the establishment of English-language education. It would create, he suggested, a small group of Westernized Indians — "Indians in blood and color" but "English in taste, in opinions, in morals, and in intellect."[6] These men would act as buffers between the British and the vast peasant society they governed. Some twenty years later, the educational dispatch of 1854 took the first steps in this direction. Universities were established in provincial capitals throughout India. Although the older cities, Bombay, Madras, and Calcutta, had had English-language schools and colleges for many years, it was only after 1854 that similar programs spread to *mofussil*, or provincial, areas. Shortly thereafter both the central and the provincial governments began requiring Western degrees as a prerequisite for employment in their offices.

The universities, however, were only examining and degree-granting bodies. They had no teaching staff and offered no courses. Preparation for their examinations was given by the private schools and colleges that began springing up even in far-flung areas. There was little control over the establishment of these programs. In fact, virtually anybody with the funds to rent space and hire teachers could open a college or preparatory school. A combination of student fees and government grants-in-aid made survival likely and prosperity a distinct possibility.

Given the uncontrolled proliferation of schools, the degree of uniformity in their curricula and textbooks was extraordinary. Degree programs throughout the provinces were virtually identical, and textbooks conformed to each other in both organization and emphasis. The reason for this was twofold: on the one hand, government funds and inspections, and the central examination system; and, on the other, intense student interest and concern.

The government could, of course, deny grants-in-aid to schools that did not pass the inspections, but a more effective weapon was the examination system. Course topics were announced two years in advance, and, at the same time, an appropriate text — "Taylor's History of India or any similar book" — was suggested.[7] Questions were usually factual and specific, requiring the candidate to list, for example, the names of the "Twelve Caesars" or "some of the chief of our liberties established by the Magna Carta."[8] Success demanded a ready memory uncomplicated by imagination or critical judgment.[9] Teachers and students, if they hoped for safety, were well advised to rely on the assigned text, or, if they had to choose an alternate, to select one which mirrored the first in organization and point of view.

Even if government controls had totally failed, the students' practical needs would have served to bring all but the most recalcitrant institution into line. The major, if not the only, concern of the student was to pass the requisite examinations: M.E. — Matriculation Examination — for entrance into college; F.A. — First Arts — on passage of half the college curriculum; B.A. — Bachelor of Arts — on completion of the whole; and, subsequently, whatever master's, law, science, or medical degree was thought necessary for the chosen career. From the point of view of students and their families, the number of passes a school obtained in the examinations and the rankings of its pupils were the first measures of its status and desirability. For private institutions, these records translated quickly into financial success or ruin. Even missionary institutions, whose motives were never primarily financial, were forced to focus on the examination subjects if they wished to attract students.[10] So intense was student interest in this matter that a school which did not emphasize the degree curricula or succeed in preparing candidates for examinations would attract few applicants. Whether government, missionary, or private, English-language institutions tended to bend their best efforts in the same directions.

Both curricula and texts provided an appropriate setting for the propagation of the message of the educational system. The British government, of course, especially in the years following the Mutiny of 1857, was determined to be neutral in matters of religion and insisted through its many institutional voices that it had no interest in interfering with the religious customs of its Indian subjects. But this commitment by no means left the educational system without an ideology or purpose. A single vision had animated public education in India from its inception and would continue to do so to the end of British rule. This vision was incorporated into the textbooks and supported, often with the most passionate conviction, by British educators and officials throughout the country.

At the heart of the ideology was a belief in the unquestioned superiority of Western culture and values. For Indian students, salvation lay only in the abandonment of their decadent traditions and acceptance of the values of the West. As A.C. Miller wrote in Seven Letters to Indian Schoolboys: "I hope that I shall not be misunderstood and that these letters may open the eyes of Indian schoolboys to some of their failings and may help them to think over matters which vitally concern them."[11] It was not, as Miller told his Bombay audience, that all Indian boys were bad or all English boys good. Indeed, he wrote, "I know very well that there are many English boys that are thoroughly bad; more shame to them because they have every opportunity of being good and every encouragement to do so . . . and it is a matter of wonder to me that so many Indian boys are as good as they are, considering the temptations that living in or so close to the bazaar offers them. But I do go so far as to say that English boys as a whole are loyal, just, devoted sportsmen."[12]

Miller wrote in the 1900s, but his theme had echoed through the halls of British Indian educational institutions throughout the nineteenth century. School texts on Indian history consistently emphasized the degeneracy of India, her culture and peoples.[13] Over the centuries, it was explained, India's climate had destroyed the physical condition of her peoples. As a result the caste system had appeared and corruption was rampant. Indians were "backward" and "effeminate." They were known for their "timidity, untruthfulness, indolence and litigitousness [sic]."[14] "They do not appear," wrote one widely read author, "to live according to any fixed standard of goodness, to act, in a word, from principle."[15] If there were good qualities to be found in the Indian character, they were quickly passed over. "This is most charming," wrote Miller in mentioning his pupils' devotion to their families, "and I have nothing more to say about it."[16]

European theories of the day commonly ascribed a shared genetic origin to the tribes which had originally peopled Europe and the "Aryan tribesmen" believed to have migrated into India three or four thousand years earlier. One writer drew this theory to its friendliest conclusion in a text for younger grade levels. The English and the higher castes of India, he said, were "like cousins of one family who have lived apart for thousands of years but have at last met once more."[17] On matters of race, it was rare for texts to be so pleasant. More often, fears and fantasies gained the upper hand, and descriptions mirrored the worst of British prejudices and stereotypes. Aryans, for instance, were often equated with Europeans; they were once, it was said, "a long-headed race of tall stature with narrow noses and fair complexion."[18] In ancient days they had been, another text claimed, "big stout white men from the northwest."[19] This particular author hurried on to explain that it was life in the enervating climate of the plains that had robbed these men of their "strength and courage" and left them to be "swept away by other tribes from the same cold northern climes."[20] In a similar vein, indigenous peoples of ancient India were often described in the unflattering terms reserved by the English for the "natives" of the country. The Dravidians had "long hair, broad noses and dark complexions."[21] "Usually of short stature," one author wrote, they were easily beaten by the Aryans and "as they were short, black and ugly and lived in the woods, the Aryans, who could not understand what they said, called them monkeys....."[22]

Most commonly, however, the textbooks invited the identification of their students not with the backwardness of the Indian past but with the enlightenment of the British present. Their most explicit encouragement was for acculturation. The English, they pointed out, had brought peace and justice to the subcontinent; they were worthy of imitation, being, with few exceptions, a noble, brave, and self-sacrificing people. Indians had remained "isolated for many ages from the rest of mankind by the physical peculiarities of their country and by the exigencies of their natural character."[23] Now, under English tutelage, this isolation could end. The efforts of the British would be to "elevate the people in their charge."[24] With their help, Indians would learn to become self-governing, and "qualified" Indians would take up positions of power and prestige within the Raj. "The Act of 1833 A.D. and the Queen's Proclamation," one of many books explained, made it "the intention of the Government to offer a large share in the administration without distinction of race or religion to natives of India who were qualified by character and education."[25] The obligatory final chapter of many texts was "The Benefits of British Rule" and provided a ready catalog of the good works of the Raj: technological advancement, peace, prosperity, increases in education, inclusion of Indians in government — all were there. Occasionally the words of the Queen herself, from the Proclamation of 1858 ("the Magna Carta of India"), would close the chapter: "In their prosperity [she had written] will be our strength, in their contentment our security and in their gratitude our best reward."[26]

During the nineteenth and twentieth centuries, the invitation to acculturate was accepted by many Indian schoolboys who saw in the attainment of Western education the prospect of financial prosperity and the hope of cultural enlightenment. But as the educated gained experience with the realities of British rule, "gratitude" often changed to bitter disappointment. Later students often believed that their advancement within the Raj was barred for reasons of race and color; at the same time they felt, inalienably within themselves, the very qualities that were so severely stigmatized by the educational system.

The prejudices of the British rulers had played their part in shaping the message of the English-language schools. Indians and Indian culture were endowed by British history books with many traits which were the obverse of the positive values held by the English. Where Englishmen were brave, manly, noble, and white, Indians were effeminate, cowardly, superstitious, untrustworthy, and black. The extent to which Englishmen found Indian indirectness and subtlety disturbing and frightening (especially when remembered in the context of the racial turmoil and violence of the Mutiny) shows in the cultural identity their textbooks bequeathed to the schoolchildren in their charge.

Psychoanalyst Erik Erikson has written in an essay on "Race and the Wider Identity" of the way in which a dominant culture can project onto a minority group all of those qualities and characteristics which it most fears and hates within itself.[27] This creates for the minority a wholly negative cultural identity. To understand how members of such a group take up this image and integrate it into their own understanding of what is negative in their being and behavior, Erikson suggests we think of the "many nuances of the way in which one Negro may address another as 'nigger'."[28] The British, while not a numerical majority in India, nevertheless controlled the subcontinent. Their textbooks provided the basepoints of what became for many Indians a core identity — a definition of themselves which they felt to be fundamentally true, even though they denied its validity and protested vigorously against it.

The educational system had the most dramatic effects during its earliest years. The first students' enthusiasm for acculturation often provoked bitter quarrels within families and castes. Particularly in Bengal, boys publicly aligned themselves with the values of the West by abandoning traditions, leaving home, or accepting caste excommunication rather than return to more orthodox modes of behavior. But the more profound effects of this amalgam of traditions came only later in the century with the fuller incorporation of Western values into family life. Slowly, over the years, the message of the West fed into the lives of children not only through schoolbooks and teachers, but through the ideas and experiences of their own Western-educated relatives. Autobiographies illustrate the ways in which Western-educated parents' experiences with the realities of employment under the Raj were being added to the sum of what their children learned as they grew. Then we can see how truly pervasive negative British stereotypes of India and Indian culture became. The complexity and contradictions of the environments which shaped authors' early years are manifest in the conflicts they remember and in the nuances of their descriptions. Particularly in the crises which sometimes seized people in the early period of adulthood, one can define the legacy of ambivalence which was the heritage of their growing years.

*   *   *

Old portraits and family snapshots of this period hint at a legacy of intricate cultural influences. The art of the photographer, one may suspect, lay in his ability to filter out of a portrait all traces of "native" culture. The surface impressions of older pictures of Indians are often impeccably Western. The pose, clothing, and facial expressions duplicate their English models. Children sit, crisply dressed in short pants and long socks; men stand, their heads half-turned towards the camera, an arm resting on a fortuitous lectern. The photographer's skill diminishes our awareness of even the presence of a deliberate item of indigenous clothing. In one studio portrait, the gentleman sits, dressed in a three-piece suit of Western cut; on the table next to him have been placed some books and a round English clock.[29] The time is 9:25. The clock, the books, the table, the suit, all engage our attention more completely than the wrapped turban of west

Indian design which rests firmly on his head. The foreign style of the whole overrides this single item of cultural identification.

But that is only the surface. So strong is culture, so pervasive its influence, that it persists in these pictures through the most determined efforts to erase it. The experience of India remains. It permeates the expression of eyes and alters, almost imperceptibly, physical presence. The pictures have a powerful resonance and they linger in one's memory, mysterious and delicate, giving a momentary glimpse into the inner reality of the world experienced by Indians under the Raj.

Autobiographies are the written equivalent of those early pictures. We look in their pages for the same resonance, hoping to understand the blending of cultural influences that shaped their authors' lives. But literature, of course, is as susceptible as art to control and manipulation. An English emphasis on empirical evidence and an Indian reticence on personal matters often combine to deflect an author's spontaneous recollections onto the safer ground of a factual recitation of events. Still, in the brilliance of an isolated passage or in the courage of a particular memory, the autobiographies do recapture momentarily the world of British India. Through a collection of these moments, one can recreate that world and can understand the various forces that shaped the life-choices of schoolboys and young men seeking to become adults in a world controlled and defined by the alien culture of the Raj.

PART I

Memories

CHAPTER

1

Memories of Childhood

PARADOXICALLY, WHILE AUTOBIOGRAPHICAL memories of childhood are brief, they often contain the most evocative and intriguing passages of the literature. Writers skip quickly over the early portions of their lives, not only because they find it difficult to remember incidents, but also because they fear to explore the emotional associations of their pasts within so public and so foreign a genre. Memories, therefore, tend to be stereotyped; the cast of characters is limited to that of a Western family. Mothers, fathers, and grandparents, the persona of the nuclear family, are the most common actors in these scenes.

Even if authors were inclined to linger over early memories, the nature of autobiography as it is conceived in India would still limit reminiscences. Childhood memories, so fleeting and ephemeral, seem incongruous within an autobiographical format that emphasizes the exact, the chronological, the documented memories of a life. In only a few books do writers consciously explore the implications of their early years and attempt to re-create its moods and memories. For the rest, the section on childhood is the obligatory portion of a memoir, necessary by Western convention, but quickly hurried through in order to reach the more concrete events of adult life. M.R. Jayakar's two-volume *The Story of My Life* runs to roughly fifteen hundred pages; the section on his childhood and education occupies only thirty of these.[1]

However censored by adult sensitivities, the memoirs do create an impression of the Indian world within which their authors grew. Childhood memories are the least restructured by Western values; the contents predate their authors' formal exposure to the values of the Raj and relate to a time of life, even within the most Westernized of families, when the child was thought too young to be restrained by explicit rules and regulations. Moreover, in these sections, authors have only their memories to guide them. Without the diaries, newspapers, journals, or letters which restrict their imaginations and bind their memories in the later sections of their books, they can produce strikingly subtle recollections, memories which capture the surroundings, moods, and emotions of childhood.

Nostalgia is the common emotional color of these childhood reminiscences. Typically, an author remembers himself, with affection, as the center of his universe, the "favorite" of all (especially his mother), the child who was indulged, petted, and adored. That memory of early childhood is dominant, and is only challenged by the subsequent recollection of the loss of this position with increased age or the appearance of younger siblings. Its centrality reflects on the structure of childhood development in Indian society. Where *infancy* usually refers in the West to a child who cannot yet walk, in India, as one psychoanalyst has pointed out, the "psycho-social quality of infancy" extends through the first four or five years of a child's life — through "the entire time in which feeding, toileting and rudimentary self care as well as walking, talking and the initial capacity for reasoning become matters of course."[2] During this period, without pressure from mother or family, the Indian child learns, at his own pace, to master those various skills and controls. The very young, it is assumed, are not responsible for what they do; as they cannot understand rules and restrictions, it is senseless to punish them for misbehavior. Adults find it extremely difficult to witness unhappiness in a young child. A north Indian proberb sums up traditional wisdom on this subject: for five years a son should be treated as a king; for ten years, as a slave; after that, as a friend.[3] This attitude combines with an observable enjoyment of childhood and children to produce an intensely loving environment especially during a child's early years.

Early memories are proud testaments to those moments of centrality and importance. "My birth in the family," recalls an eldest son, "was heralded by scenes of great pomp."[4] An heir to a small kingdom remembers how "all his servants saluted me and the more honourable people sitting on chairs stood up" when he was taken to pay his respects to his father.[5] Perhaps the quintessential phrasing of a childhood memory belongs to a famous musician: "My mother was very much attached to me when I was small," he writes, "because I was the baby of the family."[6] For the first six years of his life, Bipin Chandra Pal remembers, "Every whim of mine was satisfied. No one was permitted to lift a hand against me."[7]

This period of indulgence and freedom comes to an abrupt halt between the ages of four and seven. Traditions, customs, hierarchical considerations of family, caste, and society suddenly come into play. Children find they are expected to understand and adhere to the complex codes of behavior which structure the lives of the adults of the family. In many communities at this time, male children are expected to begin an apprenticeship in the work which they are destined to do as adults. "A

Bania youth," Morris Carstairs notes in his study of a north Indian village, "demonstrates his 'putting away childish things' by working long hours in a family shop and by displaying an appropriately serious attention to money matters."[8] In Brahmin or Rajput families of that area, the changed status of the child is symbolized by a special ceremony; a male child puts on a "sacred thread" and is thereby born a second time into the adult responsibilities of the community which he has already physically entered.

A boy especially may find his sudden separation from the indulgence of the world of women, and immersion in the disciplined world of men, difficult to bear.[9] In his father's world, there are clear hierarchical principles, and a paternal figure who judges his behavior but, by tradition, maintains an attitude of distance and formality towards his son. The rupture of the early union with the mother is one of the most intense crises of Indian childhood. The changed treatment at this age, the prolonged "infancy" which preceded it, and the subsequent restraints imposed on life may account for the lifelong nostalgia with which authors look back on the warmth and centricity of the world of their earliest memories.

Later in life, beyond childhood, intense friendships or special attention may recall memories of this earlier state. Schools and families both produced these moments: "Truth compels me to say," writes a former schoolboy, "that I was one of the most favoured students of the professors,"[10] A south Indian recalls that he was the "pet" of his sisters and brothers.[11] D.K. Karve was drawn to his close friend, Mr. Joshi, whom he saw as the embodiment of a boldness and cleverness which he himself lacked. Another college boy had a special friend to whom he was attached "in a way which I can scarcely explain"; "I loved and admired him intensely," he recalls, "even his very words. In fact everything about him moved me to the depths of my being."[12] Authors remember these special relationships with almost equal poignancy whether the "other" involved was a mother, teacher, guru, friend, or, in one case, a dog. "I had one friend, the Alsatian Frieda," one author writes about a lonely boyhood. "I loved her dearly. If I were sitting somewhere alone, she would not leave me."[13]

A desire for one special "other," a longing for one true friend, and a unique quality of intensity pervading friendships — all have been seen as refractions of the early "symbiosis" between mother and child on later adult life and personality.[14] Erik Erikson, in commenting on the intensity which frequently attached to friendships with Indians, suggested that the longing for a one-to-one relationship, as well as the desire for fusion underlying much traditional philosophy and religion, could be related to certain qualities of life in extended family units.

... The deep nostalgia for fusion is reborn, it seems from generation to generation, out of the diffusion of the mother in the joint family, in which she must respond to each and at the same time all, and thus can belong to the individual child only in fleeting moments and to nobody for good or for long.[15]

Children certainly watched with great intensity the portioning out of the affections of their parents. The seventh child of thirteen children played a game with his siblings where he divided a rupee into portions representing shares of the affections of their mother. He gave one particular daughter "eight annas" (half) and divided the rest into shares of "four annas, two annas, one anna, two pice, one pice and three of one pie each," leaving himself "only one of these pie shares."[16] Another author admitted he was "painfully anxious" to discover any element of favoritism in his mother's behavior towards her children, adding proudly that while "she was extremely fair to all her children, she did, I think, give me that extra affection that was necessary to establish faith in myself."[17] At least one modern study has commented on the striking absence of sibling rivalry within Hindu families, but while relations between brothers and sisters usually indicate mutual affection and concern, traditional wisdom also recognizes the potential for more ambivalent feelings.[18] The second memory of one Bengali (the first is of an early illness of his mother) is of the birth of a brother when he was five or six: "I loved him like anything and belied the popular legend that there are always jealousies among succeeding brothers or sisters."[19] But indeed the birth of a younger sibling could destroy a favored position. As Subhas Bose, the ninth of fourteen children, noted gloomily, the "youngest child did, of course, come in for an extra dose of fondling, but an addition to the family would soon rob it of its title to special favours."[20] One autobiographer was the first male child in his family to survive: "I was therefore looked upon as a precious gift," he recalls, "and was cherished as such until two more brothers, Gokal Chand and Balmokand, were born."[21]

Ruth Benedict has described in a study of Japanese society how the pattern of growth allowed freedom and spontaneity only to the very young or the very old.[22] Traditional Indian society imposed something of the same limitations. Between childhood and old age, social customs severely regulated behavior. The inhibitions and restrictions of adult life, we suggest, played a role in allowing elders to enjoy and encourage mischievousness in the very young, nostalgically reliving, through that behavior, their own early days of freedom. Even fathers could be ambivalent about the growing self-control and discretion of their sons, preferring a younger child's spontaneous honesty to an older's acquired deference. "You see," said a Rajput prince to Morris Carstairs, "he is learning. He says what he thinks will please his father. He really prefers the

town but he says Deoli in order to please me." And Carstairs noted, "as he
spoke he stared thoughtfully and unaffectionately at his elder son."[23]

Authors do imply that as children they were immune from discipline,
even perhaps subtly encouraged to be naughty. But they couple these
memories with recollections of harsh penalties at school and paternal
violence at home. One man claims that on hearing he had played hookey
from school, his father gave him "several lashes from his horse whip."[24]
(His grandmother, he adds, was "furious" at this.) Jawaharlal Nehru
remembers himself as a spoiled and pampered little boy, but also as a
child terrified of his father's terrible temper.[25] Someone else describes his
father's strict discipline, but adds, more cheerfully, "I always managed to
evade his vigilant eye."[26]

School attendance, it would seem, brought even more hardship. The
bitterness of memories suggests some conjunction between the age at
which a child entered school — usually five or six — and the age at which
his treatment within the family began to change. "Those were the days of
cruel punishments for children," recalls one author, describing how he
had to be carried crying and kicking to school.

> I had often to stand in the hot sun and read my lessons if I had not
> prepared them on the previous night. My brother fared no better. He
> used to be constantly in the sun, reading aloud while tears trickled down
> his cheeks.[27]

The indulged position of the child was lost to the schoolboy, who could be
beaten or made to stand in the sun for an infraction of the rules. In later
life, a brief experience that evoked the earlier freedom brought deep
happiness. D.K. Karve cherished the memory of a summer spent at his
family's home during his college years: "Father and mother were very
considerate," he wrote, "and they treated me indulgently as they began to
entertain hopes that I might achieve something to raise the status of the
family."[28]

One residue of early childhood is the almost universal affection with
which autobiographers remember their mothers. In clinical work, one
analyst has said, Indian children — especially boys — experience their
mothers, on the surface at least, in a positive way.[29] In autobiographical
memories, also, mothers are almost invariably gentle, religious,
soft-voiced, and beautiful. They are loving and indulgent in their treatment
of their children. After all, asks one Punjabi author, "Who can fulfill the
demands of a boy of eight except a mother?"[30] Mothers appear only briefly
in autobiographies; they are most often found weeping over the
impending departure of a child (the author) for some far-off place. The
behavior of Lal Behari Day's mother, on the occasion of his departure at
age eight to study in Calcutta, was only slightly more dramatic than most.

As he lay beside her the night before he left, she wept the whole night through. On the morning of the day itself, although relatives warned her it would be inauspicious, she could not control her grief. As her son walked from the village, having been instructed on no account to look behind him, he still heard the sound of her sobbing. "I afterwards learned," he concludes with no touch of unhappiness at the thought, "that she was carried away by main force from that pathetic scene by my aunts."[31]

Far from implying criticism of the mother, such stories are told in ways which indicate how fully this behavior met cultural expectations. These memories not only provoke no guilt, but even seem to provide some reassurance of the continued love and involvement of the mother. The recollections of writers whose mothers died while they were young illustrate how crucial this aspect of a mother's role was to the equilibrium of traditional culture. Although extended families, with their numerous male and female elders, have sometimes been thought to mediate the importance and influence of the biological parents in the life of the child, autobiographers whose mothers did die while they were young vividly recall their sense of isolation and deprivation at the time. Due to an illness of her mother, one Punjabi woman had been raised by her maternal grandmother; but she was still devastated by her mother's death and the father's subsequent indifference. Repeatedly she tells her younger sister: "We have no home."[32] Another author remembers with amazement his childhood reaction to a sickness of his mother. "I lightly drew my breath in those days, what did I know of death?"[33] A third specifically recalls the sadness of his "motherless" childhood and underlines his sense of loss through repeated descriptions of female relatives who "mothered" him or treated him "like a mother" in his youth.[34]

Autobiographical portraits of mothers illustrate the positive conscious memories of their children. Yet numerous observers of Indian society have noted the deep ambivalence which surrounds the image of the Indian woman — and mother — both in traditional stories and in accounts of contemporary life. A woman is "Devi," a goddess, the giver of all goodness; but she is also "Kali" (a goddess particularly worshipped in Bengal), the destroyer, the dangerous one. In this form she is unpredictable — an uncontrollable sexual temptress insatiably demanding from men the semen which traditionally is equated with male strength and power. "Fire is never satisfied with fuel," runs one proverb, "the ocean is never filled by the rivers, death is never satisfied by living beings and women are never satisfied with men."[35] Morris Carstairs suggested that this duality characterized Rajasthani children's impressions of their own mothers. Usually warm and indulgent, they could become suddenly and inexplicably distant, even dangerous, under the restrictions of customary behavior (in the presence of grandparents, for instance, or at the time of the menses).[36] The dangerous and threatening mother, theorizes one psychoanalyst, lives in the unconscious of Indian children, especially boys.[37] Her origin can be found — as can that of the positive conscious memories — in the intense closeness between mother and son during the first five years of the child's life. "The son's predicament," writes Sudhir Kakar, is extreme

> [because] although he unconditionally needs the physical and emotional sustenance that at first only his mother provides, he is profoundly wary of the intensity of his feelings for her (and of hers for him) and unconsciously afraid of being overwhelmed and 'devoured' by her.[38]

The figure of the mother, Kakar asserts, is "omnipresent in the psyche of Indian men." In fantasy, both in myth and clinical work, she is both the "nurturing benefactress and threatening seductress."[39]

In these conditions, it is not surprising that open criticism of a mother by her son is extremely rare. Women, however, are more realistic in their recollections of their mothers. Nehru's sister remembers clearly, for instance, her resentment at her mother's preference for the older brother.[40] A south Indian woman bitterly resented her mother's constant efforts to terminate her education and force her into marriage.[41] When a son criticizes, however, he invariably points to his mother's failure to live up to traditional expectations. One author from the Konkan in west India is critical of the paucity of his mother's affection for him. His own love is transposed to an aunt in whose house he was raised. She was his "second mother"; the "ideal of an Indian woman," she was "simple, hard-working and ready to be of service to everyone."[42]

Several Bengali authors do complain of their mothers' treatment. Subhas Bose recalls that he felt distant from both his parents during childhood; his mother, he noted, had a "strong will," "keen sense of reality and sound common sense." In their house she clearly "ruled the roost."[43] Bipin Chandra Pal's mother was "remarkably reserved and contained"; he writes, "I do not remember to have been treated by her in my early infancy much less in my later boyhood with outward fondness. In this she differed from most mothers that I knew. . . ."[44] Pal repaid his mother throughout his childhood with a repeated fantasy. For many years, he recalls, "indeed until I was quite a young man of fifteen or sixteen I could never free myself of the idea that she was not my mother but only my stepmother."[45]

The harshest criticism of a mother is undoubtedly Nirad Chaudhuri's. In *The Autobiography of an Unknown Indian,* Chaudhuri complains that his mother was a chronic hysteric. A woman whose illnesses ultimately weakened her health and "undeservedly saddened my father's life and troubled ours," she was hard towards her children and unreasoning in her attitude towards their father.[46] "In actual fact," he writes, "he [the father] seriously weakened his splendid constitution and went very near ruining his worldly career for her sake. Yet she was always complaining of his conduct towards her."[47] In her treatment of her children, she was "businesslike."

> If we groaned too much in times of illness or expected to be made much of, we were quickly and firmly told to go to sleep instead of making things worse by complaining. . . . No one who has not observed the behavior of little children in India can have an adequate idea of the range of expansion of their mouths in self-pity and hope of external pity. The luxury of self-pity as well as sympathy was severely rationed in our case.[48]

But her greatest flaw, in her son's eyes, was her "egoism."

> Her expectations from life as distinct from her expectations from the world appeared to be limitless. They were all grasping emotional demands made exclusively on her husband and children.[49]

And this is the central theme to which autobiographical criticism of mothers inevitably return: the degree to which the mother failed (or her child believes that she failed) to provide those qualities of indulgent attention and sympathy traditionally associated with her maternal role.

The deeper strains of ambivalence only appear in two autobiographical descriptions of a mother's death. One author is from the Bombay region, the second from Bengal. The first author was an educational administrator, and the details of his career make up the major portion of his autobiography. The fictionalized style of his book's two-page preface, entitled simply "Mother," is in striking contrast to the impersonality of the rest. He recounts the death of his mother from plague when he was a year and a half old. The family were farmers; the setting, their home in a small Belgaum district village; the year, 1901.

> Suddenly the woman groaned, opened her eyes and said to the youngest child [the author], "Dadana, I am going to die, feed here (pointing to her breast) for one last time." The child was only a year and a half but was wiser than his years. There was a clash of instincts; the filial instinct said yes, but there was a deeper and healthier instinct that said no. As the child hesitated, turned away, the dying mother smiled and said, "Oh, then you won't miss me. . . ."[50]

The father stands silently by, only speaking to promise the mother that he will not remarry and will remain on good terms with the neighbors, promises he made, the author tells us, "as he loved her and the children immensely. . . . These were her last words and in a few minutes closing her eyes forever she passed into eternal silence. The woman was my mother and I her fourth and youngest son."[51]

The second memory also takes place in a small village setting, but this time in Bengal. Father, mother, and child are placed in opposition to each other, and the memory resonates with pain and bitterness. The author was perhaps four or five at the time. His mother lay dying in the hut where she had just given birth to a new child. By tradition, the baby's birth had placed both the hut and the mother herself in a state of ritual pollution.

> I vividly remember what happened then. My father stood with me on his arms in the door of the house where the baby was born. My mother called me again and again to go to her saying, "Come to me, I will give you something." But my father would not let me go. The house was believed to be unholy owing to the birth of the child. The day of its purification had not yet come. If I went into it I should have to take a bath. But that could not be as I was suffering from fever. So the dying mother's wish to have her child with her in her last moments was not fulfilled. I have remembered this cruel affair with deep pain and anger all my life.[52]

The resolution of the first memory, where the mother passes smiling into "eternal silence," is absent from the second. The first was not, it turns out, a true memory at all, but an account of his mother's death told to the author by a widowed aunt over and over again during his childhood.[53] The second author, though, never forgave his father. His anger constantly intrudes into the autobiography in allusions to the father's hypocrisy and in frequent comparisons between the father and the eldest uncle (father's brother), a man who was not "a slave to custom."[54] As an adult, the author joined the Brahmo Samaj (a Bengali religious reform organization) and obtained a sort of posthumous revenge on his father by refusing to perform that parent's death ceremonies according to orthodox customs. His memory of his mother's death may owe some of its form to a later integration of childhood memories into the adult identity of a religious reformer. In either case, however, both memories present powerful images of the child in relation to his parents. Both put into a kind of visual shorthand the dynamics of family life — showing us each child pulled both towards and away from the mother. Both also illustrate, each with its own regional emphasis, the potential danger of a mother's longing for her child.

Traditional society balanced maternal indulgence against the greater severity of male authorities. "My disposition," writes one Punjabi author whose mother died when he was young, "was too sensitive to submit to the authority of my brothers, shorn of the sympathy and understanding of my mother."[55] Almost all observers of Indian culture, and most autobiographers, describe the Indian father as a remote and distant figure. "I always thought of him as an immortal," wrote the daughter of Keshub Chunder Sen.[56] Another writer's father "used also to sing to us and he talked with us at all times, yet we seemed never to lose our awe of him and in spite of our intimate family life, he always remained to us a kind of god."[57] Out of respect for their parents and by general custom fathers were expected to refrain from fondling or expressing affection for their sons in public. One man told Carstairs that, even in the privacy of his home, he was afraid to be affectionate to his young children for fear that they would cause embarrassment by running to him in public.[58] "I have often found," wrote a Bengali who denied that this was his own situation, "that there is sometimes an impenetrable wall interposed between father and son, the father is held in terror — a sort of frigid reserve is maintained between the two — the mother or the family friend has to intercede on the part of the latter as a go-between whenever the latter has to approach the former...."[59]

As boys could expect to remain for much of their lives under the domination of a father, traditional village education prepared them for these roles. In the Bengali *pathsala* ("village school") he attended as a boy, Lal Behari Day spent much of his time learning to write letters which were invariably addressed but never sent to the father. In them, Day recalls "I was made to beg my father to send money soon, as we were supposed to labor under pecuniary difficulties and the other boys were made to write precisely to the same effect."[60]

Fathers, then, were figures of power and authority with whom it was not appropriate to become too friendly. Although Subhas Bose might write that he yearned for a more "intimate" relationship with his parents, the actual response to the observation of intimacy between fathers and sons was likely to be discomfort.[61] A Rajput boy, son of a princely Rajasthani house, described in his diary his uneasiness on observing the companionship which existed between another Rajput and his sons:

> They joke together and often use such slang words (though not in anger) between themselves as I would blush to utter even before my companions or even subordinates.[62]

The congeniality of this relationship did not justify it in his eyes. "There is no doubt," he wrote, "that they live in great harmony between themselves, yet to a certain extent, I do not like their mode of living. According to our customs, sons should have respect and restraint towards parents...."[63]

In contrast to the restraint required of father-son relationships was the intimacy allowed between nephews and uncles. Anthropological studies have shown that an uncle, particularly a mother's brother, may often provide the open expression of affection and support traditionally denied within filial relationships. Uncles could be turned to in times of crisis — they might help with money or intercede with parents or provide a refuge for a boy who found life at home intolerable. Several writers affectionately described their uncles as men who, they paradoxically recall, treated them "like a son." As Y.G. Bonnell, a South Indian Christian, wrote, contrasting his uncle with the father who had died when he was eight: "I knew little of *My* father personally; but *I* know much about *My* father's brother ... *I* think highly of *My* father, as we his children are respected because of him. But *I* esteem *My* uncle highly as *I* know his real worth...."[64]

Within this context, however, autobiographers will seek out strands of memory which deny the totality of their father's remoteness. Fathers are often remembered with great affection as the tutors of one's early years. "At an early age," one man wrote, "my father created in me a taste for mathematics. He first taught me geometry in a third class railway compartment, showing me straight lines and right angles on the side of the carriage...."[65] P.C. Ray interpreted the concern of the English historian James Mill for the education of his famous son John within this same tradition: "One thing especially struck me," he wrote of the son's early life, "James Mill had taken the precaution of not sending his gifted son to any public school and himself acted as his friend, guide and philosopher...."[66] Ray, whose autobiography obliquely railed against a father who had squandered the family fortune and reduced his sons to penury, insists on this family portrait:

> The relations between my father and us (i.e. myself and my brothers) were most frank and cordial. We picked up more information on every conceivable subject by direct conversation with him than through mere book learning. And we were allowed the utmost latitude in approaching him and cross-questioning him.[67]

(That latitude was easily exceeded, however. One day, Ray, seeking perhaps to "test" his father, asked him the geographical location of Sebastopool. "What! ... you speak Sebastopool!" the father exploded, "I almost see with my own eyes the siege of the city by the English!"[68]) In regard to tutoring, a Punjabi woman remembers affectionately her father's efforts, but twice makes the point that "teaching ... never lasted long, for he would give it up in a few days."[69] Indeed, tutoring is not so much remembered for its educational value as for the symbol it provided of the concern and involvement of the father with his child. These memories serve a dual purpose: they indicate the father's advanced intelligence (he is knowledgeable in the subjects of the West) and also his warm concern for his son.

Similarly, paternal consideration, not only for the physical care and education of a child, but also for his ideas and opinions, becomes a further mark of a father's affection. "It is no exaggeration to say," recalls Rabindranath Tagore about his father, "that in my early childhood I hardly knew him. He would now and then come back home all of a sudden and with him came foreign servants with whom I felt extremely eager to make friends."[70] But however physically and emotionally distant, the father was consistently respectful of the ideas and actions of his sons.

> To the end of his life, I have observed, he never stood in the way of our independence. Many a time have I said or done things repugnant alike to his taste and his judgment; with a word he could have stopped me, but he preferred to wait till the prompting to refrain came from within. A passing acceptance by us of the correct and proper did not satisfy him; he wanted us to love the truth with our whole hearts; he knew that mere acquiescence without love is empty.[71]

Frequently authors couple a memory of their father's restraint with an assertion of his love. The Bengali Lal Behari Day recalled that his father loved him "excessively" but was "too wise" to spoil him with fond affection.[72] Morarji Desai remembers his father as a man "who was not accustomed to expressing his thoughts ostentatiously," but, he adds, "I had always a feeling that he had great affection for me."[73] Sudhir Kakar, in his study of Indian childhood, emphasizes that fathers forced by tradition into a remote and distant role may still be struggling to express a very real love for their sons.[74] Where custom prohibits a father from indulging his children or openly expressing love for them, other actions may become idioms for an exchange of affection. It is as if society compensated children for the distance it imposed between them and their fathers by encouraging them to see, in other behavior, indications of continuing paternal affection and concern. Attentions, such as tutoring, concern for one's physical well-being, or respect for one's ideas — indeed any departure from the traditional distance expected to characterize a father's behavior — will be understood by sons as a measure of his support, love, and care. It is a love that they frequently (and not always defensively) assert, they "always have a feeling" lies just beyond the remoteness of the traditional facade.

In autobiography, as in life, it is accepted that a son will defer to his father. The absence of direct criticism of fathers in autobiographies is evidence of the continuing power of traditional patterns of deference. Only in Bengali autobiographies is this pattern even conditionally challenged. "One day," writes Nirad Chaudhuri, "with my own eyes I saw the spectacle of a grown-up son (a retired captain of the Indian Medical Service) flying with a cudgel at his decrepit father, roaring 'I'll scatter your brains today, you bloody son of a bitch!'"[75] Chaudhuri, whose relations with his own father were troubled, notes that although tradition required love and respect, many Bengalis of his acquaintance exhibited an extreme and often violent hatred for their fathers. Another man, he reports, having heard of his father's death, "went into such rapturous antics of delight that the very servants implored him in the name of decency to restrain himself."[76]

Deference and the masking of criticism, in most autobiographies, indicate more than the simple persistence of ancient custom. They signal the intensity with which boys identify with fathers, seeing their own well-being and success reflected in their fathers' lives.[77] A father is not lightly criticized, for an accusation against him will soon rebound onto his sons. Even in Bengal, where protest is most likely to find a public forum, a father's wrongs receive little more than indirect reference or expression. Sitanatha Tattvabhushan, whose mother's death, when he was four or five, lived in his memory, describes his father in terms that tremble on the edge of sarcasm. At various points in his autobiography, he recalls how his father worked with his hands (a low-caste occupation); how he was a religious hypocrite, neither observing nor believing in traditional religion, but keeping his son from a dying mother to conform with social custom; how he died while away from home from having eaten foods that he probably should have refused.[78] When a father does fail, and his failure is (however privately) acknowledged, the bitterness clinging to a son's recollections reflects the closeness of the association and identification with the father.

Typical of the ambivalence with which a father may be remembered, and the discretion with which he may be described, are the memories of Surendranath Banerjea. Banerjea's father according to his son and a sole biographer had been a well-known "medical practitioner," one of the first in Calcutta. The son recalls with care the father's fame, his concern for the career of his child, and his own great grief on hearing, while in England, of his father's death. Scattered through the book, however, are passages of less certain meaning: references to the extremism of the father's generation, and several striking descriptions of the effects of alcoholism.

Banerjea was proud to have been an early advocate of the Calcutta Temperance Movement. (His family, Kulin Brahmins, would have had a natural predisposition to abstinence.) With obvious distaste he remembers one occasion when he found a group of his friends "lying on the floor in a state of more or less hopeless inebriety."[79] Even more vividly he recalled a brief encounter with some low-caste people in a shop.

> I saw half a dozen of men and women lying dead drunk on the floor of the shop. Another band of about a dozen men and women, all belonging to the lower classes, in varying stages of drunkenness, began dancing around me in wild delirious excitement. I apprehended violence and I slowly and cautiously retraced my steps from the shop, resolved that, so far as in me lay, this thing must cease.[80]

What Banerjea does not tell us is that his father, Durga Churn Banerjea, was said to have been an alcoholic.[81] His patients were reputed to bring him liquor to induce him to accept their cases. The small Western-educated elite of Calcutta would, of course, have understood Banerjea's comments on temperance and even "extremism" in the context of his father's reputation. That Banerjea does not discuss it or directly allude to it in his memoir is consistent both with the style of autobiographical writing and with his own insistence on his affection for his father.

Criticism of one's father, disguised or open, finds few parallels in non-Bengali autobiographical writings. In other regions, conflicts between father and son, if they exist, are yet more deliberately buried. The Punjabi jurist, Meharcand Mahajan, was "rejected at birth" and exiled from his father's house for the first twelve years of his life because the father feared a prophecy that he would die if he viewed the face of his son.[82] In relating the story of his banishment and return, Mahajan allows himself no more than one brief irony. "At the proper hour," he writes of the father's decision, after twelve years, to risk looking upon his son, "the inauspicious son was placed in the lap of his father and 500 brahmans were fed."[83] The father did not die. He lived to choose for his son both a career and a second marriage that went against the son's own inclinations. But these decisions, Mahajan insists, were for the best. He is openly bitter only that his own sons do not yield to his will as readily as he once yielded to his father. The willingness with which a Bengali such as Bipin Chandra Pal expands both on his bitter estrangement from his father and on their subsequent reconciliation is foreign to the temperaments of other writers.

Far more common is the subdued regret which colors the memories of one Chitpavin Brahmin from the Konkan area of Bombay. R.P. Paranjpye left his father's house during childhood to live with the family of his cousin D.K. Karve. "I, my parents' third surviving son, was taken completely out of my father's hands by Anna Karve and from my tenth year onwards hardly stayed in the family house."[84] Following his cousin's advice and against what he knew to be the wishes of his father, Paranjpye studied not Sanskrit but Latin and traveled overseas to complete his education at Cambridge. He remembers clearly his early closeness with his father, a closeness he specifically emphasizes in his autobiography, and is sad, rather than angry, about the friction that later developed between them. Of his father and their relationship, he recalls:

> He was always calm and even tempered. Was not at all demonstrative and bore all his troubles philosophically. I knew he did not like my going to England for study, though he became more or less reconciled to it when he heard of my success. Although he himself scrupulously followed the rules about food and drink in every detail, he never asked me what I had done while abroad though I suppose he suspected that I had not observed all the injunctions. When I returned from England in December 1901, I did not perform the customary *prayaschitta* as I did

not feel that I had committed any sin; he did not press me to do so either. But during his lifetime whenever I was at Murud, I always sat for meals apart from other members of the family. I never took part in any religious ceremonies which he performed, but I gave him whatever money he wanted for the purpose.[85]

In regions outside Bengal, both the restraint of fathers and the public self-control and submission of sons contributed to the suppression of conflict.

The autobiographical literature covered by this study includes two striking memories of the death of a father — one famous, the other virtually unknown. Mohandas K. Gandhi's account of his father's death is, of course, the famous one.

> The dreadful night came. . . . It was ten thirty or eleven p.m. I was giving the massage. My uncle offered to relieve me. I was glad and went straight to the bedrooms. My wife, poor thing, was fast asleep. But how could she sleep when I was there? I woke her up. In five or six minutes, however, the servants knocked at the door. I started with alarm . . .
> "What is the matter? Do tell me."
> "Father is no more."
> So all was over! I had but to wring my hands. I felt deeply ashamed and miserable. I ran to my father's room. I saw that, if animal passion had not conquered me, I should have been spared the torture of separation from my father during his last moments, and I should have been massaging him and he should have died in my arms. But it was not to be. It was my uncle who had this privilege.[86]

The second memory was written almost fifty years earlier. Its author, Lal Behari Day, was a Bengali who had been brought to Calcutta in the 1830s to attend school. He eventually became a convert to Christianity and a proselytizer in its cause. But at the time of his father's death, Day was only a schoolboy, perhaps ten years of age, attending an English-language program and sharing living quarters with his father in a Calcutta hostel. "As I was the son of his old age," Day recalls affectionately, "he loved me excessively, although he was too wise to spoil me with fond affection."[87] Day, for his part, was obedient and attentive. "I do not remember that he ever applied the rod to me, as I was invariable [sic] obedient to him — indeed, I do not recollect that he ever spoke angrily to me."[88] He spent most of his time in his father's company. "As I was not fond of play I was always besides by [sic] father, excepting when I was at school, and both morning and evening I had the inestimable privilege of listening to his advice in all matters relating to the conduct of life."[89]

The father's death occurred suddenly one evening during the December cold season of 1837.

The sick room was crowded with many anxious relatives and friends. Some change took place in the patient which made the physician look grave. The people in the room began to whisper to one another. Two men were sent, as I understood from the conversation which was carried on in a low tone to buy a bier. I was told to leave the room and go upstairs to my bed. I said I would not go, but sit up all night besides my father. I was forced to leave the room and I went away weeping. Repeated watchings for many nights, great heaviness of heart and constant weeping had exhausted my system and I fell soon asleep. Suddenly about midnight or rather towards one in the morning I was roused from sleep. By that time all had been over. I saw my father's lifeless body stretched on the khat. I gave a sriek [sic] and wept bitterly and reproached myself for having been quietly sleeping while my father was struggling with the last enemy. But it was not my doing. I had been actually forced out of the room, though I should have infinitely preferred sitting by him and rubbing his parched lips. . . .[90]

Both memories share certain elements: the dying father, the son absent at the time of death, the sharpness of remorse. Gandhi's father died when his son was sixteen, and that son's account poses the obligations of filial devotion and love against the indulgence of adolescent sexuality. The title of the chapter marks Gandhi's failure: "My Father's Death and My Double Shame." Lal Behari Day, on the other hand, was much younger, certainly preadolescent, at the time of his father's death. His memory, perhaps also the product of a less complex sensibility than Gandhi's, has the ingenuous quality of a younger boy. Nevertheless, though it is exhaustion, not lust, which sends him from his father's side, the obligation to be there and the loss of the moment of intimacy still lives in his memory. Not even his protestations of innocence — "I had been actually forced out of the room" — succeed in undercutting the bitterness of his self-reproach.

Once again, we must turn to students of Indian psychology for the insights into traditional culture which will illumine these autobiographical fragments. Sudhir Kakar records a clinical experiment in which 80 percent of Indian boys shown a picture of a covered figure on a bed identified it as that of a father who was either dead, ill, or recovering from an illness. Those fantasies, he suggests, not only reflect unconscious oedipal jealousies, but a deep anger in these boys against a father "whose paternal presence was a childhood blur."[91] In the years immediately following a boy's separation from the maternal world of early childhood, he suggests, the reassuring presence of a father is crucial. In this period, the father must provide emotional support and an image for his son to identify with as he gradually finds his place within the new surroundings, obligations, and increasing restrictions of the male world. But just when the son most needs his father's support and sustenance, tradition decrees that the father must remain distant and aloof. The family unit must remain paramount in the father's loyalties and custom has contrived to ensure that no single relationship (not husband to wife nor mother to son nor father to son) will arise to challenge the supremacy of the family unit. "The unconscious anger of sons," Kakar writes, "against good but 'intangible' fathers, their individual paternity muffled in the impartiality required by the extended family is one of the major themes in Hindu personality."[92]

The crisis of the Indian boy comes on his entrance into adult (and male) society and his introduction to the rules and regulations that will shape his conduct in adult life. If he successfully negotiates this crisis, throughout his life his behavior will be informed by a sensitive awareness of the symbiosis of family life. The intensity of early nurturing, combined with the sharp discipline of later childhood, will produce a self more "familial" in its orientation.[93] Throughout his life, happiness will lie in a yielding to familial responsibilities, in an identification with family status and prosperity, and in a careful negotiation of family regulations.[94]

In the adult society he enters, all figures of authority, whether gods, politicians, or parents, must be approached with deference. The ideal superior is "one who acts in a nurturing way so that his subordinates either anticipate his wishes or accept them without questioning. . . . high-handed attempts to regulate behavior through threat or punishment such as personal rejection or humiliation, are likely to lead to open defiance or devious evasion on the part of the subordinate."[95] Humble, unquestioning submission on a boy's part will be most likely to induce a helpful response, but it is equally necessary for authority, in its turn, to be sympathetic and attentive.[96] Within this traditional framework, children learn the means and parameters of initiative, protest, and resistance.

In their book *The Modernity of Tradition,* Lloyd and Susanne Rudolph describe Gandhi's technique of *self-suffering* as a tactic that echoes long-standing traditional practices. In the traditional custom of "sitting dharna," the aggrieved party fasted on the doorstep of the one who had wronged him, remaining until either his grievance was settled or he died of hunger. In a similar fashion, the Rudolphs point out, Gandhi when young protested a family decision by refusing to eat his favorite fruit for a season — in later life he would strike out against British policies or the actions of his own countrymen by fasting, even, if necessary, to the point of death.[97]

Autobiographies indicate that similar tactics were used by children to draw attention to needs or to protest decisions of their parents. Withdrawn behavior, "secret" crying, silence, refusing to eat — all were used to signal distress.[98] One man recalls how, after being scolded by a teacher, "I wept more bitterly than the boy who was caned. And went to bed early without taking my dinner that night. For weeks I was ashamed to look at his face. And was not communicative even in class. I answered questions very rarely and when I did answer my words were very few and my eyes were fixed on the ground. My unhappiness made my headmaster unhappy. He took me aside and tried to pacify me."[99]

The most common protest was the refusal to eat, an act which served immediate notice that something was seriously wrong. One writer remembers the day his father was preparing to set out on a trip; good food was being prepared for the journey. "I got scent of this trip," the author recalls, "and went on a hunger strike. When mother discovered what all the fuss was about, she persuaded father to take me also with him!"[100] In an account of a boyhood trip to Calcutta, one hunger strike succeeded in overcoming another. The author was traveling by boat from his village, and the trip involved stops along the way to prepare food on the banks of the river. But the boy's fear of tigers, heightened by the teasing of the boatmen, made him refuse to go ashore for meals.

> I protested against the practice but no one listened to me. In the night I refused to take my meal and went to bed.[101]

This protest immediately precipitated a second.

> When almost all others had taken their meals, Mr. Kundar [his guardian] roused me and said that if I fasted, he also would do so. This compelled me to go to the riverside and sit for a meal.[102]

A stronger form of protest was to leave home. According to one study of Indian families in Mysore, this is a frequent if extreme means of displaying unhappiness with a family situation.[103] Accounts of running away appear mostly in Bengali autobiographies, but one Punjabi author Bhagat Singh, does recall his efforts to secure better treatment for himself at home. "My childhood was manhood practically," he begins, in explanation. He was expected to do both cooking and household chores in his family. "When I refused to do my share of the work I was treated unkindly by both of my parents. The result was my open revolt and when I saw that nobody cared to find out why I was becoming peevish, I attempted twice to run away from the house of my parents to search for any work that might fall my lot and thus escape from home tyranny. On both of these occasions, I was caught and brought back... Thenceforward I had greater freedom...."[104]

As significant as the behavior is the response it evokes in elders. Parents will most often respond to the self-suffering of offspring with immediate sympathy and aid. Although family relations are hierarchical in their structure, as Sudhir Kakar notes, the "*mode* of the relationship is characterized by an almost maternal nurturing on the part of the superior, by filial respect and compliance on the part of the subordinate and by a mutual sense of high personal attachment."[105] The cultural emphasis on self-control and the containment of grievances leads to nonverbal protests and legitimates self-inflicted suffering as a way to call attention to the unhappy conditions of one's life. Bhagat Singh's "open revolt" was not a verbal complaint at all, but first a social and then a physical withdrawal from family life.

Tactics learned in childhood carried over easily into adult life. Gandhi's political strategy was only the most well-known example of a widespread pattern of adult behavior. In its most extreme form, of course, self-suffering led to suicide. Only two days before the wedding of his son, Morarji Desai's father killed himself by jumping into the family well.[106] The family, Desai insists, had no idea of the motive for his act, yet his father, a quiet and "uncomplaining" man had been in a state of melancholia for more than a year. His death illustrates the need for family members to react swiftly and sympathetically to early signs of distress.

The suicides most frequently mentioned in autobiographies, however, are those of women, particularly daughters and sisters. The death almost always occurs in the in-laws' village and is invariably ascribed to neglect or ill-treatment of the girl by her husband's family. Under the best of circumstances, the first years of a girl's marriage were a time of terrible stress and tension. She was isolated in her husband's family; her status was low and the work required of her — at least before the birth of her first child — was often the hardest and least pleasant. She was expected to cover her face before her elder in-laws and avoid speaking directly either to them, or, in their presence, to her own husband. As one woman remembers, solicitude for the difficulties of her position caused well-meaning in-laws to urge food on her in huge quantities and insist on its consumption.[107] In less happy circumstances, the usual signs of distress — silence, refusing to eat, and sitting by one's self — might be carelessly interpreted as normal behavior for a young bride. Suicide, for girls whose marriage conditions appeared hopeless, could be both the first and the last overt avenue of protest.

Throughout the subcontinent, departures from one's parents' house were a common form of protest, but nowhere were they as willingly embarked on or as thoroughly enjoyed as in Bengal. Bengalis engaged in the publication of their grievances to an extent unheard of in other regions. In Bombay, for instance, the first boys to be English-educated broke caste customs secretly in an organization which was hurriedly disbanded when its existence was discovered.[108] In Bengal protest was less hesitant. A much repeated although perhaps apocryphal story described rebellious students throwing meat into the courtyard of a local Brahmin.[109] The story captures the style of Westernization in that province. Widow remarriages were publically and unrepentantly celebrated in Bengal, and Bengali life histories frequently record how open defiance of orthodoxy led to dramatic breaks with families and the public departure of sons from their parents' homes. While initial contacts with Western culture precipitated conflicts and confusion in all areas of the subcontinent, the form these conflicts took in Bengal was that province's own. An older regional style of protest made its reappearance in the context of nineteenth-century events. The rebellions of Young Bengal, which in the West would be naturally interpreted as the product of adolescent energies, were actually a Bengali variation of the use of self-suffering as a means of protest.

Indeed, this same pattern appears in Bengali autobiographies where Westernization is by no means the issue. Debendranath Tagore (the father of the famous poet Rabindranath) had a younger brother greatly in debt. "Grieved and offended" over his elder brother's refusal to pay his debts, the younger boy, Tagore recalls, "left our house in a huff" and went to stay with an uncle.[110] Even after Tagore relented and agreed to pay some of the bills, the brother would not return. "I too had better leave home," the elder wrote, sensitive to the public rebuke implicit in his brother's behavior, "and never come back."[111] The second son-in-law of Khetter Chunder Ghose "was in the habit of frequently leaving his father's house upon some mis-understanding or other" and living under his mother-in-law's protection in their house in Hogulcorrea.[112] Even on her death bed, Ghose's wife continued to worry and "as if to exculpate herself from all blame in the matter exclaimed, 'Moorari's father Russick Lall Bose is wrong in blaming me as the cause of estrangement between him and his rebellious son.'"[113]

Ghose himself in his younger days used this same tactic to protest the excesses of his employer. He had worked as a clerk and writer in a Calcutta-based British firm, a job he detested but was unable to leave because of pressure from his father.[114] The source of his misery was the bad temper of his employer, Mr. MacKeay.

> Notwithstanding the care which my employer took to see that my nervous temper might not make my stay in his office troublesome to me, that gentleman's natural irritability of disposition sometimes burst out in expressions that did not at all make me in love with my service in his office. And this would compel me sometimes to resign my post, which I considered as very irksome. He was of course always kind enough to send me his head Baboo to pacify me and thus reinstate me in my post.[115]

The bitterness which often colors memories of conflicts between fathers and sons is lost in the genuine sorrow which suffuses one Bengali's memory of his opposition to the wishes of an uncle. The author, having joined the terrorist movement, had been sent to Benares. His uncle was tremendously upset — "He loved me like his own son" — and traveled north to bring him home. The sadness of their meeting reveals the greater warmth and intimacy possible between nephews and uncles. The uncle argued and objected; the nephew kept silent. "His objections were really very genuine. I had no answer to offer."[116] But he could not agree to return. When the uncle had to leave, he gave the boy money for a ticket but the money was returned. "He was enraged. I accompanied them [uncle and cousin] from Benares station to Kashi station and got down there, bidding them goodbye, silently touching his feet."[117]

Regional differences in styles of protest are paralleled by differences in other family matters. Bengalis more than others comment on a mother's failure to meet children's expectations and couple affectionate praise of a father with oblique but biting criticism. Most often it is Bengali autobiographers who record public departures from parental auspices or family, caste, school, or office quarrels. Within the nationalist movement, Bengalis, more than other Indians, were openly critical of the Gandhian style of protest and Gandhi's personal power and influence; and throughout the British Raj, Bengalis, more than Indians from other areas, seemed to provoke the most intense fury among British officials.

In explaining their anger, the English turned often to words like "weak," "timid," and "effeminate." But the pattern of behavior revealed in autobiographical memories suggests otherwise. It was not, one suspects, any excessive pliability on the part of the Bengalis which irritated the British, but on the contrary, their relatively more aggressive manner of opposing British authority. The Bengali version of self-suffering — in both children and adults — was by a considerable degree more open than that of other regions. Bengalis allowed themselves a (relatively) freer expression of anger towards those in authority. Gandhi's dominance in the nationalist movement, for instance, was not unquestioned by Indians from other areas; they also were sometimes unhappy with aspects of his rule.[119] But in other areas the Mahatma's passive resistance spoke to patterns of behavior rooted deep in childhood. The fundamental "rightness" of his method, that is, the degree to which it echoed older habits and beliefs, silenced more critical perceptions of his power. Discontinuities in regional styles of protest left Bengalis free to disassociate themselves from the Gandhian movement, and allowed them to publicize their criticisms of both the leader and his methods.

*   *   *

Childhood, then, shapes the patterns of adult life, placing them almost beyond conscious reach and control. Autobiographical memories of childhood reveal the rich world of traditions that shaped the psychic structures of the Indian child; through them we can recapture an awareness of the earliest influences and understand the ways in which early structures shaped later lives. The internal dynamics of Indian family life balanced the restrictions of orthodoxy and the remoteness of a father against the early adoration and indulgence of a mother, even adding, on occasion, the compensatory warmth and affection of an uncle. Children learned to negotiate this world, to tune themselves to the nuances of familial relationships, to bend to the ubiquitous hierarchies of authority. In adult life, in worlds beyond the joint family, older patterns of behavior would persist and the modalities of relations between Indians and the English, indeed between Westernized Indians themselves, would be shaped by childhood training. The world within which children first lived and grew marked out the boundaries of their lives. As they grew older they would leave their homes, moving out into the schools and occupations of the British Raj, but keeping with them always the boundaries of their earliest days.

CHAPTER

2

Schooldays

SCHOOLBOYS WHO ENTERED the English-language educational system of the Raj were quick to respond to its invitation to acculturate. The middle and late years of the nineteenth century witnessed the formation of scores of associations and student groups — many of which hoped to remodel India and Hinduism in the newly discovered image of the West. Newspapers, journals, and magazines proliferated in the great administrative centers of Calcutta, Bombay and Madras. In Calcutta, students were reported to have thrown meat into the courtyard of a Brahmin; in Bombay young men of different castes joined together in secret to break caste restrictions. In north India a great reform movement began, the Arya Samaj, perhaps the most indigenous in vocabulary and style of all the nineteenth-century reformist groups.

"The Life of the Educated Native: What It Should Be" — this was the title of a lecture published in Calcutta in the 1870s. It posed a question to which many were seeking the answer. Much of the writing by Western-educated Indians in this period repeated the themes of the history textbooks. Hinduism had decayed from an earlier and vital past; it had become caste-ridden and unegalitarian. Indians had grown weak and intolerant, idolatrous and superstitious. A "New Dispensation" was needed: a reform of caste, a program of physical and political nation building to be taken up under the tutelage of the British. *Rationalism* and *Enlightenment* were words with magical connotations, and when students spoke them, their enthusiasm underlined the hope of recapturing these values in a renaissance of the ancient Aryan past.

For the present, the way to that past clearly led through the adaptation of English customs. The physical symbol of acculturation was most often the Western suit, just as its educational equivalent was the proper intonation of an English accent. In the 1880s, a Bombay student caused his teachers worry; his inaccurate accent was a sign that his education had been incomplete.[1] Dress was equally a matter for concern and self-consciousness. "I started on this trip in pure Indian costume," one author wrote of a journey to Europe in 1911, "though the eyes kept gazing on my Indian uniform I managed to pass through in full dress to London via Paris. In London, however, I made a sudden change to European dress. I bought everything readymade in all a hurry."[2]

Photographs from these years attempt to present acculturation as an accomplished fact. Where the status and education of a subject had already placed him in the higher echelons of British power, a photographer might even conspire to complete his Anglicization. One author, being photographed for the Indian Civil Service (the elite administrative corps or the Raj), was surprised to find that he had turned out fairer than the Anglo-Indian being photographed with him — "though he was very fair and I chocolate black." "Sir," was the explanation, "you are a sub-collector, whereas he was only a deputy collector. Should you not be made whiter than he?"[3]

For a student to become a *sahib* was a project which united dress, language, education, and employment. In this effort, families at least initially, were in full and enthusiastic support. From their point of view, the primary goal was economic; better employment was open to those who carried the credentials of the acculturated. Along the way, however, families might add older signs of status to the "Western" ambitions of their sons. The non-Brahmin grandson of a wealthy Bombay advocate, for instance, was urged by his grandfather to study Sanskrit in college.

> The teacher in charge of Sanskrit studies in my class was a conservative Brahmin ... and my insistence on offering Sanskrit in spite of his declared wishes and pressures made him very angry.[4]

As punishment for his temerity, the boy stood in the hallway for a week.

For Brahmin students, in contrast, it was the study of Latin that carried higher social prestige. Surendranath Banerjea studied Latin during his Calcutta school days.[5] On the west coast of India, Dhonde Karve urged his cousin to take up Latin in school, rather than the Sanskrit courses that the boy's more traditional father would have preferred.

But the British always defined acculturation in terms more elusive than the acquisition of proper clothing, accent, or the classical language of the West. "Personally," wrote A.C. Miller in *Seven Letters to Indian Schoolboys,* "I should far rather hear that one of my boys had done some noble action than that he had won the best scholarship in India. . . . A boy's character is far more important than cleverness at work."[6] On the uncertainties of deportment and character, then, one's endeavor might easily founder. But which actions were sufficiently noble to render one fully Anglicized? This was always the open question. Macaulay, after all, had said that Indians could become English in thought, culture, and feeling. It was in search of the final elements of that transformation that the newly

Western-educated founded newspapers, edited magazines, and joined the innumerable associations and speaking-clubs which proliferated throughout the nineteenth century. "I produced an essay on the coconut tree," wrote one young South Indian schoolboy in 1839, "which I am happy to say underwent little or no criticism."[7] Other topics in his club, the Native Improvement Society of Bombay, were more controversial. The same student reported on a debate that resolved whether "Alexander or Caesar was the greater person" and (in a more private setting) on a discussion of female education in which "almost all gave their opinions in favor of education and supported their arguments very satisfactorily."[8]

An educational experience that covered such a great range of topics with equal enthusiasm for all was, of necessity, less focused on substance than on style. Students read, discussed, and debated the subjects that they and their teachers imagined were at that moment being similarly considered by their English counterparts. The effort to transmit an entire cultural gestalt was fundamental to the English-language schools, and it was just this ability that was used in the 1880s to argue for the exclusive use of European teachers.[9] While the missionaries who put forth this view doubtless had other motives in espousing it, it was, nonetheless, true that the teacher in the Western schools of the Raj was the key transmitter of a foreign cultural style. Similarly, his students were attempting to master not so much a curriculum as an entire way of life.

The establishment of Western education in nineteenth century India had not been a uniform process. Some provinces, such as Bengal, took the lead early and made English education widely available at all levels, primary through college. In the *mofussil,* on the other hand, in the United Provinces or the Central Provinces, for instance, even by mid-century there were few schools in existence at the college level. This unevenness was not entirely the result of government manipulation. The early availability of English programs in the capital cities of the early Raj did, of course, reflect the greater administrative needs for skilled English writers in those cities; but also, in order to establish a program of English education, one needed to convince Indian parents and families that such education would be beneficial. By mid-century, while officials in Bengal worried aloud that too many young Indians were being attracted to Western education, their counterparts in more outlying areas continued to construct stipend programs and low fee structures to entice local families into newly established educational institutions.

Depending on where one lived, then, one could acquire an English education with greater or lesser ease. In the larger capitals, a Western education might demand no more than gaining admission into a sequence of schools, paying the requisite fees, and passing the stipulated examinations. In the *mofussil,* however, or even in the capitals of more "backward" provinces, the acquisition of a knowledge of English could require considerable effort and ingenuity. Families had to be ready to shuttle children from village to town to city as the resources of local or provincial schools were exhausted; they needed the ability to arrange housing and food, sometimes in unfamiliar territory, and the willingness to risk a child's conversion to Christianity by enrolling him in the missionary school, that might often be the only available source of Western education.

The autobiographies indicate that families willing to make this effort were ones in which traditions of literacy were already well established. "My father," one man remembers, "a fairly educated person (well versed in Persian) knew the usefulness of the requirements of education fairly well."[10] Most authors had fathers literate in at least one language, and although none of these authors were Muslim, Urdu and Persian are the languages most commonly mentioned; Sanskrit is a somewhat rare and infrequent third. Adaptability and a willingness to bend to political realities predated the coming of the British in India. Families that, under Muslim rule, had tutored sons in the official language of the court, now turned their children's efforts toward the study of the language of the nineteenth-century rulers. The history of one family's cultural adaptation appears in almost archaeological layerings in an autobiographer's memory of the early ceremony which inaugurated his educational career. The ceremony began, the author remembers,

> with the family priest chanting Sanskrit *Slokas* which of course nobody understood in those days except perhaps a few pundits present on the occasion. I am speaking of nearly seventy years from now when the study of Sanskrit in Bihar, even amongst the literary classes to which my family belonged had fallen into complete decadence.... Accordingly, after the Muslim *Maulvi* had caught hold of my hand and made me write out on a slate the first few letters of the Perso Arabic alphabet (in which Urdu is usually written) the senior most of the Pandits made me similarly write out the first few letters of the deonagri [sic] alphabet....[11]

Not until the next day, however, was the ceremony concluded. At that time, the writer recalls, "the teacher of English was called to make me go through the similar process of writing the Roman alphabet [as] I had been made to do previously in the case of the Urdu and Hindi scripts."[12]

Throughout the nineteenth century, the conviction grew steadily stronger among literate families that English education was essential to future prosperity and status. As early as the 1830s, a boy of thirteen had been sent to study in a mission school at Navacol; subsequently his father accompanied him on a much longer journey, from the tip of South India to the city of Bombay, in order to enroll the boy in Elphinstone school, one of the earliest English-language schools on the subcontinent.[13] By the end of the century, it was common to pool family resources to enable at least one son to acquire an English education. A survey of the caste connections of those attending Fergusson College in Poona during the late years of the century shows how both caste and family connections were mobilized to provide support and living arrangements for students coming into the city from the *mofussil*.[14] One man, a boy when his father died in 1894, remembers being returned to school by his elder brother. The father had said "more than once on his death bed that we should continue our English education even if we should go begging in the streets for our bread."[15]

The older languages — Persian, Urdu, or Sanskrit — had been studied with tutors brought into the village or home. A short chapter of Rajendra Prasad's autobiography details the exploits and pomposities of the *Maulvi Sahibs*, Muslim tutors, hired by his family in his boyhood.[16] Hoodwinked by the children whenever possible, often the butt of family elders' jokes or ridicule, these men were a variety of servant. Village teachers could inspire awe in their pupils — Lal Behari Day lived in terror of the man who ran his village *pathsala* and "could never look upon him without trembling."[17] But whether dreaded or teased, tutors were under the supervision and control of family and village elders. When Debendranath Tagore's Sanskrit tutor in Calcutta began (as the father thought) to fill his pupil's head with religious ideas inappropriate to the eldest son of a prosperous merchant, the father expressed his disapproval. Tutor and pupil continued their lessons — but only in secret.[18]

English education, on the other hand, demanded new patterns of behavior and took place largely outside the village domain. Except among the extremely wealthy, private tutoring could not compete with the more systematic education of the institutions of the Raj. One author's father could not afford to send his sons away to school and attempted to import an English-language teacher after the older fashion of education. His one ambition, the son writes of the father, "was to teach us English."[19] A "Middle-Passed gentleman, knowledgeable in both Urdu and English" was finally located and employed, but remained only fourteen months before leaving for "more money" elsewhere. Two years of searching produced a second tutor, less qualified but with a "practical" knowledge of English. He remained only a year and a half. "Here is an end," the author concludes, "to my so-called study."[20]

In the early years of the nineteenth century, the decision to educate a son in English could mean a long and arduous journey to an unknown part of the country. It took Lal Behari Day five days to travel by foot and boat from his village in west Bengal to the city of Calcutta.[21] Once there, however, Day was fortunate to be able to live under his father's protection while attending school. For other boys, even much later in the century, the effort to learn English might mean a long journey and residence in lodgings in the provincial town or city that had the needed programs and institutions. Fortunate boys lodged with brothers or cousins in local hostels, or stayed in the homes of relatives, caste fellows, or guardians. Living arrangements were frequently disrupted. A young Bengali living in Sylhet in a house belonging to a fellow villager was called home when his uncle was accused of murdering the house's owner.[22] Students shifted from lodging to lodging, town to town, as relatives or guardians came and went, as financial situations altered, or as they advanced through grade levels and outstripped the resources of the local school. In 1896 one Punjabi youth, age seven, was first enrolled in a school in Nurpur. He remained there six years; then his father sent him, first briefly to an Arya Samaj school at Dharamsala, and then, shortly after, to the District Board High School at Palampur. In 1905 he was shifted once again, this time to the Central Model School in Lahore.[23] There, at least, he could remain. For by the 1900s, Lahore was the home of Punjab University and the center of numerous educational institutions. He attended Government College through a bachelor's degree and went on to law school in the same city.

Throughout this period we see relatively young children sent off to attend schools that were, frequently, far from home. Departures, of course, were moments of pathos; mothers, in particular, could be relied on to become thoroughly distraught. The children, however, (as they recall these scenes years later) seem strangely undisturbed, and often excited and happy about the impending exile. Of course, children were rarely, if ever, sent away to school alone. As in the case of Rajendra Prasad, two brothers, one older and more responsible, might take lodgings together, the younger attending lower school, as Prasad did in Patna, while the elder enrolled in a college. With the graduation of the elder Prasad, however, the entire household was broken up, the elder boy departing for medical college in Calcutta, and the younger returning home to his village school.[24]

Home traditionally was always more than just the residence of one's parents and perhaps this made the peripathetic life-style of students less disturbing. Nirad Chaudhuri remembers three places he called, with slightly altering connotations, "home":[25] his ancestral home, the village of his father's family; his mother's village, the place of his maternal relatives; and Kishorganj, the town where the father worked and the family actually lived. As a child, Chaudhuri recalls, he spent considerable time in all three places.

Nor, within a traditional context, did children necessarily remain with their own parents during most of their childhood. They might stay for a time with grandparents or favorite relatives in the home village of either their father or mother. For that matter, during the nineteenth and twentieth centuries, parents, particularly fathers, by no means always lived at home. In numerous Western-educated families, the exigencies of employment as a government official or teacher separated the father from his family, and allowed his return only when vacations and holidays made the journey possible. One author remembers with delight his father's departure for a post in a distant village. He begged to be allowed to go along and was. They lived together, apart from the mother and the rest of the family, for two years.[26] Once a child had reached school age and passed beyond the years of his closest ties with his mother, it was not necessarily assumed that his biological parents would be the only people with whom he lived. One Indian Civil Service official, whose job involved frequent transfers, debated sending his children to boarding school to "stabilize" their education. The only argument came from an outsider, a neighbor "missionary lady" who made the rather Western point that children should not be sent away from home at a tender age as that "would deprive them of the benefits of the parents' society and guidance."[27]

Children may have enjoyed educational sojourns in part because they were pleased to see themselves as the protectors and enhancers of their family's future well-being. Both they and their relatives would naturally assume that much of that future prosperity would depend on successfully completing their schooling and securing prestigious and profitable employment afterward. Children away from home could also feel compensated for the separation by the close attachment they might form with the male elder who might become their new guardian and by some additional measure of freedom. When Pradip Bose went to London as a student (although certainly no longer a child), he became aware of a wonderful newfound privacy. "Nobody interfered with my life; nobody offered advice; nobody worried about me; nobody asked me awkward questions. I had never felt so free in my life."[28] Planning to stay one year, he remained for three. The ability to stay away and apart from one's family for long periods of time was not unusual among Indian schoolboys of all ages.

But if the peripatetic demands of the new education were not disruptive, other qualities were. The independence of the British educational system from village life demanded a renegotiation of relationships among all parties in the system — students, families, teachers, and even the schools themselves. Centralization of examinations, government inspections, and grants-in-aid isolated schools from the control or influence of village families. There were, of course, exceptions; and the smaller the village, the greater the influence of local people. Primary and even secondary teachers commanded little pay and less status in the institutions of the Raj. It was common practice to hire a child's teacher for private tutoring, with, perhaps, an expected quid pro quo at the examination time.

Powerful families within a village still maintained something of their former stature vis-a-vis local teachers, but their influence was on the wane. Autobiographical fragments imply that on occasion the transfers which moved boys from school to school or district to district were a search for a more congenial educational environment. It was not uncommon to move a boy, if, for instance, he was doing badly in his academic work. One author, whose progress in school was not good, recalls being "literally externed to Mymensingh, where I was admitted in the City Collegiate School."[29] When Rajendra Prasad faced possible failure in the local school examinations, his brother advised the family to transfer him.[30] Another writer remembers his father's reaction to poor academic performance: "My father ... worried about my proper studies. That is why after about two years I had to leave Daulatkhan and come to Commilla."[31] When students complained about teachers who disliked and abused them, parents were powerless to interfere. A Bihari boy who had chosen to study Sanskrit (for "patriotic reasons," he maintains) became a target for the *pandit's* malicious humour. "He would often say 'Why do you not join the Persian class instead of trying to learn Sanskrit which your forefathers never learned.'"[32] The solution, in this and similar cases, was to transfer the child from the class, or even from the school. Neither village influence nor family status in *mofussil* areas were sufficient to protect a child in school or to guarantee his educational success.

A second result of the new educational system were the cultural storms that broke, again and again throughout the nineteenth century, over students and their families. Conflict between the authority of the school and that of the family could burst into the open, with the child uneasily caught in the middle. When one of the teachers in Rajendra Prasad's school in Patna wished to give him a double promotion, Prasad's elder brother, thinking it unwise, opposed the idea. "Do you understand the problem better than myself?" asked the principal, and the promotion was given. Prasad was initially proud of his success and glad of the honor. But later, transferred to another school and deprived of the protection and support of this teacher, he began to worry that "my brother's views on my double promotion were sounder than those of the headmaster."[33]

Teachers in the Western schools, particularly those from abroad, were unlikely to be concerned with their pupils' maintenance of traditional forms of behavior and propriety — or even to look upon these forms with much favor. The Hunter Commission, sent out in the 1880s to investigate the state of education in British India, reported that in Bengal the "shyness" of native boys was "often mistaken for sullenness or incivility." British teachers may have deliberately been encouraging what they saw as more forthright behavior, for in Madras parents complained to the commission that education tended to make students disrespectful towards their families.[34] The commission's response was a herald of things to come. It would certainly be the duty of teachers to "check any exhibition of this spirit," they agreed, but "they should not encourage any return to the cringing servility which sometimes characterized the old school."[35]

In opposing family wishes, teachers could rely on a certain degree of natural influence over their pupils. Traditionally barred from openly affectionate relations with their fathers, Indian boys often turned for support and intimacy to other male figures in their lives. Schoolteachers slid easily into a quasi-avuncular role, nurturing, protecting, and playing confidant to their charges. To have been the *dux* of the class, the favorite of one's teacher, is a memory almost as frequently claimed by autobiographers as that of being their mother's special favorite. Authors recall with affection teachers who lent money, provided books, and demonstrated concern for their welfare. The headmaster of the Oriental Seminary in Calcutta used to walk his pupil Khetter Chunder Ghose home every evening after classes, standing outside the house until the boy, who was morbidly afraid of ghosts, was safely inside.[36] The British supervisor who replaced the famous Alexander Duff at the missionary school attended by Lal Behari Day took a special interest in the boy from the time Day insisted on a double promotion. "Sir," Day pleaded on the occasion of the supervisor's visit to his class, "please examine me and if you don't find me fit, don't promote me." Dr. Ewart, he continues,

> then examined me in the books of the fifth class and finding the result satisfactory he put me at once into that class and kind and fatherly man that he was he began to take such an interest in me that he used now and then to come into the class purposely to see how I was doing and I shall never forget the divine smile with which he looked at me one day when he saw me sitting near the top of my class.[37]

Nor, Day concludes, "was this a mere fancy of mine, for Dr. Ewart later described to me his feelings on this occasion in after years when my relations with him became more intimate."

The enormous attraction students often felt for teachers was analogous to the love one traditionally would have for a *guru*. The *guru* ("teacher") was a special religious mentor with whom one had a unique and exclusive relationship, an authority figure who also gave open encouragement and support. Unlike his modern counterpart, a *guru* could be relied on to encourage his pupil's development in directions likely to agree with traditional social and family values. Subhas Bose attached himself with great fervour to a visiting *sannyasi* during his most rebellious adolescent years. The holy man's teachings urged that each day begin with a *pronam* ("the touching of the feet of the superior") to both mother and father. Bose dutifully carried out the letter, if not the spirit, of the instructions.

> With a supreme effort of will I mastered myself and marched straight to my father in the morning. I made obeisance as instructed by my preceptor. I can still recall the scene — how my father was taken aback. He asked me what was the matter, but without uttering a word I marched back after doing my duty.[38]

The particular vulnerability of Indian boys to warmth and attention from a figure in authority was likely to meet in their teachers a corresponding devotion and concern. Where the teachers were missionaries, students might be fortified against their own susceptibilities by a certain cynicism about motives and intentions. But where the message that the teachers brought was not conversion to Christianity but assimilation to Western ideas and values, no skepticism undercut the affection. Hence, relations between pupil and master often took a more intense and personal turn. Such was certainly the case with Henry Derozio, a teacher in one of the earliest English-language schools in Calcutta. Derozio, who was himself of mixed racial background, became an anathema to the orthodox of Calcutta society as a result of his supposed ability to turn students against caste, religion, and family. In the end he paid for his reputation with his job. In his efforts to acquit himself of one of numerous charges against him, he wrote a letter to his school supervisor, outlining his version of the rebellion which had been laid to him.

> About two or three months ago [he wrote] D. Mukherjee informed me that his father's treatment of him had become insupportable and his only chance of escaping it was to leave his father's house. Although I was aware of the truth of what he said I dissuaded him from taking such a course telling him that much should be endured from a parent and that the world would not justify his conduct if he left his home without being actually turned out of it. He took my advice although I regret to say only for a short time. A few weeks after he left his father's house and to my great surprise engaged one other in my neighborhood. After he had completed his arrangements with his landlord, he informed me for the first time of what he had done. When I asked him why he had not consulted me before he took such a step, he replied, "Because I knew you would have prevented it."[39]

The greatest fear of parents, particularly in the early years of the nineteenth century, was that their children would convert to Christianity. Mission schools were therefore regarded as the most dangerous. Lal Behari Day recalls that he was turned away from the prestigious Hare School because of his previous attendance at a missionary institution. "All

Mr. Duff's pupils are half Christian," he reports Hare saying to him, "...you will spoil my boys."[40] Parental fears were one reason for the growth and success of a number of Indian-supported private colleges in these years. If economic realities dictated enrolling children in English-language schools, then parents wanted institutions where, they hoped, their boys would learn just enough of the Western curricula to ensure economic success but not enough to cause a cataclysmic transformation of their ideas and beliefs. By mid-century, parents had learned that, in addition to Christian conversion, they had a second foe. They would do well to be equally worried about cultural conversion, the violent attraction to Western ideas and ways which sometimes seized students in the course of their education and turned them against the traditions and orthodoxies of their families.

It was true that the particular danger (or strength, depending on one's point of view) of the educational system lay in this attraction. The combination of the textbooks' invitation to acculturate and the special attentions of a teacher led students into a new identification with the substance of their education. Where they wished to secure their new Western identities through word or deed, the result was a sharp escalation in family conflict, public rebellion, and private evasion. Bengali schoolboys who were the first in their families to become Western-educated repeatedly left home in those years, often quarreling with parents or elders over matters of traditional practice and custom. Surendranath Banerjea's father ran away from his own father over a matter of orthodox behavior, and other life histories record similar disruptions.[41] One boy's family reportedly chained him within the house to prevent his leaving home.

The resistance of Young Bengal to orthodox customs had become legendary in India by the end of the nineteenth century. But outside Bengal, first-generation students expressed identifications with modern ideas and values through more muted behavior. In Kerala, the traditional Nair parents of K.P. Menon enrolled him in a Christian English-language school. Along with the English language, Menon learned several new ideas about the evils of superstition and idolatry. "I spoke vehemently," he recalls, "at the Rising Star Literary Association regarding the absurdity of such beliefs."[42] Unfortunately, the meeting was being held on the veranda of the family home.

> My father and mother overheard my speech with horror.... My father waited for the members of the society to depart and gave me a sound scolding. That was the end of my youthful crusade against superstitions. Thereafter I was content to follow them when it was convenient for me to do so, even though I did not believe in them.[43]

In other regions students tried to ameliorate the demands of older traditions and newer principles. Unorthodox beliefs were likely to be espoused in secret — or, if forced into the open, to be accompanied by mild action and a self-abnegating meekness. When Dhonde Karve was a student and teacher living in Bombay, he and his friend Mr. Joshi were both "intellectually and emotionally" in favor of widow remarriage.[44] But when his first wife was living and "the question of openly dining with people who had married widows turned up," Karve recalls, "I used to tell Mr. Joshi that I would not go in for it, because it would not appreciably help the cause of widow marriage, while it would do great harm to the good work that I was doing in [my home village of] Murud."[45] Karve eventually found himself married to a former widow and his behavior towards orthodox people was significant:

> I tried to disarm opposition by conciliatory words and deeds.... Whenever I visited my friends and relations, I offered to wash my dish and clean the place after my meals. And often actually did so.

"These ways of mine," he believes, "had a beneficial effect."[46]

If the educational system precipitated conflicts between students and their families, it also profoundly restructured the lives of the students. A boy's growth within a traditional village environment, as Carstairs suggested in looking at a Rajasthani village, was marked by two major breaks.[47] The first separated him from the world of infancy and indulgence and subjected him to the rigors of family and caste regulations. Later his status would shift again, not on the occasion of his marriage (which did not much alter his position within the extended family), but at the birth of his first child. This second change was less abrupt than the first, resulting mostly in increased prestige within the family hierarchy, but it altered his position nonetheless. Although the birth of a son did remain an event of sufficient importance to be deliberately noted in autobiographies, its significance had been largely subsumed by other, more modern, events. By the age of sixteen or even earlier, most autobiographers were no longer immersed in the society of their village homes. They had come under the influence of a different pattern of life — one which often required attendance at schools far from home, concentration on mastering curricula and passing examinations, and concern about winning suitable employment after graduation. Especially for those whose education continued beyond the Matriculation (college entrance) Examination (and that includes the majority of these authors) the new concerns became the focus of their lives.

"I met my fate," writes one author referring to his marriage, "after finishing my educational career."[48] Western criticism of early marriages in India had circulated almost from the arrival of the British. By the late nineteenth century, families were more and more frequently coming to agree, in practice if not in theory, with the foreign views. In his family, this author asserts, "we never marry in the midst of scholastic study."[49] Indeed, the demands of education and family fears of the potentially weakening effects of both sex and study combined to make it increasingly difficult to decide when to arrange the marriage of a son. If the boy was to be sent abroad for study, it was best to see him safely married before he left home. But if he was to remain at home and continue his education, it was feared that the presence of a young wife would threaten his health and distract his attention.

Indigenous Indian beliefs long associated celibacy with power, sexual activity with the depletion of a man's strength and vigor. A newer conviction held that prolonged intellectual activity — study, office work, and reading — could prove similarly exhausting. "Excessive preoccupation with study during the summer holidays," one man remembers, "told on my health and brain and I was advised complete rest and cessation of study."[50] Uncontrolled or unrationed, intense mental effort might bring on a serious illness. Therefore, if, during adolescence, the demands of marriage were combined with those of education, a boy's health could be in danger. Gandhi is only the most famous autobiographer to make this connection; he believed that his early marriage to Kasturbai competed with and ultimately damaged the energy and attention he could devote to his studies.[51] Another man, remembering his reluctance to marry even when he was eighteen, said he had feared that marriage would disrupt or possibly terminate his educational career. Indeed, his elder brother, he noted, had been totally given over to family life after an early marriage.[52] By the late nineteenth century young men themselves were buttressing a traditional ambivalence to marriage with these newer arguments. The age of marriage among the Western-educated probably rose in direct proportion to the seriousness of family ambitions for a son.

Western education did not only create new problems for families looking towards their sons' future; it also added an entire constellation of new fears and tensions to the lives of students. Increasingly throughout this period, school succeeded in dividing the lives of schoolboys into segments marked out by major degree examinations. From primary school through college and beyond, one's record accumulated. Passing the examinations was important, but never enough. The degree of success achieved, how high one had ranked among other students (first class, second class, etc.) might later become a major determinant of one's life and success. Each examination passed with distinction moved one's ultimate goal of prestige and power within the Indian ranks of the Raj a little nearer. Success in this, of course, was always more than an individual matter. The future prosperity and status of one's entire family was at stake.

While caste and economic wealth continued to be important determinants of family position, by the middle years of the nineteenth century, as one Parsi writer noted, even the Seths, the highly prosperous merchants of Bombay, were becoming aware that these alone no longer guaranteed the security of a family. Education was also becoming a necessity.[53] Only after he had passed the Indian Civil Service examination in London and gained entrance to the top administration of the country, did R.C. Dutt write home to his people that his career was set for life.[54]

As experience with the importance of examinations grew, students took ever more drastic measures to ensure their success. Cribs and epitomes (outlines) of assigned texts proliferated; stories of marathon study sessions began to circulate. Students talked of studying through the night, walking back and forth while reading to keep themselves awake.[55] As exams approached, fear and panic would start to spread. Suddenly, just fifteen days before a test, one student recalls, he fell into a terror. "Somehow or other I felt I did not know anything. I did not read a word within the last ten days. Whole days would pass in uneasiness or fright...."[56] Before his B.A. examination Nirad Chaudhuri ran up and down a ladder hoping he would fall, break something, and escape the ordeal.[57] Others took refuge in ritualistic preparations. One boy bought himself an entire set of new clothing to wear for his exams.[58] Another, after one failure, became convinced that he would pass only those examinations for which his father had paid the fees.[59]

Perhaps caste structures and definitions had partially eliminated the concept of occupational failure from the traditional mental vocabulary of Indians. For students did not always immediately grasp the potential for failure which lay within the British school system. For the first two years of college, Morarji Desai was completely unworried about examinations.[60] Impervious to the panic of others, he thought their fears, particularly those of a Maharastrian friend, unnecessary and irrational. Then, in one paper in his intermediate examinations, he made a mistake, and suddenly, faced with the prospect of failure, he understood in an instant all he could lose. Subsequent exams found him in a state of total apprehension, which easily equaled, if it did not surpass, that of his friend.

In another part of the country, a failure in the Matriculation Examination precipitated a partial breakdown in a young South Indian Christian:

> *I* went home after the examinations were over and *My* behaviour appeared very queer to all. *I* was weeping and wailing now and then....
> *I* sought solitude so as to mourn *My* failure and avoided the roads and pathways. *I* was not communicative but very often shouted: "The Fellow Who Failed in Matric."[61]

Examination failures threatened more than the economic aspirations of students. They struck at the emerging sense among the Western-educated of who they were — or rather, who they might be able to become. The loss of one's growing identification with the West added to the sharpness of academic defeat. One could neither turn back to older forms nor, now, go on to more modern ones. "B.A. Failed" Indians began to appear, people who appended both earned and failed degrees to their names, for in doing this they retained some portion of their Western identification.

*   *   *

During the nineteenth century, the Western-educated in India were a developing elite. By the twentieth century, their elite status rested on the multiple bases of caste connections, educational degrees, and high-status jobs within the range of professions which had grown up under the auspices of the British. Education was the requirement for membership in this new elite; it was the precondition for economic security and social status under the Raj. The security of high-caste status, a family's power within a village, the birth of a first son — all these were not unimportant, but they were no longer the crucial determinants for a Western-educated boy's life. Students faced life-determining problems in other contexts and in a sphere of activity beyond the village world.

The introduction of Western education into nineteenth-century India added, to the growing years of Indian children, particularly boys, a period between childhood and adulthood similar in many of its demands and stresses to Western adolescence. Traditional society provided individuals with predetermined adult identities and occupations, but young Western-educated Indians had to come to terms with new sexual, educational, and occupational situations and choices. They could anticipate and imagine future adult roles and begin to understand the cost, in terms of older ideas and childhood loyalties, at which such roles might be won. As a result, they could come to fear both the future loss of a newly imagined identity, and perhaps equally strongly, its successful attainment.

This new period in a child's development appeared in a society where traditional identities were increasingly under attack. The growing power of the Raj devalued older roles and patterns, robbing them of their once firmly held prestige and security. Older caste roles could no longer serve as the defining principles of life. At the end of their educational training, young men would have to become something. But the questions were: What would they become and who would they work for? What work would they do, and at what cost would this be achieved? Trying to answer those questions, schoolboys reached for solutions that, as often as not, brought them into conflict with their families. Where indigenous traditions, newer values, and childhood loyalties were sufficiently confused, the questions seemed impossible to answer. Many boys found themselves poised on the edge of adulthood, immobilized by the conflicting pressures that whirled around them. Yet neither conflict, confusion, nor postponement eliminated the need for decision. For schoolboys raised in the multiple traditions of home and classroom, the necessity of resolution was absolute. It was the sole condition of their growing up.

CHAPTER
3

Growing Up

IN THE 1930S AND 1940S psychoanalyst Erik Erikson formulated his concept of identity and elaborated and developed it in his subsequent work. Working with World War II veterans and with young people just emerging from adolescence, Erikson found certain repeated patterns of behavior and attitudes among those who were unable to form, or re-form, in the case of the veterans, a clear identity. These people had several characteristics in common. Generally, they were unable to work or concentrate, although at times they worked compulsively, to the point of illness, on irrelevant activities. They experienced what Erikson called a "diffusion of time perspective," an acute sense of urgency and lost opportunities, combined with a diminished awareness of the significance of immediate time. Physically, they slowed down and moved, in his phrase, as if "through molasses." They were unable to establish intimate relationships, and experienced intense feelings of isolation.[1]

Normally, Erikson theorized, one would come to some definition of one's adult identity towards the end of adolescence. All previous strands of memory, experience, and expectation would be pulled together and shaped into a coherent psychic unity. Identity was the sense one had of being continuous over time — the successful merging of what one had been in the past, was at the moment, and would be in the future. It was a feeling of wholeness, certainty, and completeness.

It was just this "togetherness" that Erikson's veterans and young patients so noticeably lacked. Some confusion normally accompanies the end of adolescence, for only out of the developmental conflicts of this period does an adult identity emerge. But what is only a stage for some, becomes a crisis for others. When no unification occurs, the result is the turmoil which Erikson eventually called *identity confusion*. In this state, there is a "split of self images, a loss of center, and a dispersion."[2] In desperation one might take refuge in a *negative identity*, adopting those "identifications and roles which ... had been presented as most undesirable or dangerous and yet also as most real."[3] Others, equally unable to resolve their confusions, might seek a period of withdrawal — in Erikson's terms a *psycho-social moratorium* — as an escape from the immediate need to commit themselves to an identity that continues to elude their grasp. But whether one remains in the grip of paralysis and confusion, seizes on a negative identity, or attempts a temporary retreat from adult responsibilities, considerable time, freedom from pressure, and some luck are all necessary before the uncertainties of adolescence lift and allow the confusions of this stage to find their resolution.

Erikson offers these concepts as descriptions of a life process experienced by all, but appearing in its most acute form in the lives of only a few. Although his theories rely on Western assumptions of individuality and autonomy, he argues that the concept of identity is present in all cultures. Children in all societies become adults. In order to do so and to be able to act with certainty in their adult roles, they must achieve a clear sense of what their adult presence will be.

Regardless of the debatable universality of Erikson's theories, they became relevant to nineteenth-century British India. The introduction of the structures of Western education and employment into India had considerably disrupted traditional patterns of life, introducing foreign values and, more important, foreign structures into the lives of Indian children. The years of childhood had come to be separated from those of adult responsibilities by a new span of time — similar to adolescence in the West — a time given over to educational and occupational preparation and testing. This period had not previously existed in traditional society, and as we have seen, the indigenous culture was somewhat unprepared for its concurrent problems and conflicts.

Children who grew up in India in the nineteenth and twentieth centuries were confronted with at least two separate cultural traditions. To become adults able to function within the Western occupations of the Raj, they were expected to integrate some part of both traditions into their lives. To organize what they had been taught into a coherent framework, they had to define roles which were no longer completely determined by traditional models — and yet not completely free of the traditional either. Their dilemma focused on the need to incorporate and then accommodate themselves to the demands of two diverse and, on some points, antagonistic cultures.

Even for those with the mildest temperaments and the most peaceful inclinations, the changes which accompanied Westernization caused tension and unhappiness. Those who were the first in their families to become Western-educated might find themselves in positions of acute psychological isolation. The need to nurture the foreign identifications of their schooldays forced some into rash actions, threatening to life itself. One widow remarriage in mid-century Bombay ended a year later in the joint suicide of the unfortunate couple.[4] Cut off from society by the iconoclasm of their act, they had been unable to survive. Less tragic, but also illustrative of the needs and problems of the newly educated, were the events which led to the widow remarriage of Dhonde Karve.

In retrospect, not even his daughter-in-law considered Karve a likely candidate for the role of a fiery opponent of orthodoxy. He himself remarked that diffidence and timidity were lifelong handicaps. Yet in 1893, while still in his thirties, Karve married a widow, the sister of a close friend, an act which alone precipitated a ten-year ostracism from the society of his village, separated him from easy contact with his family, ruined his attempts to organize a district association in his home village, and started him on what became a lifelong involvement with the cause and conditions of Hindu widows. Commenting in his autobiography on the effects of his marriage, Karve noted mildly that at the time he had come to realize that life was more "serious" than he had previously thought.[5]

Karve had been the first in his family and one of very few in his village to complete an education through the college level. Born into a Chitpavin Brahmin community of the Konkan, in the small village of Murud along the west coast of Bombay Presidency, he had studied first in his home village. Later he had gone on to a variety of English-language schools and colleges in Bombay city, ending finally with a B.A. degree from Bombay University. With the degree, however, had come a growing sense of isolation. He felt increasingly alienated from the people of his village and equally unhappy with solitary living arrangements in Bombay. The latter he managed to alter by creating an ad hoc joint family out of the members of his own immediate family and those of a close friend, Mr. Joshi.[6]

But his estrangement from Murud impressed him as a different problem, one common to a growing number of educated people in that region. "Many of the inhabitants of the Taluka," he writes in his autobiography, "were well educated and in service away from their native villages. Several of them used to spend the summer vacation in their native places. Some others who were educated and used to read Marathi newspapers remained in their villages to look after their small holdings."[7] Out of this assortment of middle-class people, Karve hoped to create an organization. "My idea," he wrote later, "was to bring as many of them as possible together, once every year in order that they should form friendly relations with one another and discuss some questions in the interest of the Taluka."[8] His plan succeeded.

> In May 1890 I sent out invitations to a number of them to meet in Murud. About forty people responded. We held meetings in the open yard of my friend's house and it was generally thought desirable to have a regular organization. Rules and regulations were therefore drawn up and an annual subscription was fixed. I bore the expense of the first meeting. I

was appointed the first secretary. The latter meetings were so arranged that we met on Saturday afternoons, spent Sunday together and dispersed on Monday morning. We had two more successful meetings at two other villages at which about a hundred people met together.[9]

"I had hopes," Karve recalls, "that in time beneficial results would ensue."[10] But the organization did not survive the turmoil of Karve's marriage to a widow. This event "only a few months before the session of 1893 fell as a bombshell in the midst of these people."[11] Karve attended the next meeting but failed to effect a conciliation. His offers to sit outside the meeting place and to prepare his own food privately were rejected and soon after this session the organization disappeared. It failed, as Karve put it, from "want of care."[12]

The intense conservatism of even the middle-class people of Karve's Konkan village was typical of much of the province of Bombay. Karve himself, while living in Bombay city during the lifetime of his first wife, had refused to break caste restrictions and dine with the families of remarried widows.[13] Yet there was no lack of sympathy in Karve, or in Bombay society, for the plight of widows, particularly the child widows whose husbands had died before their marriages were consummated. These children, widowed as early as seven or eight years old, were barred forever from marriage and motherhood. They spent their lives, when fortunate, as appendages to the households of either their in-laws, parents, or brothers and sisters. There they would do whatever house and kitchen work they could, fasting often, shaving their heads of all hair, wearing no ornaments and (in the most orthodox of settings) dressing only in a single garment of white cloth.

Even the orthodox found pathos in their condition. Among Western-educated communities throughout India widow remarriage was one of the most volatile reform issues. In Bombay in the 1890s, Karve remembers, there was "an emotional song in Marathi describing the miserable condition of widows, blaming society for allowing old men to marry young girls and appealing to it to allow widows to marry again."[14] Both Karve and his friend Mr. Joshi liked the song very much. "We often discussed the subject," he remembers, "and intellectually as well as emotionally I was entirely in favour of widow marriage."[15]

Newfound Western principles fed Karve's intellectual commitment to the idea of widow remarriage. But it was only chance and a characteristic inattention to those around him that propelled him into a personal role in the on-going drama of social reform. Karve was both timid and diffident. He enjoyed benevolence, was a frequent donor to public organizations, and his household often held relatives and near relatives whose educational careers he directed and aided. But charity came most easily to him in impersonal settings; his character combined public generosity with a propensity towards private emotional restraint. A reticent and reserved man, he inspired respect and sometimes affection in those closest to him — but neither response was untinged by criticism. To one of his daughters-in-law, a perceptive author and well-known sociologist, his personality was revealed best through metaphor; he was like a tree, she wrote, which shelters others but is not itself responsive to them. He was not selfish, merely unaware. "Even when he is eating something," Iravati Karve wrote, "and there is a dish full of it before him it never occurs to him to give some to a child who is standing by looking expectantly at him."[16]

Karve's weaknesses, of which he was somewhat aware, account for his close and dependent relationship with Mr. Joshi, a man he had known since the early days in Bombay schools. While others found Joshi "flashy" and calculating, even cruel at times to the point of sadism, to Karve he epitomized self-confidence and activism.[17] At the beginning of their acquaintance, Karve writes:

> He saw that I would be a proper companion for him and called me to read with him. . . . My shy and retiring nature kept me confined to my studies. I could not make friends and practically did no extra reading. My friend Mr. Joshi was of a different nature. He would make friends with clever students and find out from them what extra reading they did. He would also visit teachers and professors and know from them what extra books were worth reading. . . .[18]

Karve believed he derived great advantage from Joshi's company. "We occasionally read together and had instructive discussions," he recalls, "especially on the question of social reform."[19]

Given Karve's age, education, and temperament, it was natural that on the death of his first wife, he was drawn to the idea of marrying a widow. He was then thirty-five. If he wished to remarry, he faced a serious dilemma, for with few exceptions girls from good families were married at, or even well before puberty. Suitable brides from his own caste background would be no more than twelve or thirteen years old. And Karve admitted that the thought of marrying a child terrified him.[20]

By coincidence, however, the younger sister of Karve's friend Joshi had been widowed some years earlier, and the death of Joshi's wife had summoned her to Bombay to help in the joint Joshi-Karve household. Indeed, since her widowhood at age eight, Anandibai had spent virtually all of her life working for others — first for her in-laws and then later, in her parents' house. When Karve was considering remarriage, however, she was no longer in her brother's home, having been given a place in Pandita Ramabai's school for women in Bombay city. Perhaps her absence helped maintain, in Karve's mind at least, the theoretical quality of household discussions on the subject of remarriage. For Karve, at home and with friends, was freely using his reformist convictions to deflect proposals during the current marriage season. "Mr. Joshi had become a widower before me," Karve remembers, "and I wrote to him that he should marry a widow and that I was thinking of doing the same."[21]

As his daughter-in-law perceived, these discussions implied no necessary or immediate commitment to action. But a visit from Joshi's father swept the situation forward with a sudden rush. Joshi himself was absent from the house. In conversation, the subject of social reform came up. With his usual imperviousness to the moods or intentions of others, Karve offered the unqualified assertion that "as far as I was concerned I had made up my mind to marry a widow."[22] Joshi's father immediately responded with the offer of his daughter.

"I cannot express in words," Karve wrote later in his autobiography, "what I felt at that moment."[23] But the same hesitancy which, at that point, under normal circumstances would have kept him safely within the bounds of orthodoxy, left him unable to withdraw. Still he procrastinated, suggesting that he needed his family's permission before taking such a step. Later he told Anandibai herself that they might have to wait a considerable length of time while her hair grew out. "When he came to ask me about marriage," she would later write, "he thought that he would have to wait several months before my hair could grow again. He did not notice that although I had covered my head with the ends of my sari, I had allowed my hair to grow."[24]

When the marriage did finally take place, social ostracism almost immediately followed. Karve and his wife were banned from his parents' home village. At the meeting which decided their fate, no one spoke for them; the other educated people were intimidated, Karve thought, by the roughness of the discussion.[25] Next summer he went alone to Murud but it proved unbearable. He could not stay with his mother or brother but had to live in a house a furlong away from the family establishment. Food was also a problem. The village Karves were forbidden to eat with him, and food had to be smuggled in through the auspices of a young cousin. Karve saw his brother, but his mother and sister visited him "only once at midnight."[26] Nor was there any shortage of village women willing to watch both houses and report any infraction of the ban.

Perhaps inevitably, the marriage had difficulties. The fact that the couple had lived in the same household before marrying produced hints and gossip. There were frequent rumors of quarrels and attempts at reconciliation. Anandibai's long life as a widow had left its mark on her character. Neither husband nor wife possessed great flexibility of temperament, and both suffered greatly from the social pressures caused by their marriage. By the end of their lives, they were living separately, although coming together on occasion to reminisce over their past. In Anandibai's view, her husband behaved "whether with me or with the children in a reserved and calculating manner." She interpreted his "single-mindedness" as a lack of interest in herself or her family.[27] She never called her husband by his first name, she recalls in her autobiography, "not because I believed in the superstition that if a wife utters her husband's name his life is shortened, but because I did not like his name."[28] Karve was scarcely less blunt. His second marriage, he wrote in his autobiography, had not been for "greater enjoyment of the world" but to further the purpose of reform.[29]

Although neither emerged unscathed from their joint challenge of orthodox culture, it was Anandibai who bore the greater share of social stigma. When her husband began his famous school for widows, she was not allowed to approach the place. Her presence, it was feared, would lead parents to believe that their widowed daughters were in danger of being married. Both Anandibai and Karve worried that if he died, no one would be willing to help support their children, so Anandibai took training as a midwife.[30] She practiced her trade and saved her earnings until age left her incapable of further work.

For Karve himself, the repercussions of his marriage were enormous. One need only recall his continual involvement with his village, his habit of returning there each summer, his constant plans for its improvement, to calculate the cost. His district organization collapsed immediately following his wedding, and even in Poona, at Fergusson College where he taught mathematics, there were some abortive attempts at ostracism. Yet Karve turned out, as his daughter-in-law notes, to possess the fortitude and endurance necessary to survive and even triumph over the consequences of his apostasy. As much from necessity as choice, he became an advocate for the cause of widows, founding a school for their education, campaigning for social reform, and fund-raising unceasingly on behalf of his students. His response to the changed conditions of his life was original, energetic, and inventive.

While a combination of circumstance and ideology had triggered Karve's marriage, in his subsequent efforts for social reform (and his own reinstatement in society), he returned to the older cultural modes of submission and self-suffering. It took, he noted, about ten years before the people of his village became adjusted to the idea of his marriage. Their eventual concession, he believed, was the direct result of the tone of diffidence he had adopted from the start. "I tried to disarm opposition by conciliatory words and deeds," he wrote in recalling his tactics. "In my lectures, I never uttered bitter words against orthodox people or pointed out their defects. I appealed to them on the grounds of humanity. . . . These ways of mine had a beneficial effect."[31]

By the end of his life Karve had become famous in both Poona and Bombay. Even today, both cities have major streets which bear his name. As one who had dared to challenge orthodox traditions and had worked tirelessly for social reform, he was an honored survivor, a reminder of a time of struggle against the strictures of orthodox society.

Social and familial conflicts beset Karve's attempts to reconcile his new Western customs, ideas and identifications with older indigenous traditions. In other parts of India the newly Western educated often faced similar problems. Particularly in the earliest years of the nineteenth century, boys, isolated from their families by the ideological acquisitions of their education, but fearful of their still undefined futures, sometimes flirted with conversion to Christianity as much from loneliness, one suspects, as from conviction. By mid-century, however, the major cities of the Raj could usually offer other alternatives. Most had a sizable student population attending various English-language institutions and at least one major Hindu reform association. In Calcutta, for instance, by the 1860s, a boy newly arrived from the countryside could always find a companion able to understand the conflicts of his position; and if he were still tempted to reinforce his newly acquired values and ideas by an open break with orthodox traditions, he could do so by joining the religious reform society of the Brahmo Samaj.

This was to some extent the case with Sitanatha Tattvabhushan, an only son whose village home was located in East Bengal. Sitanatha lost his mother at an early age. As she lay dying in the hut where she had just given birth, she called to him over and over, "Come to me, I will give you something." Years later that scene and his father's restraining grip still lived in his memory. As an adult the memory of his father's "irrational" compliance with tradition became the force behind a lifelong commitment to the reform movement of the Brahmos.

During his childhood, Sitanatha had twice been exposed to the ideas of the Samaj. When only thirteen, and a student at Dacca, he had heard the famous Brahmo leader Keshub Sen. Understanding little, he nonetheless felt himself in the midst of "a storm, a storm of feeling."[32] In his home village, his cousin (the eldest son of his father's eldest brother) had been his "first guru," initiating him into the ideas of the Samaj and helping him, he recalls, to give up his belief in idolatry and become "a worshipper of God."[33] But it was only when he moved to Calcutta to join his cousin in a college run by Keshub Sen's brother that Sitanatha came under the continuous influence of the society.

The Brahmos had a variety of tactics for engaging the energies of their younger members. There was, Sitanatha recalls, a *Chhota Samaj* ("little society") attached to the main organization. This was for younger boys who might feel "shy and unwilling to speak in the presence of elderly Brahmos more advanced in spiritual life."[34]

> Everyone had to keep a diary [Sitanatha recalls] and in that they had to record the substance of the Sunday sermon and the Mandir and that of the conversation which took place in the Samghat.[35]

At weekly meetings all recited what they had done the past week, and each was asked "What is the special object of your life?" This question was so compelling that years later, as an autobiographer, Sitanatha was still composing his answer.

At first both cousins lived in the household of an uncle (father's brother) who ran the family business in Calcutta. But the boys' association with the Samaj did not pass unnoticed. Although the eldest uncle, who remained at home in the village, was willing to tolerate the cousins' interest in the Brahmos, the Calcutta uncle, for both financial and religious reasons, was not. In true Bengali fashion, events soon escalated into an open break. His uncle's treatment, Sitanatha recalls, "soon grew into regular persecution."[36] Whenever the boys needed anything, they "had to hear many bitter words. He clearly let us understand that he did not like our staying with him."[37] Finally the older boy abandoned his medical studies and left the house. Sitanatha "lingered for a while with difficulty" but ultimately left his uncle and rejoined his cousin.[38]

Further difficulties followed. The Calcutta uncle determined to exclude Sitanatha from a share of the family property; his financial position grew steadily worse until finally he too was forced, as he explains, to abandon his schooling. On his father's death the extent of his rebellion became obvious for he refused to perform the orthodox version of his father's *sradh* ("death ceremonies"). By tradition, only after the eldest son had performed this act would his father's spirit be at peace. Alarmed by his refusal, family members traveled to Calcutta hoping to argue him out of his decision.

After leaving their uncle, the boys moved to a hostel attached to the Brahmo college and supervised by Mitra Lal Bose. Bose became Sitanatha's special protector and friend. "I felt," he later wrote, "that he took special care of me. I often spoke to him of my doubts and difficulties and obtained his deep sympathy and attention."[39] Bose was with him when his family arrived. As Sitanatha remembers, "Mr. Bose's politeness to them was evidently meant to show that my refusal to accompany them was quite voluntary and that there was no persuasion or compulsion in the case."[40] A generation earlier, the same role might easily have been played in an English-language school by a Derozio or a Duff. The Brahmos — as they often claimed — may well have saved many young men from conversion to Christianity. It is questionable, however, whether orthodox relatives took much comfort from their intervention. For the orthodox, traditions were almost equally disrupted by either Brahmo- or Christian-influenced disaffection.

By the twentieth century, the Brahmos had declined in both vitality and membership. Young men such as Subhas Bose or Nirad Chaudhuri, whose fathers had, in their time, been attracted to the Samaj, no longer considered it important to their lives. Sitanatha wrote in his autobiography, in the 1940s, that even "young people born in the Brahmo Samaj scarcely attended it."[41] By the twentieth century, the Western-educated had grown in numbers, and their unquestioned financial success obviated the need for organized protection against the orthodox. The newly educated were no longer so easily isolated, either within families or in small *mofussil* villages. Their numbers were too great, and contact with others like themselves was facilitated by the numerous journals and newspapers in existence. Conflict between the old ways and the new could be somewhat diminished by limiting one's associations to like-minded and similarly educated people. But even more important, the establishment of the Western-educated as the Indian elite of the British Raj had begun the process that was to establish their behavior and ideas as the new orthodoxy.

As exposure to Western ideas deepened over several generations, identification and self-definition became increasingly bound up with the ideology and values of England and the West. The clarity with which first-generation students could perceive that their struggle lay between the ideals of the West and the demands of their families vanished. But attempts by first and later generations to fit their children into the framework of another, and on occasion hostile, culture produced its own measure of ambivalence and tension. Furthermore, as Western values became integrated into the lives of Indians, all memory of the foreign origins of those values vanished. British stereotypes of India became accepted as definitive. The negative identity projected onto Indians by the spokesmen of the Raj took on an independent life of its own. "I am an Indian who is trying to be a man," writes one author, quite unconsciously accepting a British dichotomy.[42] Another autobiographer remembers a teacher in his school who disliked his pupils — as the teacher had lived many years in India, the autobiographer explains, he "knew how black the hearts of Indians were."[43]

Central to British criticisms of India was the accusation that Indians were "weak." This, of course, took on many meanings: the climate was debilitating; morality was lax; courage and assertiveness were wanting. "The sedentary habits of the higher classes" of Indians, many Englishmen would have agreed, were among the worst of their faults.[44] The Hunter Commission in its report urged that regular physical exercise would have especially good effect upon the minds and bodies of most Indian students. We therefore recommend that physical development be promoted by the encouragement of native games, gymnastics and drill and other exercises suited to the circumstances of each class of school.[45]

Indian schoolboys were by no means indifferent to these charges. Gandhi, who disliked games and whose father had him exempted from after-school sports, still felt uneasy at this dereliction.[46] Subhas Bose, looking back on his childhood, believed he "should not have neglected sports": "By doing so I probably developed precocity and accentuated my introvert tendencies."[47]

It was not uncommon for sons of Western-educated fathers to undercut their own dislike of sports with assertions of their fathers' enthusiasm. "Father saw to it," one man writes, following a common theme, "that I developed a good physique and took regular exercise both at home and in school."[48] Remembering that his father would buy any gymnastic equipment his sons might want, Nirad Chaudhuri pointedly confesses, that if "in my youth and manhood I had not the strong constitution he desired for me, it was because I neglected his advice and in matters of physical culture pursued the bad old traditions."[49] If a father was enlightened, it would seem, his son's dereliction became a more individual and less significant failing.

Indeed, not only in sports, but in many matters, the "strength" of a father was terribly important. The importance of family status to both children and adults and the intensity with which a son identified with his father's success or failure made the father's position, vis-a-vis his British superiors, a matter of great importance. Children watching or hearing about their fathers' humiliation, were themselves made "smaller"; similarly British criticisms and stereotypes were taken to heart by schoolboys, for they raised questions about their fathers' power and strength of character, and by reflection, about their own strength as well.

One author recalls the following exchange between his father and a British official. The British officer, driving carelessly, had hit the carriage of the Indian.

> My father was naturally very angry and striding up to the European said, "I shall prosecute you for rash driving if you are not more careful." Now my father was a man with a magnificent physique, tall with great breadth of shoulders and possessed of immense muscular strength, while the European was a slight, undersized man. The latter flushed, grew red in the face, looked at my father's athletic figure and then drove away without a word.[50]

We enjoy the reversal in this account even as we question its accuracy and acknowledge how thoroughly actual experience probably contradicted it.

Indian fathers, working in jobs which gave them high status and economic prosperity within their own communities, were frequently required to swallow insults and criticisms from their British superiors. Fathers seem to have accepted this treatment as part of a necessary, if unpleasant, apprenticeship. But the autobiographies of men who, as children, watched their fathers receive this treatment show considerably more ambivalence. In this one memory, at least, the small weak Indian of British lore has grown into a man of "magnificent physique . . . and possessed of immense muscular strength"; the European has shrunk, until he fits exactly, both physically and psychologically, the stereotype applied to Indians.

Images of weakness and strength, success and failure were of profound importance throughout the life of Prafulla Chandra Ray. His autobiography, *The Life Experiences of a Bengali Chemist*, illustrates how the issue of a father's status and the new pressures of British education could complicate life within a Western-educated Indian family. The resulting mélange of identifications and associations could, at the very least, significantly alter a child's life.

Ray's family came from the eastern section of Bengal Presidency, from the village of Raruli. They were landowners there, and, from time to time, local officials. The great-grandfather, according to family legend, had held a government post so lucrative that the rupees from his territories had been brought to the village in covered basketloads.[51] Succeeding generations, however, saw the dissolution of this prosperity. Ray's father and grandfather often quarreled, and the family tragedy was that the old man had died without revealing the location of the family fortune. Searches were made everywhere; the father even dismantled the house in his quest for the money. But the treasure, if it had ever truly existed, was never found.[52] The family might still have remained prosperous, had Ray's father been careful and provident, but he ran up debts in abundance, using family properties as collateral and even, on occasion, selling lands held in the name of his wife to pay his creditors.

The tension between Ray's father and his grandfather started when the father was sent as a boy to study in the English-language schools of Calcutta. Fearing that his son was adopting too many Western habits, the grandfather called him home, ostensibly for his help in the management of the family estates, but in reality to remove him from the dangerous ways and companions of the city. But even his short stay in Calcutta was enough to sustain the father's lifelong identification with the ideas and values of the West.[53] It was from his father, Ray recalls, that he learned, "when almost a child" that "beef eating was quite in vogue in ancient India," and

it was from his lips that I learned for the first time in my life when a mere boy of such works as Young's *Night Thoughts* and Bacon's *Nova*

Organum. He was a regular subscriber to Tattvbabodhini Patrika and Vividhartha Snagrahbh, the journal conducted by Rajendralal Mitra, *Hindu Patrika* and Amrita Bazar Patrika. . . .[54]

Even his brief taste of urban society left Ray's father permanently dissatisfied with village life. He "whose mind had been formed and character molded on Hafeez and Sadeeq and some of the masterpieces of the English literature" often complained "of the society of the village gentry into which he was thrown. . . ."[55] Boredom and anger, perhaps, as much as ideological conviction prompted the father to attempt his own social reform movement. In the midst of his own father's village, he successfully convinced a local villager to marry a widow. Preparations for the ceremony had actually begun, only to be stopped by the grandfather's precipitous arrival. An "orthodox Hindu," the grandfather had been "simply shocked by the enormity of the crime about to be perpetrated."

He ran to Raruli post haste with relays of palanquin bearers and peremptorily forbade the approaching nuptials. My father had to submit to his dictates and the program fell through.[56]

Ray was angry at a father who had lost for his sons both the economic and the psychological security of a high-caste landed family. But his anger alternated with an attraction to the Western learning which was also part of his inheritance from the man. When the family moved back to Calcutta, Ray tells us, he continued to prefer the company of simple villagers to that of his father's friends. His comment is meant to reflect equally on his father's bad judgment and his own good taste. But at the same time, he cannot stop speaking of his father's Western accomplishments: his library, his education, his "enlightened" attitude towards his sons — all are measures of his standing and importance in British India, and, by reflection, of the importance of his sons.[57] "He was very much in advance of the average rural gentry. . . .," Ray writes, forgetting that he has earlier considered this a fault. "He was therefore naturally anxious that his sons should have the benefit of the best education available."[58] Neither his father's substantial indifference to the family's welfare nor the reality of financial ruin could provoke Ray into repudiating his Western inheritance.

Poverty and enlightenment were joined to a personal history of chronic illness. Dysentary and insomnia became the physical companions of Ray's life, appearing first when he was only twelve or thirteen. This was just four years after Ray's family moved to Calcutta and he had been entered in the Hare School, the most prestigious and competitive of the English-language schools in the city. Previously, he insists, he had enjoyed "splendid health, good appetite, sound digestion."[59] Suddenly an attack of dysentary appeared, so virulent that he was forced to leave school and return for nine months to the family village. After seven months the acute stage of the disease passed, but

> I became a permanent valetudinarian and my digestive organs were impaired. I grew weaker day by day and my natural growth during the period of adolescence was thus arrested. . . .[60]

At sometime in that period, Ray stopped sleeping through the night. He was, he remembers in another connection, a "ferocious devourer of books" and when "barely twelve years old" would frequently get up "at three or four o'clock in the morning so that I might pore over the contents of a favorite author without disturbance."[61]

Later this would become insomnia, and it, as well as dysentary, would plague him the rest of his life. "In its milder aspects," Ray recalls, "it [dysentary] has been my lifelong companion since 1875."

> I became a victim of indigestion, diarrhea and later on of insomnia. I had to submit to the most rigid observation of the rules of diet and regimen and for the sake of sharpening my appetite I had always tried to follow a regular routine of walking in the morning and evening.[62]

Returning to Calcutta after his illness, Ray did not reenter the Hare School. Instead, he joined the less prestigious school of the Brahmo Samaj. At the end of his first year, he did not sit for examinations, explaining that as he planned at the time to return to the Hare School he did not think it fair to win the first prize at this other institution. Among the year-end awards, however, there was no prize at all for him — "I could not of course claim one," he adds philosophically, "as I had absented myself from the examinations."[63] But the authorities of the school awarded him "a special prize of general all round proficiency," and the next year Ray stood first and "won a basketload of prize books."[64]

Ray never did return to the Hare School. He remained with the Brahmos and after graduation moved on to college courses in the less competitive Metropolitan Institution, which had ties to the Samaj. There he took the science program (a course which was frequently underenrolled in other provinces) and won a scholarship to travel abroad and study in Edinburgh.[65] It was from that Scottish university that he obtained his doctorate in chemistry. "Of course I knew it to be a foregone conclusion," he says of his degree examination in Edinburgh, "I was the only candidate for the year and was in close touch with my teachers. They knew well the progress I had made. . . ."[66]

Degree in hand, Ray delayed his return to India. He stayed several months in London, seeking in vain to secure a position within the Indian Educational Service. (That service, he writes in his autobiography, was closed to Indians: "No doubt a few solitary exceptions were made, but they

were exceptions and no more. . . .")[67] Again and again he applied for help
to a particular English official — finally the man asked him outright: "How
long can you hold out?"[68] Ray left the interview practically in tears.
"Realizing the hopelessness of my situation," he writes, "I made up my
mind to return home."[69]

In India a year of unemployment was ended by a temporary position
in the chemistry division of Presidency College. There he remained until
late in life, neither promoted nor demoted, and, on at least one occasion,
resisting an attempt by British administrators to move him out into an
administrative post in the *mofussil.*[70]

In saying good-by to his mother on his departure for Britain, Ray had
promised to restore the family fortune if he were successful.[71] But when he
returned to India, he did not even notify his people of the time of his
arrival. He stayed in Calcutta with friends ("My purse was empty. . . .") and
went only for a few days to the country village where his family had retired
after the decline of their fortunes. Some long-standing estrangement
undoubtedly existed, for even during his absence, Ray wrote only to a
brother in Diamond Harbor, and it was through this brother that his family
received whatever news they had of him. It may be that Ray avoided his
family because he had failed to establish himself in England.

The autobiography reserves its most bitter tones for those Ray regards
as successful in the eyes of the world. Marwaris from other regions, he
frequently reminds his readers, have robbed Bengalis of their economic
heritage, reducing them to the level of wage laborers and clerks.[72] The
British school system is equally criticized: its classes were uninspiring; its
teachers, without perception; its examinations, blatantly unfair. A boy's
progress "in a [dull] school," Ray wrote, "is apt to be slow even if he is far
and away the best boy in the class" for

> it is by no means the case that a boy who is known as the dux of his class
> is really the most promising boy, although an ordinary teacher with his
> narrow vision may pronounce him to be such.[73]

Recalling his failure to obtain a scholarship in the entrance examination,
Ray recalls, "I myself took the matter cooly and have always laughed up my
sleeve at the brilliant products of the University who sparkle for a moment
and disappear in the midst."[74] After all, he concludes, "a volume can be
written on *examination as a test of merit*. Of course, I shall be told that so
and so got a high appointment due to his brilliant academic career. But an
accountant general is at best a glorified clerk. . . ."

Ray never succeeded in reestablishing for himself the unassailable
security of position and status that his family had once enjoyed during his
childhood in Raruli. From his early days in Calcutta primary schools
through the years of his tenure in the university system, success — or the

feeling of success — eluded him. Whatever the objective truth of his past, his memories are constantly edged with uncertainty, anger, and defenses. A bachelor all his life, small and thin, Ray's only interests were his university work, his writing on Indian chemistry, and the establishment of an indigenous chemical and drug company. But those interests barely competed with his preoccupation with his health. By the end of his life, when he wrote his autobiography, his illnesses had become the core of his existence, around which all other matters revolved.

In old age, Ray deduced the pattern clearly: reading and study were inseparably linked with illness and insomnia. Too much reading led to insomnia; insomnia produced indigestion and then dysentary. "I had to practice rigid abstinence as regards my appetite for reading," he writes, for "...such efforts carried on after eventide would involve serious consequences in the shape of keeping me awake almost the whole night."[75] Careful scheduling could keep the situation under control.

> During the last half century [he reminisces] in consideration of my health, I have had to abstain from any and every kind of mental labor after five in the afternoon, except when I have sojourned in the cold climes and even then I have only indulged in reading light literature for an hour or so before going to bed.[76]

Only in England, ironically, did his condition improve. On a return trip to England after many years absence Ray had worried "that on reaching London I might get worse." But England cured him. "I had however been barely twenty-four hours at a hotel there," he writes, "when I forgot all about my stomach complaint."[77]

Both Ray's illness and the self-control he used to keep it in check provided valuable identification with Englishmen similarly afflicted and separated him from Indians unable to follow a program of similar self-discipline. "It will now be understood," he writes, following a description of the diet and exercise with which he combats his maladies,

> why I characterized my being a prey to the obstinate malady as a blessing in disguise. . . . Overwork of the brain plus sedentary habits cut short the life of Keshub Chunder Sen, Kristos Das Pal and Telang, Vivekananda and other victims of diabetics [sic]. They were carried off before becoming fortyfive or fortysix and even earlier, i.e. at a time when an Englishman considers himself almost in the prime of life. This represents a loss to the country which it is impossible to overestimate. Readers of Froude's Life of Carlisle will remember that the Scottish philosopher and sage while a student at Edinburgh had to suffer excruciating pain in his stomach and was also a life-long victim of insomnia. And yet by strict observance of the laws of health and by taking regular exercise he not only lived to an advanced age, but could labor

prodigiously in the intellectual field. Herbert Spencer was an even worse sufferer. I might quote several other instances but I must stop here for fear of being guilty of digression.[78]

This description, however, was far from digression. An identification with the lives and sufferings of British heroes was a necessary part of Ray's lifelong effort to relocate himself within his society. Cut adrift from a single source of cultural identification, Ray had been able neither to find his way back to older traditional moorings, nor to feel himself safely ensconced within the new establishments of the Raj. While a student in Edinburgh, he had momentarily laid aside his chemical work to compose an essay for a contest on the topic "Indians and Nationalism." In his essay he wrote: "From the moment an Indian begins to think for himself, he probably begins to be ashamed of himself."[79] Probably he meant to refer to his countrymen's lack of independence, but his comment could stand just as well for his own ambivalence and the self-doubt which characterized his life.

To the extent that Indian boys measured their self-esteem and well-being by that of their families and their fathers, Ray, as both a child and a young man, had faced particular problems. His own father had thrown away or lost much of the family's traditional status, and in spite of Ray's uneven efforts to rehabilitate that reputation within the autobiography, we may guess that the father had traveled in somewhat questionable Western circles in Calcutta. Ray's accounts even of his successes as a schoolboy seem touched by failure. As an adult, his effort to undo his father's failures did not succeed. He did not — as he once promised his mother — restore the family fortune, nor, although he had a foreign degree, did he do much (until very late in life) to renew the family's flagging prestige.

In the 1920s Ray became something of a hero to the growing nationalist movement of Calcutta. His career at Calcutta University seemed to the nationalists clear evidence of the way in which the British government had ruthlessly suppressed Indian talent, refusing recognition and high positions even to internationally trained and recognized scholars. When private donors established an "Indian" scientific institution and stipulated that the staff were to be Indian nationals, Ray was one of the first to be appointed.

If the nationalists saw in Ray's life a struggle against the power and prejudices of the Raj, we may see it also as a life immobilized by fears and ambivalence — the unsuccessful result of an attempt at acculturation. A painful sense of failure clung to Ray which not even the recognition which came to him as an elderly gentleman did much to dispel. The illnesses that followed him throughout his life were in some sense his most certain achievement; they were the outward symbol of the cultural conflicts that had shaped his life.

*   *   *

As students began to respond to the new structures of childhood and the message of the educational system, it became apparent that the changes produced in their lives and self-images would bring numerous problems. Family conflicts were inevitable. There was a basic contradiction in the way families urged their sons into Western institutions, only to respond with alarm to the changes that resulted. The contradictions of the educational system was yet another problem. The encouragement to become Western implied the ultimate enjoyment of full equality with English rulers. High-caste Indians, for whom traditional identities had once ensured both economic security and social status, felt deeply the absence of the latter and longed to reestablish the earlier security within the context of the Raj. But the rhetoric of a Macaulay and the promises of a Proclamation did not alter the reality of life in British India. Acculturation never made one a Sahib as the British were. It did not give one entrance into British society, nor, in most cases, employment at the upper levels of government. Nor did it free one from the negative images and stereotypes that British rulers had enshrined in textbooks and Indians increasingly accepted as an integral part of self-definition. Even Macaulay, while promising that Indians would become English in taste and opinions, noted parenthetically that they would have to remain Indian "in blood and color."

The fact that Westernization — or rather Western education — did not bring with it full acceptance within the Raj was a source of some irritation to many newly Westernized Indians and of even greater bitterness to their children. The first rush of enthusiasm for Westernization faded later in the nineteenth century with the growing awareness of the degree to which its promises would remain unfulfilled. Disillusionment did not bring rejection of Western values or educational skills; the economic value of an English education was too firmly established for this. But schools and their promises were approached with growing cynicism.

As the early attractions of English-language education waned, the years of childhood became a time of multiple and often contradictory influences. Children were exposed, at one and the same time, to the demands of orthodoxy, the ideals of the West, negative stereotypes of India and Indians, and the bitterness of parental frustrations and lost hopes. And even as people grew more cynical about the roles they would be able to play within British India, they grew less aware of the roles which British images of India were playing in their own lives. Foreign ideas entered children's lives from many sources — from schools and teachers certainly, but also, in Western-educated families, from fathers and elders. As these ideas merged with traditional family lore, people became less able to distinguish the foreign values in their upbringing from the traditional and less certain of their relationship to either. In the early and middle years of the nineteenth century most children entered English-language schools from exclusively traditional backgrounds, but by the twentieth century the family traditions of many students were a mixture of indigenous and Western values. Those who were the first family members to obtain a Western education had faced loneliness and social isolation; later generations in a family had to face an increasingly confused array of identifications, ambitions and loyalties accumulated during their growing years. Boys negotiating the path to adulthood were loaded down with the baggage of an ambivalent youth, and lives were sometimes destroyed when the weight of those contradictions proved too heavy to be borne.

PART II

Identities in Crisis

CHAPTER

4

"Surendranath" or "S.N." Banerjea?

THE AUTOBIOGRAPHY OF Surendranath Banerjea, a prominent Bengali nationalist of the ninteenth and twentieth centuries, reveals the way in which diverse influences in childhood could disrupt later attempts to forge a cohesive and integrated adult identity. Ambivalent loyalties and conflicting identifications were a central problem in Banerjea's life. His efforts to bring together the disparate and often contradictory directives of two cultures ended in a crisis that destroyed his first career, almost at its very beginning, and produced a period of confusion and despair. His problems illustrate the dimensions of difficulties shared by many of his countrymen; his solution to his own dilemma provides an instructive model for the successful regeneration of a life.

Born in 1848 into an orthodox high-caste Brahmin family in Calcutta, Banerjea was the son of one of the first students to attend Hindu College. His father, a highly Westernized "medical practitioner," had determined that his son should also receive the best Western education possible. So Banerjea was sent to Doveton College in Calcutta, a school for Anglo-Indian children. On receiving his B.A. in 1868, he was sent to England to compete in the Indian Civil Service examinations. It was expected that success there would start him on a career in that prestigious administrative organization, the Indian Civil Service or ICS, which ran the government in India. At first, Banerjea was denied admission to the examination on the ground that he was one year beyond the legal age limit. Protests to various officials were unsuccessful, but finally Banerjea won his claim through an appeal to the London courts. He immediately took and passed the examination, returning to India in 1871 to receive his first appointment in the service.

Within two years, however, Banerjea had been charged, tried and permanently dismissed from the ICS. The charges against him dated to 1872. It was alleged that as an assistant magistrate he had postponed a decision on a charge of theft for nine months and subsequently dismissed the offender in an attempt to hide the long delay. Banerjea attributed his problems to the hostility of the English officials under whom he worked, a hostility which, he claimed, had intensified after he successfully passed a language examination a senior English colleague had failed. In 1873, on learning of his dismissal from the service, Banerjea again traveled to England to appeal his case in the courts. There he remained for thirteen months, living outside London, traveling into the city periodically to attend to his case and subsequently to seek admission to the Bar.

Neither effort was successful. He failed to gain a reversal of the decision, and the London Bar was also closed to him. He then decided, the autobiography tells us, to return to India and devote himself to public life. He would become a spokesman for the Indian peoples, the defender of their rights against the arbitrary power of the Raj. Reaching home in 1875, he became, in the next seven years, a well-known public speaker, a teacher at the Metropolitan Institution in Calcutta, the founder of the Indian Association (a political organization), coowner and publisher of the *Bengalee* (a Calcutta newspaper), and the founder and principal of a college in Calcutta later to be named Ripon College. He maintained these activities until his death in 1925.

Over the years, Banerjea became a prominent figure in Bengali and nationalist politics. In 1883, he was arrested and briefly imprisoned for statements appearing in the *Bengalee*. He participated in the protests over the partition of Bengal and was arrested and fined in Barisal in 1906. Active in both national and Calcutta city politics, he became president of the Indian National Congress in 1895 and again in 1902. He was a member of the Bengal Legislative Council from 1893 to 1901.

As the twentieth century proceeded, Banerjea found himself under increasing attack from younger nationalists. He was shouted down in 1907 at the Surat Congress and, late in life, when he accepted an appointment as a government minister, he was sharply criticised, both for accepting the appointment and for his subsequent actions as minister. By the end of his life, his influence had waned, particularly in Calcutta where he lost an election for the Legislative Council to a younger and more militant nationalist faction. He died in 1925, the same year that his autobiography, *A Nation in the Making: Being the Reminiscences of Fifty Years of Public Life*, was published.

Banerjea's own explanation for the events of his life roots his commitment to the public and to political activism in the high-handed treatment meted out to him by British officials. "Were others to suffer as I had?" he asks, describing his feelings in 1875. "They must, I thought to myself, unless we were capable as a community of redressing our wrongs and protecting our rights, personal and collective."[1] But the emergence of

Banerjea's public conscience and consciousness has other roots and may be understood in psychological as well as political terms. Certainly the British were eager to bar him (and indeed all Indians) from the ICS, and they were embarassingly quick to expel him.[2] But granting the existence of a harsh and antagonistic bureaucracy, the question must then become, to what extent was government aided in its actions by the conflicts and confusions of the young man himself?

Banerjea's autobiography yields persistent clues to the origins of his later conflicts. Two patterns of imagery and associations run through the book, and Banerjea, although identified with both, sets them clearly in opposition to each other. On the one hand, there are the qualities he associates with Hinduism and Brahminical status: mildness, tolerance, and unyielding orthodoxy. On the other hand are the associations linked to the West and Westernization: rationalism and modernity, militance, extremism, and violence. These characteristics have an early origin in Banerjea's life. They can be traced to his childhood, when the contrast between Western and Indian culture and values were presented initially through the medium of two generations of his family. His grandfather was an orthodox Hindu, scion of a Kulin Brahmin family that had "maintained [its] purity with proud and inflexible consistency."[3] A sharp contrast to the grandfather was Banerjea's father, a Western-educated doctor, and one of those whose "alienation from the faith of their fathers was complete and even militant."[4]

The father had received "the best kind of English education available at that time."[5] He had been an early student at Hindu College and a pupil of David Hare. Banerjea emphasizes the effect this education had on him. "His culture," he writes, "had dispelled from his mind the orthodox ideas fostered by his domestic environment."[6] As a young man, the father had once run away from his father's home, "to avoid the displeasure of my grandfather for an outrage against Hindu orthodoxy."[7]

A child of this family conflict, Banerjea's allegiances are divided. But, setting down his memories, he sides most often with his grandfather. The conflict, he explains, was the result of a meeting of East and West, but his father's ideas had little effect on the family. "Tolerance," Banerjea goes on, "is engrained in the Hindu nature; and in those days, so long as we were not interfered with in our religious beliefs and practices, we did not mind what others around us, it might be our own kith and kin, said or did."[8] Yet later in the book, when Banerjea speaks of extremism and militance, attitudes that he has already identified with his father, there is a note of criticism in his remarks.

Still, *A Nation in the Making* was written in Banerjea's old age. As a child and young man, we may wonder, with whom did he identify? An indication of the double loyalties aroused within his household appears when Banerjea tells us that as a five-year-old, attending the local Bengali school, he insisted on being treated both "with the consideration due to my Brahminical rank and the fame of my father."[9] His attitude towards his father, while often critical, is as frequently admiring, and when he learned of his father's death, it was, he tells us, one of the "saddest moments of my life." His ostracism by caste people after his return from England in 1871 was due, he is sure, to jealousy "of my father's fame and of my recent success."[10] There are also intriguing glimpses of a much younger Banerjea trying on attitudes towards England and the West which he must have identified with his father. He remembers writing to that parent from England in 1868, praising the English custom of seaside vacations and complaining of "its absence among our own people."[11] Later, in Sylhet District as the new assistant magistrate, Banerjea signed himself "S.N." and was known for his Anglicized habits and dress. Even his wife, it was reported, was seen out in English riding costume.[12]

In Banerjea's early twenties, in the years between 1868 and 1875, the first fruits of the conflicting loyalties and identifications of his childhood began to appear. By training he had been intended for employment within the British Raj; his father's memory was closely associated with this goal.

> Great physician that he was, he was an even shrewder judge of men; and in 1853, when I was barely five years old, he drew up a will, a copy of which subsequently fell into my hands, in which he directed that I should be sent to England to complete my education. From the days of my infancy he had formed the idea that education in England would be helpful to me in life.[13]

His family's plan to send Banerjea to sit for the Indian Civil Service examination directed him towards the most prestigious employment open to Indians in their own country. Normally, an appointment in the ICS would have secured his position for life — and at an appropriately high level, in terms of both status and income, for one from a Kulin Brahmin background.[14] But in the seven years which followed, there arose a series of obstacles and then disasters to these hopes and expectations. By 1875 Banerjea had been finally and irrevocably dismissed from the service. His defence against the government's charges, his appeal in London, his attempt to be called to the Bar — all failed. "My name was duly put up [for the Bar]," he recalls in an account which still echoes an earlier exhaustion and despair. "An objection was, however, raised from what quarter or by whom I knew not, nor did I care to enquire then, nor do I even now. . . ."[15]

"My friends declared that I was a ruined man."[16] Their assessment was not overly pessimistic. Between 1868, when Banerjea first journeyed to England, and 1875, when he finally returned to India, the decline in his prospects and expectations was extraordinary. By 1875, two years after his dismissal from the service, he could expect (and his comments indicate he knew this) that the British held a file on him that would block his acceptance into most avenues of prestigious and profitable employment within the Raj. The future looked bleak, and he admits as much when he praises his wife's loyalty in this time, saying that she stood by him "in this dark crisis, and never thought that ruin and confusion had seized us."[17]

Elements of Erikson's pathography are present in Banerjea's account of his life in the period from 1868 to 1875. The entire period is bound together in his memory into one continuous stream of events, a stream which reached its culmination in thirteen months of withdrawal and desperate reading in a small English community outside London. "During these thirteen months," Banerjea writes:

> I shut myself up in my lodgings in the village of East Molesey near Hampton Court. . . .From ten o'clock in the morning after breakfast till dinner time at eight o'clock in the evening I was incessantly at work, reading books that I thought would inspire me with fervour and equip me with the capacity for that which was to be my life work. I used to make copious notes with indices and these are even now in my possession. Occasionally I used to run up to London and see friends and consult as to what should be done in order to be called to the Bar. But it not be exaggeration to say that I was immersed in my books and got no higher pleasure than in the companionship of the great masters with whom I was then in daily communion.[18]

The intensity of Banerjea's isolation in England, his urgent reading and note-taking, his clear sense (in part, of course, completely realistic) of lost opportunities — all are reminiscent of Erikson's descriptions of patients in the throes of identity confusion. Then too, it is intriguing to learn from an account by a friendly Englishman appended to the autobiography that Banerjea's dismissal was attributed to a "certain laziness which was alleged to be his leading foible."[19] How are we to understand that "laziness" when compared with the earlier energy of a student who had passed the ICS examinations and the later stamina of an orator who could speak on occasion for four hours at a stretch? Indeed, the records of Banerjea's trial and dismissal from his Sylhet post show that his condition while there was close to paralysis. The inability to decide a case of theft was no isolated incident. Although it was the immediate cause of his dismissal, by the time charges were brought against him his chronic procrastination at work had become a major irritant to the British official who was his superior. Banerjea's own court clerk, in testifying against him at the trial, admitted that the young man devoted a great deal of time to his work and frequently (in defiance of regulations) took papers home in the evening. Yet he still seemed to make little progress in his cases.[20]

The curiously long series of struggles by which Banerjea got himself into and out of the Indian Civil Service is, in the end, his own testimony to the underlying confusion and ambivalence in his life at this time. Banerjea, after all, did not act realistically in the light of what he and others knew to be the prejudices of British officials in India. Indeed, in Sylhet, even while Banerjea barraged his supervisors with memo after memo in his own defense, they wrote privately to one another lamenting his lack of candor, his "want of moral tone."[21] Earlier, in 1868, when Banerjea was first excluded from the service examination, another Indian found himself similarly situated. While Banerjea took the matter to appeal and, ultimately, to court, the second man allowed his case to drop. It was a more realistic, if less courageous, course of action. Had Banerjea's goals been more certain, or his ambitions less conflicted, perhaps he could have chosen more carefully where and when he fought. Alternately, having pursued his rights and obtained them, he might have been better able to keep what he had won.

The idea of public service, Banerjea insists, came to him in London, out of the depths of great despair: " . . . the gloom that surrounded me was dispelled in a new vision that opened out to me in the prospective glories of a dedicated life of unselfish devotion in the service of my country."[22] After his return to India in 1875, and for the remainder of his life, he would take on the task of representing a newly invented Indian public. He would become the spokesman who demanded the representation of Indians within the existing institutions of British government. This concept of public service became the central theme around which Banerjea rebuilt his life. With astonishing quickness — within seven years — he became a public orator, an educator, a newspaper editor, political organizer, college principal and public critic of the British bureaucracy in India.

Erikson has argued that when a man finally comes to a firm sense of his own identity, of who he is and what he will be able to do, he experiences a surge of energy and acts with a sureness which belies his earlier paralysis.[23] The swiftness and originality displayed by Banerjea in the re-creation of his career may signal the resolution of his personal crisis. Although we see his stay in East Molesey as marked by isolation and withdrawal, Banerjea insists that this was a time of triumphant hard work and preparation. He places his triumph at the beginning of his stay in England, and not the end. But if we argue with his timing, we cannot argue with the triumph itself. For whether Banerjea came to a sense of himself and his future capabilities at this period of his life or only later, and more gradually, after his return to India, it is certain that by the end of this period he had come to a new understanding of what he could be and what he would be able to do in his life. "All that I had in view," he explains, denying that there was a financial motive behind his management of the *Bengalee*, "the sole inspiring impulse was to serve the public ends with which I had completely identified myself."[24] With his return to Calcutta and the commencement of a series of new occupations and commitments, he had reached the end of a long period of identity confusion and conflict.

To understand the dimensions of Banerjea's problems and the significance of his success, we should look further at the implications of the conflicting identifications present in his childhood. What did these early examples teach him about what he should try to become in later life and what he should absolutely avoid? What is, after all, the negative identity of a young child who is conscious enough of his caste status to complain at age five of his teacher's lack of respect? Or of one who, again as a child, felt an intense desire to see his neighbour, a young widowed Brahmin girl, remarried? Heated family conflict surrounded this subject for on the issue of the girl's remarriage, Banerjea remembers, "my grandfather was violently opposed to it; my father was as eager in its support." He himself could "never pass her house as a boy without the liveliest emotions."[25]

In British India, as we have seen, textbook images of Indian weakness, lack of principle and energy came to form the core of a negative identity accepted by many Indians educated in the British system. The textbooks, however, also offered a positive alternative — escape from an "Indian" identity was possible through assimilation to the culture and values of the West. Banerjea and other children growing up in this period faced the necessity of combining the educational system's code of conduct with that of orthodox society. For Hinduism was also a source for authoritative cultural guidelines, and its representatives were as eager as any spokesman of the Raj in insisting on the absolute application of its rules.

For Banerjea the problem was even further complicated. The debate between indigenous and foreign values had been fought within his family compound, and its spokesmen were his father and his grandfather. The grandfather and the family he represented offered the security of extremely high standing within traditional social structures. His father, the extremist and rebel, had achieved fame in contemporary Calcutta. Yet the grandfather's caste status no longer could guarantee social and economic security in British India, and the father's fame may have verged on notoriety, for his fondness for liquor was well known. Surendranath's choice was by no means easy. One may, in fact, wonder if there were any points (beyond agreement on the desirability of Western education) on which the identity of the grandson of a Bengali Kulin Brahmin and the son of a Western-educated Indian doctor could be united. It is not surprising that to some extent Banerjea never chose, but merged elements of both identifications within a third alternative. His solution was the invention of a third identity, a new role for himself — that of a public representative of India. It was a role in which he could be both a Western-educated Indian and an Indian in opposition to the West.

By 1875, circumstances had forced Banerjea to abandon the destiny intended for him by his father. The "S.N." Banerjea of Sylhet days had begun to merge with an earlier "Surendranath." But there are indications in the autobiography that throughout his life Banerjea continued to struggle with questions of what he could and could not be.

Although he could not return to being simply the grandchild of a high-caste Hindu family, Banerjea's identification with Brahminical status was always important to him. He speaks fondly of those who look to him as a *guru* and is appreciative of people who show respect by "taking the dust" of his feet. High-caste status was a source of continuing reassurance and comfort. Approached by two young revolutionaries intent on the assasination of a British official, Banerjea was taken aback. He dissuaded them from the attempt, he explains, and then "clinched the matter by saying that they must swear [not to do so] by laying their hands on my Brahminical feet."[26]

Banerjea's education, his father's intentions and convictions, and the economic and political realities of existence under the Raj all combined to place him permanently beyond the boundaries of orthodox society. Even while he toys with the themes and motifs of older ways, he consciously separates his own way of life from traditional patterns. He describes orthodox society as rigid and condemns the barbarity of forbidding the remarriage of widows. Later he speaks of the futility of trying to pretend that old traditions can be re-created as if there had never been a break with the past.

Elements of his father's Western ideology have invaded Banerjea's sense of obligation and structured his feel for the general fitness of things. Although admitting that he loves to sleep — "Sleep has been my greatest enjoyment" — he is at pains to demonstrate his capacity for work.[27] Even on vacation, he assures us, he does not remain idle: "I believe in a rest cure, diversified by moderate work."[28] When he was a member of the Bengal Legislative Council, he recalls:

> The sittings of the council often extended from eleven A.M. to five P.M. with an interval for lunch. . . . It reminded me of the time when I was competing for the Indian Civil Service. Often I would be at work till one o'clock at night preparing myself for the work of the council which was to meet at eleven o'clock on the following day.[29]

Banerjea's dismissal from the ICS had, of course, originated in a charge of laziness and malingering. Even in his later years, he was still reviewing and responding to those charges.

Hard work led on several occasions to illness. After completing his assignments for the legislative council, Banerjea came down with an attack of "brain fever." Later in life, the strain of a visit to some flooded areas in north Bengal was "too much for me. I had an attack of fever followed by broncho-pneumonia, which at one time caused grave apprehension among my medical friends. . . ."[30] Touring Calcutta as a minister in the 1920s, Banerjea met opposition and hecklers wherever he spoke. The effort precipitated "an attack of fever and it took me months before I could shake it off."[31]

One of Banerjea's most serious illnesses seized him in the 1890s when a scandal threatened to close the law school of his college. The school had been accused of granting degrees to students who had never attended its classes, but the matter was raised while Banerjea was away on a political mission in England. "While I was away," he recalls with that touch of paranoia which is never far from the autobiography, "materials were being readied for a deadly blow at the college."[32]

The task of saving the law school obsessed him. In a rare moment of introspection he admits that all his life he has periodically been absorbed in one thing to the exclusion of all else.[33] Now the college took all his energy.

> My friends vied with one another in giving me parties and entertainment, but the central idea in my mind was 'how to save the college from impending ruin.' I had built it up with my life's blood. It was a highly efficient and successful institution. I was now confronted with the crisis of the gravest magnitude.[34]

The school was ultimately saved by the intervention, Banerjea tells us, of one who had "known my father and admired his genius and personality."[35] But close upon the resolution of the crisis came a severe illness.

> The strain and worry through which I had to pass in connection with the Ripon College controversy, coupled with the work for the Congress which was to meet in Calcutta in December 1890, brought on an attack of pneumonia.[36]

The illness was so sudden, Banerjea recalls, "and I was so little prepared for what was coming, that I had actually ordered my carriage to be got ready to take me to a dinner party . . . just as I was about to start for the dinner, I felt feverish. . . . The diagnosis was bronchitis. I was ordered to bed and for over a month I lay there a helpless patient."[37] The Calcutta session of the National Congress continued without him, and Banerjea, whose earliest reputation in Calcutta had come from his fiery Town Hall speeches and participation in political meetings had to endure "the agony of a bitter disappointment that I should be shut out from the joy of work that was so congenial to me." "They held a Town Hall meeting," he recalls sadly, "but I was not there."[38]

The Ripon College incident revived earlier conflicts with the British and threatened, if only temporarily and symbolically, the identity which Banerjea had created with so much energy since his return to India years earlier. Linked in his memory of the crisis are familiar themes: laziness and hard work; sickness and health; failure and success. With the onset of illness, comes a momentary hiatus in his most cherished role as public spokesman and Town Hall orator. Old fears and associations transformed this minor incident, in Banerjea's eyes, into a new struggle for survival.

For a man in his early seventies, the age at which he writes his autobiography, a certain preoccupation with illness is understandable. Yet sickness, as such, does not interest Banerjea. Indeed, the only time he mentions bad health in his autobiography is when it can be attributed to hard work, tension, and strain. A multiple association of illness, hard work, physical health, and achievement runs through all the autobiography's episodes of personal sickness and becomes most explicit in the account of the Ripon College incident. These themes, of course, were a major preoccupation of the school textbooks which frequently attributed the physical weakness and moral decadence of Indians to the deleterious effects of the climate. Yet the pattern of associations comes together in a curiously personal way in the description Banerjea gives of the character of his father. A "medical practitioner," a successful man, his father was, Banerjea tells us, greatly concerned with physical health, for "being a doctor, he realized that health is the basis of all success in life."[39]

Banerjea's autobiography was written between 1915 and 1925, the latter date being the year also of his death. The book offers us an old man's view of his childhood and later life. During the time that he was writing, Banerjea was much troubled by criticism directed against him by younger and more militant nationalists — both those he would have labelled extremists and those who were followers of Gandhi. His autobiography is full of oblique and not-so-oblique references to those critics. He tells us, in one breath, that in his own youth he was aggressive in his opposition to British rule in India; in the next, we hear about his total commitment throughout his life to nonviolence and noncooperation. The contradictions reflect no more than the attempts of a beleaguered politician to explain and justify his actions to an audience increasingly unsympathetic to or perhaps merely uninterested in the point of view he represented. Banerjea was particularly bitter over what he saw as the failure of those around him to honor him in his old age. Additional offices had been added to the new Calcutta municipal bureaucracy (added, we might note, by Banerjea himself) in the expectation that they would be given to "a few elderly men who would not care to face the risks of an election."[40] Instead these appointments had been turned over along political lines to those whose party had been victorious in the recent Calcutta elections — "young men," Banerjea notes with particular irritation, who "might easily have contested seats."[41]

In his young days, soon after his return from England, Banerjea himself (as he keeps telling us) might easily have been called an extremist. An influential leader among Calcutta students, he gained a certain notoriety as an agitator. Jailed in the 1880s for contempt of court, he explicitly encouraged students to protest his conviction, and notes with approval that "in the demonstration that followed the passing of the sentence, they [the students] took a leading part in the fashion common among young men all over the world, smashing windows and pelting the police with stones."[42] But in the last years of his life, Banerjea seems to have wanted a resolution of his quarrels with the bureaucracy and the British. "It is charged," he writes near the end of his autobiography,

> that in public life I am no longer what I used to be and that I have changed my colours.... In the first years of my public life, it was all opposition — strenuous, persistent and unremitting. But when at last the government showed signs of an advance to meet the popular demand and took definite measures towards that end, my opposition gave place to a readiness for cooperation.[43]

The acceptance and approval of the British had always held great importance for him. In the quintessential symbol of acceptance, Banerjea spoke in the 1920s before the Rotary Club of Calcutta. He was deeply moved. "When I rose to address the gathering which was large and enthusiastic," he recalls, "I felt that I was not merely an Indian but a Rotarian."[44]

As an old man, Banerjea no longer understood the younger nationalists. Their demands seemed unreasonable; their view of India's future, threatening. Elements of Western culture were so thoroughly integrated into his view of the world that when Banerjea tries to discuss the possibility of actual independence and separation from England, he seems almost beyond words. The noncooperation movement, he says, wants to cut Indians off from the source of their sustenance.

> The sap that feeds humanity is to be cut off from us and we are to flow down the stream of life, unfed, unsupported by the culture, the art and civilization of the rest of mankind, rejoicing in our isolation, taking pride in our aloofness. To me the thought is intolerable.[45]

Banerjea links the destructive aims of modern extremists to the earlier demands of his father and his father's generation. Images of young men in revolt against their elders (as perhaps the memory of his father's rebellion against his grandfather) draw his sharpest criticism. He is quick to castigate both the pro-Western Indians of his father's day and the "extremists" of his own. As his father had cut him off from traditional Kulin status and community, these young men would deprive him of his hard-won position as a minister, a Rotarian, a subject of the Raj. In a complex passage looking back on both familial and national history, Banerjea identifies his own behavior and position with that of his grandfather and the Hindu tradition. The spirit of tolerance, he says, "the heritage of our people," has disappeared.

> Extremism is of recent origin in Bengal. Our fathers, the first fruits of English education, were violently pro-British. They could see no flaw in the civilization or in the culture of the West. They were charmed by its novelty and its strangeness.... It was obvious that this was a passing phase of the youthful mind of Bengal; and that this temperament had concealed in it the seeds of its own decay and eventual destruction. In due time came the reaction, and with a sudden rush, and from the adoration of all things Western, we are now in the whirlpool of a movement that would recall us back to our ancient civilization and our time-honoured ways and customs, untempered by the impact of the ages that have rolled by and the forces of modern life, now so supremely operative in shaping the destinies of mankind.[46]

Perhaps the critics of his last years did not understand the forces that had shaped Banerjea's early political behavior or caused him, in the end, to long for reconciliation with the power of the Raj. The internalization of British culture and values which took place in his childhood left him dependent on a continuation of links with the British. The source of Western culture and values had been within Banerjea's own family. Although unable to realize the more complete Western identity and career which he believed his father had intended for him, Banerjea had adapted to his father's influence by incorporating many of that parent's values and beliefs in his own adult identity. The "representative of the people" who emerged from the ruins of Banerjea's first career was, on the surface, critical and suspicious of British rule in India; yet he was bound to a deep reliance on the presence of the Raj, and the ideals and values it represented. In this sense, Banerjea emerged from his struggles a more deeply Westernized man (or a less traditional Indian) than his father. The more spontaneous and superficial enthusiasm for Western culture and style possible for the father (and typical of the very first young men exposed to Western education) was lost to his son. Banerjea's adaptation was deeper; his attitudes, more ambivalent; his loyalties, more divided; and, as a result, his confusion and his conflicts, more acute.

CHAPTER

5

The Path of Rebellion

I am now at the crossways and no compromise is possible.[1]

THUS SUBHAS CHANDRA BOSE WROTE to his brother in 1921 in a letter he includes towards the end of his autobiography. Having passed the examinations for the Indian Civil Service, Bose was to be appointed to a post. But against the advice of his father and his older brother Sarat, he rejected the appointment and stepped out on a path of "wholehearted dedication" to his country's cause. He was, he thought, the first Indian to refuse a post in the service.[2]

Bose wrote his autobiography, *An Indian Pilgrim*, in the 1930s while he was living in Europe. Ostensibly an unfinished work, it concludes with his rejection of the ICS at the age of 24, adding only a short chapter on ideology, "My Faith (Philosophical)." But in dramatic and episodic terms the book is certainly complete. It is the record of Bose's passage from childhood into adult society, the story of how he became himself.

Within this drama, his rejection of service is the final act, committing him, in his own eyes and perhaps also ours, to the "pilgrim's path" of struggle and self-sacrifice. "Life loses half its interest," Bose wrote in 1921, "if there is no struggle."[3] While this opinion reveals an adult spirit of energy and independence, it also reflects that particular adult's tendency to find his strongest and most complete self in moments of struggle and rebellion. It is the growth of both qualities — independence and rebellion — which the autobiography, however unconsciously, records.

"The earliest recollection that I have of myself," Bose writes of his childhood years, "is that I used to feel like a thoroughly insignificant being."[4] The "sixth son and the ninth child" of his parents, Bose felt "lost in the crowd" of his large family, yet at the same time under pressure to "live up to the level" of those who had come before.[5] He yearned for "a more intimate contact" with his father and mother and envied "those children who were lucky enough to be on friendly terms with their parents."[6] His father "usually had a cloak of reserve around him and kept his children at a distance"; even his mother, while "more humane," was held in awe by most of her children.[7]

Although the Bose family were Bengali, they lived in Cuttack, the capital of Orissa. Bose's father was a lawyer and a prominent figure in local society; for part of his career he was a government pleader and public prosecutor. Along with others of his generation, Bose recalls, his father was "a-political"; he had "a high standard of morality" but was not "anti-government."[8] The mother was the daughter of a wealthy Calcutta family, a family, her son points out, that had "attained a great deal of prominence by virtue of their wealth and their ability to adapt themselves to the new political order."[9] Both parents were sympathetic to the reform movement of the Brahmo Samaj. The father had been educated in the Albert School in Calcutta, a Brahmo institution; he was personally familiar with the Brahmo leaders of his time and had once even considered conversion. Portraits of Keshub Chunder Sen adorned the Cuttack house.[10] During their stay in Orissa, however, the family's religious practices had become more eclectic. Bose's father was head of a local Theosophical society there, and he had been initiated on separate occasions by two *gurus*, one a Sakta and the other a Vaishnava.[11]

Individual attention is necessary, Bose asserts in looking back on his childhood, otherwise "The growth of personality suffers."[12] He himself, deprived of this attention in his early years, had become "introverted," abnormal, and precocious; feelings of insignificance and lack of worth had only been exacerbated by the first school he attended, a Christian establishment intended primarily for English and Anglo-Indian children.[13] The curriculum focused on English subjects and much time was spent in memorizing passages from the Bible. Education was less valued than character. Deportment and sports were the keys to self-esteem and the means most likely to unlock the admiration of teachers and fellow students. Bose suffered as a result.

> As I did badly at sports and did not play any part in the bouts that took place and as studies did not have the importance which they have usually in an Indian school, I came to cherish a poor opinion of myself. The feeling of insignificance — of diffidence — to which I have referred before continued to haunt me.[14]

Bose remained in this school until his eleventh year. Only at the end, he writes, did he begin to have "a vague feeling of unhappiness, of maladaption to my environment and a strong desire to join an Indian school where, so I thought, I would feel more at home."[15] Instead of remaining after classes to play with schoolmates (a practice frowned on by his parents) he took to returning home to work in the family garden. In the end his neglect of sports "probably developed precocity and accentuated my introvert tendencies."[16] Young children, he suggests reflectively, should not be exposed to Western values and culture at too early an age. Introverted children "are bound to suffer" and "the reaction against the system and all that it stands for is bound to be hostile."[17]

We may wonder if prejudice and discrimination in Bose's school played any part in increasing his sense of diffidence. His description of his failures in this Anglo-Indian environment — his shyness, inability at sports, and smallness — closely parallels textbook criticism of Indians, criticism which the teasing of Anglo-Indian schoolmates may have echoed.[18] Bose, himself, however, has another, more metaphorical, explanation for his feelings: "Having joined in the lower standard," he writes of his years in the school, "I had probably got into the habit of looking up to others and of looking down upon myself."[19]

In 1909, Bose moved to an Indian school. He was immediately aware of an increase in social and psychological stature.[20] In the Indian environment, educational accomplishments counted more than character or ability on the playing field. In addition, in the new school a greater value was given to parentage. Traditionally, of course, the Bose family standing was high, but not exceptionally so. But caste status was augmented in Cuttack Indian society by the mother's Westernized Calcutta connections and the father's local influence and position. Where Bose's Indian heritage brought low prestige and a negative self-image at his first school, in the new situation Bose's family connections, combined with his natural abilities, brought him attention, deference, and a feeling of importance. As an adult Bose rejected his parents' political and social accomodations; as a very young schoolboy he may have been ashamed of their Indian background. But in the middle years of his education, it was through identification with both his father and his family that he gained new importance and inceased social status.

Bose's autobiography deliberately emphasizes his growth as a political man, his movement away from the apolitical morality of his father and family, his acceptance of a deliberate anti-British, nationalist position. But unconsciously his writings reveal another change as well: the growth of his identity as both a "Pilgrim" and a rebel. The autobiography records the story of one who, even as he asserts his commitment to the ideals and values of those in authority, assumes characteristics and behavior anathematized by those same authorities. In adolescence and again in later life, Bose was to repeat this pattern. His rebellion would always be explained and justified by reference to the values of those against whom it was directed.

"The loss of a sense of identity," Erik Erikson has written, can be expressed through "scornful and snobbish hostility towards the roles offered as proper and desirable in one's family or immediate community."[21] When a positive identity proves too elusive, adolescents may retreat to a negative image and temporarily cling to a negative identity, one which incorporates identifications and roles which have been presented during "critical stages of life and development ... as most undesirable or dangerous and yet also as most real."[22] But for young people growing up in a country dominated by a foreign power, this negative identity can become even more confused. The dominant culture projects onto the community all those images and elements it most fears within itself, insisting that this represents the totality of indigenous identity. Individuals may identify with the negative definition presented by the dominant culture even as they consciously reject it. Adolescents, in their struggles to reach the stability of adulthood, may respond in even more convoluted ways. They may incorporate elements of the dominant culture's negative identity in their own developing identities, while at the same time, through their behavior, they seek to assert their possession of the very qualities the dominant culture's definitions have denied to them. In just this way Bose, throughout his life, reversed the stereotype which had been bequeathed to Indians by British culture. He chose, on one level, to be something that British culture, British officials in India, and even his own family regarded as most negative — rebellious, a bad student, and a "violent" Indian. At the same time, he freed himself from the charge of bad character, lack of principle, and weakness — the negative identity of an Indian under the Raj.

"A state of acute identity confusion," according to Erikson, "usually becomes manifest at a time when the young individual finds himself exposed to a combination of experiences which demand his simultaneous commitment to physical intimacy (not by any means always overtly sexual), to decisive occupational choice, to energetic competition and to psycho-social self-definition."[23] For Subhas Bose, the age of thirteen marked the beginning of a long and difficult period in his life: "I was at this time," he writes,

> entering on one of the stormiest periods in my psychical life, which was to last for five or six years. It was a period of acute mental conflict causing untold suffering and agony which could not be shared by any friends and was not visible to any outsider. I doubt if a growing boy normally goes through this experience, at least I hope he does not. But I had, in some respects, a touch of the abnormal in my mental makeup. Not only was I too much of an introvert, but I was in some respects precocious. The result was that at an age when I should have been tiring myself out on the football field, I was brooding over problems which should rather have been left to a more mature age.

"The mental conflict," he continues, "as I view it from this distance was a two fold one."

First, was the natural attractions of the worldly life, and worldly pursuits in general, against which my higher self was beginning to revolt. Secondly there was the growth of sex consciousness, quite natural at that age, but which I considered unnatural and immoral and which I was struggling to surpress or transcend.[24]

Emerging sexuality, the approach of college, and the possibilities of adult employment and responsibilities may well have raised in Bose's mind questions about the role he would play as an adult, a man, in Indian society. Images of strength and weakness had a central importance throughout his life; in adolescence, by his own account, they held particular significance. Before the age of thirteen Bose had been a "good" boy, obedient to his parents, returning home after school as they wished, staying within the family compound. But the years of his adolescence witnessed an increasing disregard of parental wishes: "I had passed the stage when I believed that obedience to one's parents was in itself a virtue. I was rather in a mood to defy every obstacle to my goal, no matter from what source it came."[25] He took, he recalls, a "peculiar pleasure" in defying his mother's "unjustified" orders.[26]

The more my parents attempted to restrain me, the more rebellious I became. When all other attempts failed my mother took to tears, but even that had no effect on me. I was becoming callous, perhaps eccentric, and more determined to go my own way, though all the time I was feeling inwardly unhappy.[27]

In letters and conversations with friends, Bose made explicit his association of rebellion and manhood. "Goody-goody Bengali boys," he reportedly told a friend, were "eunuchs." Bengalis would never become manly "unless the so-called good boys are totally uprooted. . . ."[28]

At the same time, a second source of unhappiness for Bose was his desire to find "a central principle which I could use as a peg to hang my whole life on."[29] Erikson has emphasized the importance of fidelity to adolescents — their need to identify ideals and principles to which they may commit themselves.[30] Again and again Bose's autobiography returns to his wish for altruistic renunciation and self-sacrifice. Initially this led him closer to religion. He studied traditional Hinduism, attempted to practice yoga, and sought out various religious men for guidance. He immersed himself in the writings of Vivekananda, a Bengali religious leader whose work emphasized altruism and social consciousness.

These interests and Bose's growing rebelliousness provoked his parents' disapproval. They commented critically on his activities, his companions, and his growing "eccentricity." He began to feel "himself" only when in the company of like-minded friends: "I began to feel more at home when away from home."[31] His parents noticed, Bose recalls, "that I was going out frequently in the company of other boys. I was questioned, warned in a friendly manner and ultimately rebuked."[32] But Vivekananda's writings taught that rebellion was not only acceptable, but essential for the full development of the self. "Nothing mattered to me," Bose remembers, "except my inner dreams and the more resistance I met the most obstinate I became."[33] It was in these years that he began self-consciously to define himself as a rebel.

Parental objections and family ridicule, however, did force Bose to follow his new religious practices in secret. Yoga, for instance, was done at night: "the best thing was to attempt it in the dark after sunset and so I did. But I was ultimately seen one day and there was a titter."[34] Yet, at the same time, perhaps in retaliation, Bose's provocation of his parents increased. Following the directions of a holy man, he committed himself to begin each day with a *pronam* ("touching the feet") to his father and mother. But he made no effort to explain his actions.

> Up till now I have not the faintest notions of what he [the father] or my mother who also had to undergo the same experience thought of me at that time. It was nothing less than a torture every morning to muster sufficient strength of mind to go up to my parents and do obeisance to them. Members of the family, or even servants, must have wondered what made the rebellious boy suddenly so submissive.[35]

Rebellion and this new interest in religion brought Bose more attention than before, but it came at a certain cost. "There was very little understanding or appreciation at home," he recalls, "of what I was dreaming at the time and that added to my misery."[36] One hears echoes in the autobiography of an unspoken wish that a wiser use of parental influence had guided Bose's life. Parents, he suggests, looking back on his own adolescence, should "be circumspect in dealing with children possessing an emotional and sensitive nature. It is no use trying to force them into a particular groove, for the more they are suppressed, the more rebellious they become and this rebelliousness may ultimately develop into rank waywardness." In his adolescent years, Bose seems to suggest, parental pressure was pushing him into a deeper commitment to the role of a rebel than he either wanted or intended. On the other hand, he continues,

> sympathetic understanding, combined with a certain amount of latitude, may cure them of angularities and idiosyncracies. And when they are drawn towards an idea which militates against worldly notions, parents and guardians should not attempt to thwart or ridicule them, but endeavor to understand them and through understanding to influence them should the need arise.[37]

Bose may have had some reason to expect greater family approval for his interest in religion. Others have described his mother as a religious woman and it is said that Bose wrote frequently to her on such matters.[38] Moreover, since Bose was interested in a religion which would unite "science and religion," he might also have thought that his ideas would have fit well with the reformist ideology of his parents.

Yet, on another level, Bose's involvement with Hinduism, and particularly his friendships outside the family, were deliberately provocative. He was both echoing and mocking his parents' ambitions. Since his growing objections to worldly concerns and his religious interests threatened to direct him away from the practical goals of education and employment, Bose's behavior posed serious difficulties to family plans for his career. Even had his family been sympathetic to a theoretical commitment to religion, they would not have wanted their son to become a *sannyasi*, or even to roam constantly about the countryside with like-minded friends. Faced with these changes in a "once promising boy," Bose's parents packed him off to Calcutta for his college years. They hoped, he remembers, that "in the realistic atmosphere of Calcutta, I would shed my eccentricities and take to a normal life like the rest of my tribe."[39]

Bose's last and most outrageous act of religiosity came during his first years at college. Religious conviction was combined with an act of protest against parents and family. Without notice, Bose left school during vacation for a trip with friends to Benares. He was looking, he explains, for a personal *guru*. "Of course," he adds, "I did not inform anybody at home and simply wrote a post card when I was far away."[40]

The card threw his family into an uproar. "My mother," Bose later wrote to a friend, was "almost mad at the thought that I had left home for good."[41] His father's attitude, more "passive," was that "things would take care of themselves." Nevertheless, an astrologer was consulted, and an uncle dispatched to a city (the wrong one, it turned out) whose name began with a *B*. Soon after, however, Bose reappeared in Cuttack. "I was not repentant for having taken French leave," he recalls, "but I was somewhat crestfallen at not having found the guru I had wanted so much."[42] On the day of his return, emotions ran high. "It seems you have come into this world to kill me," his mother cried. "I would not have waited so long before drowning myself in the Ganges only for the sake of my daughters have I not done so."[43] His father openly wept.

After I had made my pronam he embraced me and led me to his room. On the way he broke down and in the room he wept for quite some time holding on to me.... Then he lay down and I massaged his feet — it appeared as if he was feeling some heavenly pleasure.[44]

A few days after his return Bose came down with a case of typhoid; the penalty, he notes lightly, for *guru* hunting and bad food. "While I was in bed," he writes, "the Great War broke out."[45] As he lay in bed, Bose also began to reexamine his ideas and values: "Was it possible to divide a nation's life into two compartments," he asked himself, "and hand over one of them to the foreigner, reserving the other to ourselves?"[46] The answer, he decided, was no. With this decision came an end to his commitment to a life of religious asceticism. Although his religious associations and activities would continue for the next two years, "inwardly I had changed a great deal."[47] Bose's religious interests had always met needs other than the spiritual and his acts of rebellion had been almost as important as the ideology they had expressed. Now he was broadening the context in which rebellion would have meaning for him. Ultimately he would abandon his religious beliefs for a fuller commitment to political action.

*   *   *

The calamitous events of Bose's third year at Presidency College confirmed his identity as a rebel on a wider scale and with greater implications than had previously been the case. Bose had been at the college for over two years, he writes, when "a sudden occurrence broke into my life."[48] Bose had reason to wish later that the incident had been forced upon him, for events led ultimately to his expulsion from school. The episode involved a professor of English at the college, a Mr. E.F. Oaten, who had, Bose recalls, a reputation for "manhandling" Indian students. Earlier in the term, one incident had already occurred, protests had been lodged, a student strike begun, and the offending teacher had apologized. A month later, however, a second offense "came like a bolt from the blue."[49] In retaliation, Oaten was attacked and beaten by a crowd of students. He was not, Bose insists, thrown down a flight of stairs nor hit from behind. (One solitary blow did come from the back, "but that was of no account.") Bose called himself an eyewitness to the attack. School authorities thought him considerably more. "Bose," the principal told him, "you are the most troublesome man in the College. I suspend you." "I said, 'Thank you,' " Bose recalls, "and walked out of the room. Shankaracharya's Maya lay dead as a doornail."[50]

University officials were no more insightful in their dealings with Bose than his parents had been. Where the parents had answered provocation with ridicule, the officials used punishment. A committee of inquiry was held. "Naturally," Bose recalls, "we expected justice."

> When asked whether I considered the attack to be justified, my reply was that though the assault was not justified, the students had acted under great provocation and I then proceeded to narrate seriatum the misdeeds of the Britishers in Presidency College during the last few

years. It was a heavy indictment, but wiseacres thought that by not
unconditionally condemning the assault on Mr. O., I had ruined my case.
I felt, however, that I had done the right thing regardless of its effect on
me.[51]

As his college record was excellent and the evidence against him slight,
Bose told a friend that he did not expect a heavy punishment.[52] "I lingered
on in Calcutta," he recalls, "hoping against hope that something favorable
would turn up."[53] But the decision was negative. Bose stood expelled from
the College.

In acting against authority Bose's behavior had closely paralleled the
moral guidelines of the British. Brave, principled, and self-sacrificing, he
had embodied the antithesis of the negative stereotype of an Indian. " . . . I
had done the right thing," he writes. "I had stood up for our honor and
self-respect and had sacrificed myself for a noble cause."[54] He was not, he
might almost have said, the rebel he seemed to be; far from an enemy of
the Raj, he was one who believed in and acted on its most cherished ideals.
Similarly, in earlier conflicts with his parents, Bose's emotions had often
contradicted his behavior. "To defy my parents in this way," he recalls of
one adolescent episode, "was contrary to my nature . . . but I was swept
onwards as by an irresistible current."[55]

The negative aspects of Bose's actions did not yet represent the core
of his identity. But the danger for an adolescent who takes refuge in a
negative identity, as Erikson points out, is that he may be responded to by
family and society as if he were in reality what he has only temporarily
become. Family, friends, and society may force upon him as a permanent
identity what was, in its beginnings, only a momentary refuge. Other, more
positive, possibilities, in the process, may be damaged or lost. "Michael A.
Jones, 20, was fined twenty-five dollars and costs . . . but he just didn't leave
well enough alone," Erikson writes, quoting a newspaper account of the
boy's arrest for reckless driving.

> "I understand how it was, with your pegged trousers and flat-top
> haircuts," [Judge] Roberts said in assessing the fine. "You go on like this
> and I predict in five years, you'll be in prison." . . . "I just want you to
> know I'm not a thief," interrupted Jones to the judge. The judge's voice
> boomed to the court clerk: "Change that judgment to six months on the
> road."[56]

In treating the boy's protest as an attack on authority, Erikson suggests, the
judge may have confirmed a criminal identity which up to that point had
only been temporarily assumed.

In Bose's case also, intentions and inner regrets were not sufficient
to mitigate his actions. Under somewhat greater provocation, the
administration of Calcutta University confirmed in Bose elements of a
negative identity only momentarily assumed. They completed, through

their actions, what parental misunderstanding and family ridicule had earlier begun. Bose saw his expulsion as a defining point in his life.

Little did I then realize the inner significance of the tragic events of 1916. My Principal had expelled me but he had made my future career.[57]

Introverted, shy, and fearful as a boy, Bose discovered another self in moments of rebellion. In protest he became a leader; in rebellion he grew in significance and importance to those around him, and the bravery and "manly" aggresssion prized by British texts and schoolmasters became his own. As he recalls:

I had established a precedent for myself from which I could not easily depart in future. I had stood up with courage and composure in a crisis and fulfilled my duty. I had developed self-confidence as well as initiative which was to stand me in good stead in future. I had a foretaste of leadership though in a very restricted sphere, and of the martyrdom that it involved.[58]

This clarity was the product, however, of considerable hindsight. In 1916 Bose found himself marked as a rebel. His educational career seemed at an end. His future was "dark and uncertain."[59] Even his own family treated him as a sort of criminal. Fearing his arrest and imprisonment, they ordered his return to Cuttack and, once there, he found that he was expected to remain. He asked to be sent abroad to study, but his father refused. "He was definitely of the opinion that I should have the blot on my escutcheon removed before I could think of going abroad."[60]

Fears and regrets followed him into exile. Bose suffered, as he had all his life, from terrifying dreams. He dreamed of snakes, of examinations for which he was unprepared, of arrest and imprisonment. "Self-analysis" cured his fears: "I would sit down at night and picture myself in a closed room full of poisonous snakes," he recalls, "and repeat to myself, 'I am not afraid of being bitten, I am not afraid of death.' Thinking hard in this way, I would doze off to sleep." Similarly, fears of house searches and arrest were made to disappear: "I had only to picture to myself house searches and arrests going on without disturbing me and to repeat to myself that I was not upset in any way...."[61]

But fortunately, within two years, what had seemed a permanent exile was transformed into a temporary suspension. Through the intercession of the vice-chancelor of Calcutta University, Bose won readmittance to the College of the Scottish Free Church Mission. "At college I led a quiet life," he recalls with what we may hear as a touch of regret, "There was no possibility of any friction with the authorities with such a tactful and considerate man as Dr. Urquhart as Principal."[62] Instead Bose turned to work. By 1919 he had passed his B.A. examination with some distinction, and his family were once again considering his future with care.

> One evening when my father was in Calcutta, he suddenly sent for me. I found him closeted with my second brother, Sarat. He asked me if I would like to go to England to study for the Indian Civil Service. If I agreed I should start as soon as possible. I was given twenty-four hours to make up my mind.[63]

He decided to go. If Bose's expulsion forced him into a more permanent commitment to the identity of a rebel than he had, perhaps, intended, the period of study that led to his success in the ICS examinations laid the groundwork for revenge in a gesture directed against both the British government and the ambitions of his own family. Bose spent the years from 1916 to 1921 reestablishing himself in the same society from which his earlier expulsion had seemed so permanent. In his family's eyes, his efforts were praiseworthy; he was reformed and rehabilitated. Whether he consciously saw his efforts as a preparation for the grand renunciation which was to come is problematic. But after five years, he was in a position to choose, on his own initiative, an identity which had earlier been thrust upon him. In this new freedom of choice, as well as in the courage of the decision itself, lay much of his triumph.

Discussing the decision to turn down the ICS appointment, Bose posed to his family two alternatives: crude self-interest or principled self-denial.

> I am now at the crossways and no compromise is possible. I must either chuck this rotten service and dedicate myself wholeheartedly to the country's cause, or I must bid adieu to all my ideals and aspirations and enter the service.[64]

"For a year," he wrote to his brother, re-creating the events of the time of his expulsion, "my future was dark and blank, but I bore the consequences bravely. I never complained to myself and today I am proud that I had the strength to make that sacrifice. The memory of that event strengthens my belief that if any demands for sacrifice are made upon me in the future, I shall respond with equal fortitude, courage and calmness."[65] His compassion for his father was supported by his understanding of how completely his decision aborted parental hopes for his future.

> Father wants to save me from this sacrifice. I am not so callous as not to appreciate the love and affection which impels him to save me from this sacrifice in my own interests. He is naturally apprehensive in that I am perhaps hasty in my judgment, or overzealous in my youthful enthusiasm. But I am perfectly convinced that the sacrifice has got to be made by somebody at least.[66]

Bose's rejection of the ICS was the culmination of a personal search for self-definition and identity. From childhood, in moments of conflict, Bose had seemed to become the rebellious, violent individual pictured most negatively both by his family and by British authorities. At the same time, however, his behavior had rid him of the negative identity of an Indian. Now, again, his refusal to join the administrative service presented the same double image of his character. The bad boy, the rebel, showed his contempt for the worldly ambitions of his family and for the most prestigious employment that the British Raj could offer. But by that same decision, Bose also clearly established his claim to qualities the British declared most valuable in men — principles, courage, and aggression. If he seems to have taken some pleasure from the effects of this act on those who had earlier forced him into the role of rebel, one may forgive him his moment of triumph. He paid well for it through all the misery and confusion that plagued his adolescent years. And he would continue to pay in his future. Throughout his life, the autobiography reveals, Bose faced continuing doubts and regrets about the adult identity he had, in one moment of his life, so permanently and irretrievably embraced.

CHAPTER
6

"Civis Britannicus Sum"

WHEN NIRAD CHAUDHURI PUBLISHED his life history, *The Autobiography of an Unknown Indian*, in 1951, he moved almost immediately from the status of a relatively unknown journalist to that of a writer with a reputation and readership that spanned three continents. This sudden fame contrasts strangely with the book's major theme: "My friends," Chaudhuri writes in his introduction, "would call me a failure."[1] The preoccupation with failure, however, was his own. Indeed it is Chaudhuri's wish to examine and come to terms with a failure twenty years past, and with the ensuing period of depression and paralysis in his life, that motivated this book, and sustains it.

Chaudhuri was born in 1897 in Kishorganj, a small village in the eastern section of Bengal, the second child and the second son in a family of eight children. His father was a local lawyer, a profession that ranked low within the hierarchies of the Raj but brought the family prosperity and status in Kishorganj. The traditional standing of the Chaudhuri family was also high, and the ancestral village of the father was no more than five miles away. Both mother and father, Chaudhuri recalls, were Brahmos by conviction. While not actually converting to Brahmoism, they sympathized with reformist ideas and were unorthodox in their own beliefs and practices.

The most serious problem of the family, their son recalls, was the instability of his mother. She suffered from recurring fits of hysteria and withdrawal. After one episode of depression in 1910, possibly precipitated by a mysterious attempt on her life, the father decided to move the family to Calcutta. There he hoped to establish himself in business and enroll his older sons in school. His efforts were, however, a partial failure; within three years, financial difficulties forced the parents and younger children to return to the *mofussil* and Kishorganj. The two eldest boys, Nirad and his older brother, remained behind to continue their education.

For Nirad, the end of college brought spectacular success, followed in a relatively short time by disastrous failure. In 1918 he passed his B.A.

examinations with his name listed first among all the candidates for the university. His triumph was so unexpected that when the news was received he asked his father to wire back for confirmation. Dreams of success began to dissolve within a year, however, with his first attempt to pass the master's examination. He sat through three papers and then refused to attend the fourth, telling his mother that he was badly prepared and had not done well so far. A year later, he found himself unable to read or to concentrate on studies. He refused to make a second attempt.

Plans for a university career were only the most immediate casualty of this decision. During the next twenty-six years, Chaudhuri took a variety of positions; at various times he was a clerk in the Military Affairs Office, a journalist and, in the late 1930s, the secretary of the elder brother of Subhas Bose. Through all these years, however, he held on to his memory of failure. He suffered from persistent depression and felt a paralysis of his will to act. Only in 1947, in the midst of the violence and chaos which accompanied India's partition and independence, did Chaudhuri's confusion begin to lift. With growing clarity of vision, he began to write his autobiography.

The book, Chaudhuri asserts, is "more of a national than a personal history."[2] His definition allows him to avoid personal details where he chooses and to focus the reader's attention more exclusively on the grand design he has evolved to explain his own and his country's past. "From a personal standpoint," he writes, "this historical thesis has emancipated me from a malaise that has haunted me throughout my life."[3] The brutality of India's partition so laid bare the Indian character that now, he feels, he is able to understand the shadows that darkened his earlier years. India's history, as Chaudhuri sees it, is a continual counterpoint between an indigenous culture and a series of foreign invasions. The indigenous culture is retrograde and dying. Periodically, infusions of foreign vitality and creativity bring it back to life. But, as the effect of each invasion wanes, so does the energy of the country. In 1947, as British power and influence ebbed, the synthesis of Indian and British culture and values that had reached its height in the "renaissance" of the nineteenth century fell into a sharp decline. Indians sank back into the decadence, chaos, and brutality natural to their country's climate and culture. Only a few individuals held on and, like Chaudhuri, continued to be inspired by the earlier synthesis. But their persistence brought them intellectual salvation tempered by cultural despair. In his own life, Chaudhuri argues, it was the dissonance between his own beliefs and the historical trends of his country that brought about his personal difficulties.

> Today [he writes] I nurse no grievance, because I have at last unveiled the genesis and growth of my maladjustment. The process was simply

this, that while I was being carried along by the momentum of our history, most of my countrymen were being dragged backwards by its inertia. We have been travelling in opposite directions and are still doing so. I can now see both the motions as from an independent point in space. I have found liberation from a nightmare.[4]

The antecedents of Chaudhuri's thesis are lost to him. He links the weak and debilitated condition of India's inhabitants to her climate, an intriguing restatement of textbook axioms with which earlier schoolbook authors would have agreed. As one nineteenth century author explained:

...in the past ages the hardy tribes which came down time after time from the cold countries of the north lost their strength and courage from living in the hot plains of Hindustan. They were swept away by other tribes from the same cold northern climes....[5]

The schoolbooks would also have agreed with Chaudhuri that Indian peoples were characterized by weakness, malice, and decadence; a main thesis of books Chaudhuri almost certainly studied in school was that India's strength and vigor could be renewed only by infusions of energy from British culture, values, and customs.

"I have only to look within myself and contemplate my life," Chaudhuri writes, "to discover India."[6] The country he discovers is the same one that earlier textbooks found. Now, their stereotypes become Chaudhuri's own; they are integrated into his view of India and himself. Consistent with his interpretation is Chaudhuri's persistent attribution of his good qualities to British ideas and values learned in his youth. Bad traits are left to India. It is as if he wishes to identify the exact degree and measure of the healthy influences (British) that have shaped his life and the retrograde forces (Indian) that have inhibited it. Having done so, he can then give due praise to the man who was the true source for all that is sound within him, the one who was the inspiration for the man he wishes he could become — his father.

It is clearly the father who is the hero of the book. He is the apotheosis, for his son at least, of the Western-educated Indian. He and he alone created the world in which Chaudhuri and his siblings grew. He gave his children their mixed cultural heritage, a world which was a cultural amalgam, where no aspect of life was untouched by foreign values, yet no aspect completely altered either. By his presence, image, and ambitions, he gave the physical and intellectual substrata of his children's lives their focus and their purpose. His commitment to the ideals and values of British culture was complete. His antagonism to indigenous lifeways was unqualified. Chaudhuri's later historical theories and his psychological conflicts can be traced to both that commitment and that antagonism.

Chaudhuri's father was from a traditional village family. He had received some English education through his mother's accidental discovery of a hoard of money. But when those funds were exhausted, his education stopped. As a result, he was qualified to practice law only at the local level. "My father," Chaudhuri recalls

> was the abandoned son of the old order. He was educated by the money which his mother had found in the hidden hoard; with all the clan behind him, he had gone to seek a new livelihood at Kishorganj with only eight annas in his pocket. He must have felt that the bond had finally snapped and he was not sorry. He must have felt, and here I seem to touch the heart of the matter and to hit the hard core of truth, that to live at Banagram was to live without working, to live also without purpose, to live only in the empty shell of the past. . . .[7]

The father's hostility to traditional ways permeated the household. "My father never explained this latent dislike," Chaudhuri recalls, "but from my young days I heard him speak of the patriarchal type of family in a deprecating manner."[8] Never openly criticizing his own father, he still "gave us the impression that the most serious vice of these families to his thinking was parental selfishness." Among his charges were the selfish hoarding of food by the male elders and the absence of "natural affections." "The women and children," Chaudhuri's father claimed, "had to take their meals in the common kitchen and live on the plainest diet while the elders savoured no end of delicacies in their private rooms."[9] Children were spoiled — that much the father conceded — but only by the women in the family, and through the "deliberate indifference" of the male elders.

Chaudhuri's mother, somewhat surprisingly, shared her husband's antipathy to traditional life. She was so adamant in her opposition to superstition, her son tells us, that she concurred in the father's decision not to allow horoscopes to be drawn up for her children. "My mother," Chaudhuri recalls in this context, "was such a reformist that after her marriage she had even refused to chew the betel leaf . . . and as a mere girl of fourteen to eighteen had for five long years defied the jeers and importunities of the whole village."[10]

The parents' hostility extended even to the father's ancestral village.

> My father personally never seemed to feel quite at home in his ancestral village. He even disliked it positively. And this dislike was shared by my mother. They visited it as a matter of duty and form in obedience to the universal habit of paying the ancestral village the homage it claimed. But when it came to the question of taking Banagram nearer to their life, they felt all their inner revulsion. They went to Banagram thrice with the intention of settling there, but came back every time.[11]

The two villages were close, and the custom of living apart from the paternal home, Chaudhuri notes, was no longer uncommon. With the death of the paternal grandfather, the matter was resolved and the Chaudhuri family remained at Kishorganj.

In matters other than place of residence, the Chaudhuri household was also unorthodox. A peculiarity of their birth, the author notes, is that all the children were born "under the auspices of our father."[12] The mother's family was poor and could not send for her before each child's birth. So after the death of the grandfather, Chaudhuri's father insisted that the children must be born in his own house at Kishorganj. Other Kishorganj families followed this practice, but

> there was perhaps a difference in the spirit in which my father shouldered his responsibilities. Instead of maintaining an attitude of detached neutrality while the women managed the affair, he appeared to take everything very actively on himself.[13]

It was the father who was the architect of the family's style of life. His house in Kishorganj was Bengali in style, composed of huts of bamboo and cane built around an interior courtyard. But the furnishings were more culturally eclectic. There were two or three beds, heavy affairs not easily moved, and a number of steel trunks in which a variety of household goods were securely locked. The father's modern spirit was evident in the presence of "a table with one single drawer, a dressing mirror, a glass-fronted cupboard and two racks with open shelves." In the cupboard were the written sources for the children's acculturation: the Holy Bible ("in Bengali"); Anandale's English dictionary; Milton's poetic works (the last lines of Satan in *Paradise Lost* were a favorite paternal quotation); "some volumes" by Burke; the plays *Julius Caesar* and *Othello*; "a few novels by Bankim Chandra Chatterjee and the works of the first modern Bengali poet, Michael Madhusudan Dutt. Books of religious songs were kept beside the mother's bed.[14]

The furnishings and literature found their complements in the decorations of the walls. Most pictures were traditional — "usually very tawdry images of Hindu gods and goddesses" — but alongside them were hung a pair of stag antlers, a colored reproduction of Raphaelo's *La Donna della Sedia*, and two pictures illustrating the victories of the British in the Boer War. These last were a continuing source of fascination through Chaudhuri's boyhood. Periodically the author would coerce his elder brother into climbing to the correct height by means of various trunks and reading off the names of the soldiers. The brother would read first the regiments' and then the commanders' names.

Standing in front of the Praetoria picture he would say, 'General Roberts, General Kitchener, General Staff, General Staff, General Staff. . . . ' 'All General Staff?' I would ask perplexed. 'Yes,' My brother would confirm. . . . It appeared to both of us that Staff was a very common surname among British Generals.[15]

The father's experiments as a pioneer and innovator went beyond the environment of the house. He was driven, his son explains, "by a passion for creating a new type of human being, a new breed, so that he might rise above his environment, have his revenge upon it, not individually and episodically but generically and for all times."[16] He was intensely preoccupied with family life and the raising of his children.

My father's originality was that he built up a Bengali-Hindu family of a different type. We never called our father brother nor our mother daughter-in-law. It was a family in which every person knew his place and his function. In fact the status of my mother was noticed by all our relatives and neighbors. The authority she wielded was considered to be a special characteristic of the little group of human beings comprised by Upendra Narayan Chaudhuri, his wife, Sushilla Sundari Chaudhurani and their children.[17]

Dissatisfied with the progress of his sons in school, the father tutored them himself for a period of two years; his son proudly attributes his self-confidence in English to his father's teaching. Exercise and nutrition were equally emphasized. Believing that all of life "ultimately rested on physical foundations," the father carefully monitored the diet and eating habits of his family.

He prescribed the kind of food we should take and the hours at which we should take it. He fixed our hours of study, our hours of sleep, our hours of exercise and play, our hours of recreation. And what was even more remarkable he never permitted us to read beyond the prescribed hour and in no circumstances were we allowed to sit up at night in order to read for examinations. . . .[18]

Yet the father was no tyrant. "I heard him say time and again," Chaudhuri recalls, "to my mother, to me, to my brothers that he would never try to influence our moral and religious opinions and even in worldly matters such as the choice of a profession and marriage he would only give us advice and take no initiative unless we ourselves wanted him to."[19] He was the only Bengali father Chaudhuri knew who kept to this view of the relationship between a father and his sons, a consistency his son attributes to his "liberalism" and his belief that "freedom by itself was as important as the ends for which it is supposed to be desirable."[20] Friends and relatives accused him of having spoiled his children.

Chaudhuri's admiration for what was orderly and regular in his childhood is unequivocal. Not only was his father aware of what would benefit the growth of his children, but, more important to his son, he had "the will power to carry out the changes he thought necessary."[21] In the "regularity" and "discipline" of his home Chaudhuri finds the greatest difference between his family and surrounding Indian households. There, he notes, "everybody ate what he liked, ate at any hour he liked, came in at any time that he liked, went to bed at any time he liked. . . . "[22] Joint family relationships inevitably got "mixed up" but in the Chaudhuri home there was no confusion: "Our family grew up as a true family — composed of the father, the mother and the children — in which each element had its due share of importance and its proper status."[23]

Ironically, the father's enthusiasm for foreign ways may have fostered in his children an exaggerated awareness of their own Indian origins. In his eagerness to ally with his father's perspective, no cultural relativism informs Chaudhuri's views. He condemns whatever "Indian" qualities he finds in himself and others. More than once negative qualities are assumed to be the residue of an Indian heritage. All Chaudhuri's own difficulties in life — his failure in the M.A. examinations, his inability to make plans and stick to them, his failure to follow in the (Western) footsteps of his father — all are explained by the dominance of indigenous traits in his character. His father's ability to identify Western values and take them as his own made him an acculturated and superior person. By implication it is the son's inability to do the same which makes him the stereotypical Indian.

In the most negative aspects of his character, Chaudhuri identifies with his mother. Her chronic hysteria, self-concern and demanding egoism made her, in her son's view, the opposite of the self-sacrificing father. "What my mother found wanting in my father I could never discover," Chaudhuri writes.

> To all appearance there was no more devoted and loyal husband to be met with anywhere; a husband who made no demands on his wife, on the contrary was ready to answer any and every demand from her. In actual fact he seriously weakened his splendid constitution and went very near ruining his worldly career for her sake. Yet she was always complaining of his conduct towards her.[24]

Nevertheless, Chaudhuri tells us, he was the "true son" of this mother, more like her in temperament and behavior than like his father.

Between 1900 and 1920, the years in which Chaudhuri grew to manhood, his family moved into and out of Calcutta, and the nationalist movement intensified. These complications added to the already confused loyalties and identifications of his childhood. The family did not escape the nationalist fervour which seized Bengal in the twentieth century. Chadhuri clearly remembers the day a gentleman arrived at their house carrying with him a bundle of silk threads. The boys were to be initiated into the nationalist movement. Their father asked them all to bathe in the river "and then in a state of cleanliness tied the thread around our wrists as a token of the brotherhood of all Bengalis."[25] The parents were too practical to destroy their European clothes, but these were packed away and Indian-made *dhotis* worn in their place. At first, Chaudhuri recalls, they felt "as coarse, heavy and thick as sack cloth."

In his family's eyes, the father was fully identified with the anti-British movement. When the school cricket trophy was found to be of foreign origin and authorities refused to replace it, the father withdrew his children from the school. He began to investigate national institutions and even to think of "developing the newly established National school in town."[26] His children responded with equal enthusiasm. The Kishorganj family sang the songs of Bankim Chandra Chatterjea, believed in the "national renaissance" of Hindu values and took definite political positions: "We always turned up our noses at the mere mention of the moderates and even before we had begun to air our contempt for them, a complete transformation had come over our spirit."[27] Nationalism even found expression in the more erratic behavior of the mother. On one journey back to Kishorganj, she was offered some water in a glass jug — "suddenly she took a violent dislike to the vessel as a foreign article and told my brother . . . to break it."[28]

The jug was dispatched against the side of a tree. The conflicting legacy it represented was not so easily set aside. The dual message of Chaudhuri's childhood — admire the British/oppose the British — surfaced later in his life in a persistent ambivalence to nationalism and its manifestations. During his college years, Chaudhuri was painfully aware, he recalls, of the existence of two subcultures in Calcutta — the world of the revolutionaries and the world of the secret police. They were "two worlds, hidden from my eyes, spectral presences investing me closely and bodiless evils shunning our sunlit existence yet tormenting it with their malign telekinesis."[29] Both worlds frightened and attracted him. He and fellow students feared the "ever present" danger that they might unknowingly become involved with revolutionary activities and be seized by the police. Yet at the same time, during his preparation for the B.A. examinations, Chaudhuri became fascinated with "the technical aspects of warfare." Page after page of his notebooks were covered with sketches of guns and planes. "I am sure," he recalls, "had my room by any chance been searched by the police, I should have been in trouble."[30]

Only three times did Chaudhuri become totally caught up in the nationalist protest — in 1906, less definitely in the 1920s, and again in 1931. Generally, he was restrained in his emotions and, even in retrospect, proud of his ability to separate himself from the "herd" who blindly followed the nationalist leaders. At the same time, he was identifying himself more and more as an academic, an identity which called for a somewhat different set of loyalties. An essay on historical objectivity, written at the end of his twentieth year, demonstrated his ability for independent thought. While it owed much (he admits) to the "ideas and even phrases" of Lord Acton, still it showed, he thinks, his ability to formulate

independently of personal example or guidance an attitude towards life which on the one hand did not grow out of the system of values I had acquired earlier in life and on the other was in complete opposition to the prevailing supernationalistic ideas and emotions.[31]

But conflicting loyalties continued to disrupt his life. In 1919 the "unruly disorder" of Calcutta protests against the Amritsar massacre disturbed and angered him. "To my great disgust," he recalls, "I saw bands of ragged street urchins throw mud and dust at the tram cars. This was my first experience with a form of rebellion against the British which was to become typical of the city . . . but even so they made me furious. . . ."[32] Yet he also could be "rocked by these tremors of passion" — if only momentarily and in fantasy. Attending a concert in Calcutta with an English friend, he was seated in one of the galleries of the theater:

Below me were thronged in tiers and rows, English men and English women in their graceful evening dress and I could hardly see one Indian. As I listened to the Meistersinger overture and the Jupiter Symphony, one violent thought kept recurring like the ticking of a clock in my mind, worked up as it was to a state of heated and excited imagination. It was the thought of dropping a bomb on the crowd below and killing the whole lot. On my way home I told this to my English friend. He only remarked "How interesting."[33]

Chaudhuri's ambivalence may have been fostered by his family's move to Calcutta, a move which challenged an earlier certainty of status and self-esteem. In the world of his boyhood, he remembers, the family's standing had been unquestioned. "We saw," he writes,

no occasion to emphasize or even refer to a thing which was so uncontested, and felt contemptuous only when a plebian tried to trot out a claim to good birth by pretending the sort of anecdotes to which we thought we only had the right.[34]

Family status — acknowledged equally in Kishorganj and in the ancestral village five miles away — was enhanced by the father's innovative adaptations of Western ideologies and materials. Inside this family stronghold, Chaudhuri dreamed of success in the outside world. From the age of twelve, he recalls, he planned to become a university professor. Within the family circle he was the "acknowledged doctrinaire."[35]

Calcutta called into question the security of those earlier years. On arrival, taking the advice of friends, the father abandoned plans to enroll his sons in the Hare school, the most prestigious school in the city, and sent them instead to a smaller, less competitive institution. He feared, Chaudhuri recalls, "we might not be able to hold our own against the boys of the bigger schools who came from the best, or rather the wealthiest families of Calcutta and were, as a rule, very turbulent and undisciplined."[36] An even greater blow was to follow. Within three years it was apparent that the father's business was failing, and the family would be forced into retreat to Kishorganj. Although everyone opposed the move, preferring even drastically reduced finances and the possible loss of the children's education to the idea of returning to the *mofussil*, the father insisted. He was "not the man to shift the burden to other and weaker shoulders," Chaudhuri writes, "and he took a decision which was consistent with his manly nature."[37]

"In appearance and manners," Chaudhuri recalls, "I was a semi-savage when I came to Calcutta."[38] With his father's failure and the sudden shock of seeing his family (and himself) in the context of the larger city, Chaudhuri retreated. He presents himself and his family as rustics. The city, he insists "polished off the rough edges" but could not break his "rustic core."[39] Although "I learned to speak the standard Bengali, yet I never gave up my dialect."[40] There is more than a little pride supporting this insistence on a rural identity. Chaudhuri retains it, almost mockingly, after long years of city residence had rendered it irrelevant. Similarly, he almost boasts of his inability to enter the elite society of Calcutta. Although he lived in the city for twenty years and belonged to a group which studied Tagore's poetry, he had only one conversation with the poet. Having met Jawaharlal Nehru, he was urged by various friends to maintain the acquaintance; he refused to do so. "The cultivation of important people did not come naturally to me," he writes, "my life was the hermit crab's life."[41]

In school in Calcutta, Chaudhuri sought refuge in an absorption in study and renewed dreams for an educational career. His way of life, he writes, came to appear "very unsocial, unbalanced and wayward in its one-sided pursuit of intellectual interests."[42] In Kishorganj, a "pioneering" father had raised his sons in the great traditions of Western civilization; in

Calcutta, one of those sons sheltered his pride and an early identification with his father in a commitment to Western modes of study. When Chaudhuri began the master's program he was delighted to discover that a course on French history had been added. To confine himself to Indian history, he thought, would be a great mistake:

> I should in the first instance be cut off from world currents and become parochial and next, make no progress beyond the second rate in scholarly techniques.[43]

The act of studying and the emotions of scholarship attracted him. The most inspiring speech he ever heard was one, he admits, he could not fully comprehend. The speaker's accent eluded him. Nevertheless, he concludes, "the impression the lecture made on me was profound."[44] For every true scholar knows, Chaudhuri asserts, that the true mark of his profession "is a capacity for experiencing the emotion of scholarship."[45]

Chaudhuri's dramatic success in the B.A. examination, he recalls, seemed to justify everything. But paradoxically, success left him even more vulnerable to the fear of failure. He had always feared tests and found preparation for them difficult. "I disliked and even dispised examinations when they were not immediate realities," he remembers, "and got worried about them when they approached." He had taken his Matriculation Examination with "no preparation," passing only, he believed, because of the solidity of his previous education. Before his bachelor's exam he had become so terrified that "on its eve I ran up and down a ladder quite a number of times recklessly inviting a fall and the consequent breaking of a limb or two in order to have a valid excuse for not going up." Now the master's examination was preceded by a period of "black unrelieved misery." He turned to drawing up plans for an Indian army and "the making of cardboard boxes in my room."[46]

Cracks in the edifice of Chaudhuri's ambitions began to appear with his withdrawal from the M.A. examination in 1920. Within another year, he would pull the entire structure down around him.

> The great adventure came to nothing. I failed to pass my M.A. examination. I sat for three papers and on the morning of the fourth told my mother that I was unprepared, had done badly so far and was not going up for the rest of the examination.[47]

It was a failure without conviction, neither spontaneous nor inevitable. Even Chaudhuri's family assumed that he would reapply and retake the tests in the following year.

But the next year the problem had worsened. Chaudhuri was signaling in the traditional Indian manner that he was in distress. "I was in a state of continual worry," he recalls, "trying to keep up the appearance of study, yet finding myself incapable of concentrating on it." He did not openly mention his troubles, but " ... as months went by I found my physical and mental strength progressively becoming inadequate.... " Under normal circumstances, his behavior might have provoked an inquiry, but, significantly, his distress coincided with preparations for his brother's wedding. Finally he was forced to raise the matter himself. "Being unable to endure the torture any longer," he recalls, he told his father "briefly but decidedly that I was not going up for the examination again and would accept whatever employment I might secure."[48]

Chaudhuri may have hoped for an energetic response to a decision which abandoned the ambitions of a lifetime. But his father "must have been anticipating some such announcement" for all he said was "all right."[49] Later, Chaudhuri would praise the "liberalism" of a father who refused to make decisions for his sons. His inner feelings may have been more ambivalent. Throughout his life, in spite of the expressed convictions of his father, Chaudhuri held on to a very traditional dependence on that parent. It was, he admits, always his father who intervened in times of trouble or economic distress — once to give money for a hobby his son wished to pursue; on another occasion to salvage the occupational disasters of his second son's life. In fact, "the last call he thought he heard," Chaudhuri remembers,

> was from me. I had written to him to give the news that I had lost my employment. But although in desperate straits I had not asked for help nor even for advice. He wrote back saying that he was sorry to hear of my unemployment and would soon come down to Calcutta and try to do something for me. He was struck dead in his chair about an hour after writing that letter.[50]

Against this evidence of continued paternal intervention and concern, Chaudhuri places his conviction that his decision not to retake the M.A. examination marked the beginning of a coolness in his father's affections. A "coldly indifferent" attitude arose, he insists, which was maintained "so consistently that it hurt me more than even an angry and continuous abuse would have done."[51] The cause, he is sure, was the injury he had given his father's plans and hopes. "Obviously," he wrote, his father "had cast out with a resolute exercise of the will all ambitions he had formed on my behalf and if any wounds were left in his mind by the operation he was not the man to make a display of them."[52]

In the period immediately following the wedding of his brother and his own fateful decision, Chaudhuri's life was one of progressive deterioration and paralysis. He managed to find a job as a clerk in the Military Accounts Department of the government. "There was plenty of good will and opportunities for me in my new office," he writes, "and I had only to work hard and make use of them in order to ensure for myself a prosperous and stable career in the service of the Government."[53] For a few months he did work hard, carefully enjoying the "most proper feelings and sentiments about my new opportunities." He was grateful for the work and relieved, he insists, that he would not remain continually dependent on his father. Having proved himself capable of doing the work, however, he soon acquired an aversion to it.

> I began neglecting them [his duties] to the detriment of my prospects... It was useless to argue with me, I remained wholly unreconciled to the Military Accounts Department and resolved to leave it as soon as I could. In the meanwhile I went on neglecting my work and not only losing the good reputation I had earned for myself in the first few months but also putting my friends in the office in an awkward position.

He was unable either to work or to quit.

> No one could have gone on like this without having to pay for it. If I was not made to do so by being turned out of my job, I had to make up in mental distress. It was of two kinds: first, the distress arising out of the aversion I felt for my work and secondly the distress caused by the consciousness of my neglect of duty. Only one of two things could put an end to it, either conscientious work in my post, or its immediate relinquishment. But as I did not possess the strength to have recourse to any one of these two remedies, the only result was that the double-edged suffering turned inward and corroded me. There never was a time in my life when I was so passively and weakly pessimistic. I thought continually of death, as if death ever helped a weak creature to find release from the punishment he was gratuitously bringing on himself through his own folly. Thus instead of death, what came to me was a sort of moral and intellectual valetudinarianism. I led a life of extreme anemia and feebleness. Yet the most extraordinary part of this feebleness was that if it made me incapable of effort, it did nothing to blunt the nerve of pain. The more complete the paralysis of my will and capacity for work, the more sensitive and quick did I become in my suffering.[54]

Chaudhuri's paralysis drew strength from his need for time. He had not so much failed in his postgraduate career as he had simply refused to succeed. Similarly, Erikson has suggested, when the problems of establishing an adult identity seem insurmountable or when people fear that too early a commitment may prove fatal to still-developing potentialities, they too may seek a momentary escape from adult roles in what Erikson has called a *psycho-social moratorium*. Through postponement, they gain time necessary for the growth and development of inherent abilities. Yet delay also carries, Erikson warns, the potential danger of entrapment.

> Then the moratorium has failed; the individual is defined too early, and he has committed himself because circumstances or indeed authorities have committed him.[55]

Chaudhuri's years of hesitation caught him, in his own eyes at least, in the identity of a failure. His insistence on the fact of failure identified him, in a minor way, with his father and, during his father's lifetime, ensured that parent's continuing help and support. In a more important sense, however, Chaudhuri's self-definition carried a second accusation more central to his life — he had not been able to carry out his father's grand design; he had failed to become a true son of his father.

This second accusation becomes explicit in his description of the crucial incident of his life: his failure to pass the master's examination. It was a failure caused by numerous weaknesses characteristic of him, but conspicuous by their absence in the character of his father. First, he was frightened. Throughout his life he had been terrified and apprehensive of examinations. Second, his health had failed. He suffered from a "lack of vitality" and at the time of the exams, he recalls, "my strength was not equal to sustaining even the routine of studies called for by an examination."[56] But third, and by far the most devastating, had been his failure of will. He was not prepared for the tests. His reading had been "too diffuse and haphazard."[57] The diffusion, however, had not come from ignorance of proper study habits. "I could," Chaudhuri wrote, "draw up plans which if executed with steadfastness would have given me not only success in examinations but also a solid founding in the subjects I was to learn."[58] But having planned, he could not act.

> I never commanded the will power to carry out my own deliberate projects. Frightened or tired out by the too exacting programme I was always taking the virtuous resolution to put through, I gave myself up to my immediate impulses and read only what I was momentarily interested in and the more I read about it, the more interested and bogged in its details did I become for the time being. Thus although I came to acquire a deep knowledge of certain aspects of certain subjects very unusual in a student of my age, taking it all in all, I did not succeed in having an even grounding in any subject.[59]

Fear, physical debility, and lack of will: could any Englishman have given a more devastating critique of an Indian's failure? Yet even though these criticisms had originated in the textbooks of the English-language schools, their source in Chaudhuri's life had been the teachings and ideology of his father. How often in the autobiography does Chaudhuri emphasize for us his father's character, strength of will, and self-control? — he who had "cast out with a resolute exercise of the will" all ambitions for the career of his second son; he who had said "a score of times that a man was nothing if he was not self-willed"; he who had emphasized throughout his son's life the importance of nutrition, exercise, and care of one's health? How much bravery was implicit in the description of the "pioneering spirit" of a father who had defied traditions and established a "true family" for his wife and children? How much courage in the acts of one who had openly supported the cause of India's independence? "If in my youth and manhood," Chaudhuri has written, "I had not the strong constitution he desired for me, it was because I neglected his advice and in matters of physical culture pursued the bad old tradition."[60] But more than his father's advice on physical conditioning had been neglected when, weakened by the Indian elements in his character, Chaudhuri had fallen back into the "bad old tradition." With his failure to study for and pass the master's examination, he had, in his own mind at least, failed to become the new man his father had intended to create. Of the period of deep depression into which this failure led, he writes, "Yet it was neither abysinth, nor lust, nor disease, nor remorse for some hideous suppressed crimes, nor unrequited love which had brought me to this pass. My new spirits were absolute. There seemed to be no cure for them."[61]

Amidst the chaos of independence and partition, Chaudhuri recast the disparate elements of his childhood into a cohesive whole. His matured talents as a writer gave this new synthesis full expression in his autobiography: "In May, 1947," he writes, "I began work on the book and I did so only when the conviction was forced on me that unless I acted promptly the demonstration of my thesis was likely to precede its enunciation."[62] To appreciate what was kept and what abandoned in the process of this reordering of identity we have only to read the dedication of the autobiography: "To the memory of the British Empire in India," Chaudhuri wrote,

> which conferred subjecthood on us but withheld citizenship. To which yet everyone of us threw out the challenge Civis Britannicus Sum, because all that was good and living within us was made, shaped and quickened by the same British Rule.[63]

In observing the murderous (Indian) passions which had engulfed the subcontinent in those years, Chaudhuri had come to a resolution. All that was Indian in origin was decadent and dying; all that was the product of contact with the West was vital and living. His perception brought new order and clarity into his personal life even as it precipitated the development of a historical thesis which dichotomized India's past. Not surprisingly, his enlightenment was shortly followed by his physical departure from India. As he hoped to leave her psychologically, he would, in fact, leave her physically. He wrote:

> As I see the matter, the generalizations of my countrymen are unconscious or subconscious, while I flatter myself that I have arrived at mine after laborious and deliberate inquiry. In any case, they are consciously held and I am fully aware of their implications. I know they are leading me away from my country and my people.[64]

In 1942 Chaudhuri had left Calcutta and the province of Bengal, the land of his birth, to live in Delhi. In the 1950s he would leave both Delhi and India to travel to England. His new consciousness of self had become even more sharply focused, one suspects, in the writing of his autobiography. If all that was Indian within him was not completely rejected, still, those "ancient tendencies" to which he was heir were subjected to the most negative scrutiny. His departure was for Oxford. There he would take up residence. His new surroundings would be alien, perhaps, in physical appearance and associations; but they might provide a more congenial atmosphere in which to live the life of the "Civis Britannicus" his father had once hoped he would become.

CHAPTER
7

Fathers and Sons:
The Second Generation

"LOOKING BACK FROM THIS LONG DISTANCE upon those early memories," writes Bipin Chandra Pal in his autobiography, "I oftentimes feel tempted to try and realize how my father felt towards me and ask myself very often have I the same feelings and mental attitudes towards my sons?" [1] Pal had broken with his father during his college years when the father objected to his membership in the Calcutta Brahmo Samaj. "He refused to accept my letters," Pal recalls. "He would not permit me to go near him, not even when, as happened during his short stay at Sylhet about the middle of 1880 he was ill and I wanted to see him." [2] They became reconciled only shortly before the father's death. Pal was left with lingering regrets, and later in his life, when he had become a nationalist, an "extremist," and even to some extent a defender of Hinduism, he found his earlier apostasy inexplicable.

Pal's inability to explain earlier attitudes sets an autobiographical tone of deep nostalgia. Memories of a childhood intimacy with his father are set against the background of a maternal relationship which was unusually cold and austere. "My father," Pal recalls, "tried so far as he could to keep me constantly near him. . . . At meal-times I used to have a seat placed for me at right angles to my father's and he used to feed me with his own hands . . . every night I slept by him, almost inside his protecting embrace." [3] In contrast, Pal remembers his mother as "remarkably reserved and contained." [4] "I do not remember," he writes, "to have been treated by her in my early infancy much less in my later boyhood with outward fondness." [5] Pal's mother was the father's second wife, married while the first, who was barren, remained alive. Even her son recognized that she suffered from her position as cowife in the father's household. But not even this, in her son's eyes, justified her peculiarly unindulgent treatment of him and "in my bitterness," Pal recalls, "oftentimes I actually believed that my own mother was dead and she was only my stepmother." [6]

Throughout the first volume of his autobiography, Pal struggles to understand how he could have allowed youthful convictions to completely shatter his early closeness with his father. In the 1860s, Pal had come from the East Bengal *mofussil* to attend college in Calcutta. He soon joined the Brahmo Samaj. But unlike Sitanatha Tattvabhushan, an East Bengal contemporary who also joined the Brahmos in this period, Pal's autobiography makes clear that his interest in the Brahmos' religious reforms overlay a nature whose inclinations were more political. Pal initially visited the society only because a close hostel friend went regularly to their meetings. He converted to the sect of Shivanath Sastri, a sect, by his description, based on a "fuller" definition of the Brahmo purpose. Sastri's group, Pal claims, opposed "current image worship and caste-domination" in Hindu society, but was also dedicated to "the modern ideals of Equality, Liberty and Fraternity." [7] Nor was the "physical side" overlooked. Members

> pledged themselves . . . to learn to ride and shoot and preach the duties
> of acquiring these military trainings and aptitudes to their fellow
> countrymen.[8]

The program prefigured Pal's later interests as a nationalist. By the time he wrote his autobiography he had moved away from the religious and reformist concerns central to the Brahmo program of the early 1870s. Nor was he himself sure any longer that he understood the motives that had originally inspired his early rebellion against his father. Somewhat ironically, given his description of his relations with his mother, Pal partially attributes his willingness to join the Samaj to her death. "My mother's death," he writes, "practically removed the bands that tied my heart and my life to my family and home. And this very considerably made it easy for me to cut myself off from the old orthodox society which I was compelled to do by openly joining the Brahmo Samaj." [9] But it was two years after his mother died, in 1877 — the same year he failed to pass the Fine Arts examination — that Pal joined the Brahmos. When his father learned what the son had done, he first withheld funds, then ceased to send them altogether. Pal withdrew from college.

The separation between father and son ended only with the father's deathbed wish for reconciliation. Pal's memories constantly reflect his sense of lost intimacy with his father. "How I wish," he writes at one point, "I had understood something of the Vaishnavic cult and culture during my father's life-time so that we could talk these deep things of life together and understand each other more intimately than what was possible in the days of my youth."[10]

Unable to explain his youthful attitudes, Pal finally takes refuge from his guilt in an ingenious interpretation of a childhood episode. When he was only a small boy, he recalls, his father bought for him at auction a set of English furniture — "A small table, teapoy, chair and easy-chair" which had previously belonged to the son of the local English magistrate. "It was a very small thing," he admits, for his father was not Western-educated and the family's life-style was Bengali. "But this had," he continues, "a great effect in shaping my character...."

> In buying the furniture of young Shaw for my use, my father unconsciously introduced a very great innovation in my life which had, I feel, a far-reaching effect in giving certain impulses to my future life and evolution. In my young days I was very partial to English ways and ideas; and I have often wondered whether the accident that led my father to bring me up while I was a boy in the use and enjoyment of the furniture of young Shaw had not something to do with it.[11]

Pal was right to seek the source of his early rebellion in the experiences of his childhood — although, perhaps, too eager to see the symbol of his conflicts as their cause. His memories of his father and the conflicts of his life offer a curious contrast to the recollections and problems of the three authors previously discussed. Surendranath Banerjea, Subhas Chandra Bose, and Nirad Chaudhuri all grew up in households with fathers who were enthusiastic proponents of the new English-language education and Western values and ideas. All three fathers urged their sons towards careers in the upper echelons of the institutions of the Raj. Pal's childhood, on the other hand, was predominantly traditional. His father, a devout Hindu, vigorously objected to the son's reformist and Western ideas. Pal's affectionate and nostalgic memories of his father contrast sharply with the ambivalence of Banerjea's, Bose's, and Chaudhuri's. The openness of his early rebellion and the simplicity of his later regrets in no way resemble the more confused emotions and psychological conflicts characteristic of the other three lives.

As adults, Banerjea, Bose, and Chaudhuri were deeply troubled by the sense that what was Indian in them was inherently inferior to what was foreign. In Banerjea, those feelings expressed themselves in a continuing preoccupation with issues of hard work and health; in Bose, through a repeated need to place himself in opposition to authority; and in Chaudhuri, in the constant denigration of all that was "Indian" in habit or character. In discussing those three authors we used Erik Erikson's concepts of identity and identity confusion to focus on and explain the central crisis of their lives. Can we now apply these same concepts to a life history as different in its conflicts and tensions as that of Bipin Chandra Pal?

The concept of identity, as we stated earlier, is essential to a description of adolescence, a stage that entered the lives of Indian children with the introduction of English-language education and British-style occupations. Only then did the demands of British institutions and the diminishing importance of traditional sources of identity combine to make the definition of an adult identity a prerequisite for movement from boyhood in the English-language schools to adult life in the world of the Raj. Questions of identity, then, have relevance to the lives of all Indians who — like Pal — shared these experiences. Identity confusion, on the other hand, may represent a critical stage in the lives of only certain of these people.

For Erikson, identity confusion defines a more or less normal phase in the developmental process that moves children into adulthood. Indeed, he emphasizes that the confusions of this stage are necessary to the process. Only where the tensions of late adolescence activate already existing problems and conflicts does the confusion become a potential life crisis. But the crises faced by some Indian autobiographers suggest that what might have been normal developmental confusion in a Western context could become more severely disturbing under the particular conditions of British India.

The negative cultural identity created by the foreign ideas, values and prejudices of the English educational system added a new element to the psychological development of some Indian children. Negative images of what it meant to be an Indian pervaded the conscious and unconscious identifications of many Western-educated Indian children and became catalysts for intense confusion, ambivalence, and self-hate. In the autobiographies of Banerjea, Bose, and Chaudhuri uncertainties about adult careers, and conflicting attitudes towards father and self are continuing motifs. It was these authors' ambivalence, more than any preexistent or specifically individual psychological problem, that precipitated the crises they faced in late adolescence. For these Western-educated Indians, and for many of the other autobiographers, identity confusion was more than a single stage along the path of normal development. It was a period of special psychological vulnerability and danger. Men, like Surendranath Banerjea, who successfully negotiated its crises and went on to later fame and success, carried the ghosts of their earlier struggles with them well into later life.

But some autobiographers did not experience this same psychological crisis — as the autobiography of Bipin Chandra Pal demonstrates. For Pal, exposure to Western education (the analogue of the English furniture he remembers) brought new sources of identification and precipitated intense family conflicts as he moved into adult life. The memory of these conflicts left Pal with regrets in his old age. But neither the ideas of the educational system nor the conflicts that beset him in late adolescence and early adulthood brought the inner confusions and psychic disintegration that threatened others. Similarly, authors like

Dhonde Karve or R. P. Paranjpye remember their rebellions against orthodox ideas and the difficulties of negotiating family relationships afterward, but their life histories do not show the deeper psychological confusion that appears in accounts of other lives. Indeed, so marked is the lack of psychological conflict in the lives of some nineteenth-century Indians that one historian has suggested that the process of acculturation presented Indians with no real difficulties but simply required that they shift gears and directions as they operated now in the world of traditional values, now in that of British India.[12]

Why did the exposure to the teachings of the English-language educational system produce two such widely differing psychological responses? The answer must lie beyond the more superficial aspects of acculturation, beyond an author's momentary acceptance or rejection of a style of dress or speech. Instead we must concentrate on the depth of influence of Western culture in the background of the author's family. We must consider how completely an author's environment might have integrated Western and Indian traditions in his childhood; how conscious or unconscious he may have been of the cultural antecedents of a turn of phrase or an item of attire. It becomes important to ask whether an author's father or uncle, paternal or maternal grandparents were Western-educated — to know how many generations back the custom of Western education extended. A child growing up in a home with an English-educated parent or grandparent will be more deeply, if less consciously, influenced by the themes and emphases of his later education, if only because some elements of it will be already familiar to him. He will certainly be more conversant with Western ideas and paraphernalia then an individual who is the first in the family, village, or caste to attend a Western school.

When we take these autobiographies out of chronological sequence and arrange them according to the depth of Western education within the generational history of the authors' families, an interesting pattern emerges. The experience of Western education created a different consciousness and, consequently, resulted in quite different conflicts and tensions for the first generation in a family to be Western-educated than it did for the second generation. It was primarily for that second generation, the sons of already Western-educated fathers, that the process of becoming an adult and the need to integrate ambivalent images and identifications from childhood into an adult identity became most complex and conflict-ridden.

Of course the penetration of Western education and culture into Indian family life was always more complex than this simple division between first and second generations allows. Autobiographies illustrate how the circumstances of joint family living could complicate a family's cultural environment. A father might work in a traditional occupation, while an uncle received a Western education and joined the Brahmo Samaj. A parent might not know English, but work for the British in a Westernized office environment. A mother might be described as a "traditional" woman, yet be the daughter of a highly Westernized and acculturated family. The usefulness of the distinction between first and second generation, however, lies in its ability to focus our attention on the cultural environment of a child's early years and not in the possibility that these distinctions might be applied to all autobiographers with equal and absolute precision.

In the autobiographies of those who were first in their families to attend the English-language schools, the Western ideas taught there appear in sharp contrast to the traditions of the author's orthodox society. Superstition was bad; rationalism was good. Through education, Indians would become Westernized, and this acculturation would be both desirable and possible. One Punjabi author recalls his indignation as a youth when an older man attempted to touch his feet in a traditional gesture of respect.

> My education and training in the American Presbyterian Mission School, Rawalpindi, had taught me to believe that it was a sin for one man to bow to another.[13]

Rationalism was a key theme in first-generation ideology. One man recalls his attempts while supervising a school hostel to instruct his wards in Hinduism as he conceived it should be. This would be, he writes, a religion "free from all meaningless rituals, outworn social institutions and unscientific beliefs — a religion based on reason as well as authority and experience."[14] A Bombay diary from the year 1839 reflects its author's sensitivity to the charges of his missionary guardians that Hinduism was superstitious and idolatrous. This boy was "glad" to read a book whose author proved that "the Hindus in reality worship only one Supreme Being. . . ."[15]

A dual preoccupation characterizes first-generation writings. On the one hand, authors had to come to terms with the demands and restrictions of orthodox society; on the other, they had to express their identification with the ideas and values of their English-language education. Whether this was resolved in accommodation or in conflict was, to some degree, determined by preexisting regional patterns.

In Bengal, as we have seen, the open publication of grievances was a style of protest that appeared in a wide variety of social contexts. When newly educated sons found themselves in conflict with their families over issues of orthodox behavior, the result might be open defiance on the part of the son, a quarrel, and the dramatic departure of the rebel from his paternal home. Bengali autobiographies report such incidents frequently;

anecdotes of the resistance of young Western-educated Bengalis to the tyrannies of their fathers' orthodoxy had passed into legend by the late nineteenth century and were well known throughout the subcontinent. The father of Surendranath Banerjea ran away from his own father's house after a quarrel about orthodox washing rituals. Bipin Chandra Pal quarreled with his father over the ideas of the Brahmos, and the father of P.C. Ray was summarily brought home in his youth to remove him from the pernicious influences of nineteenth-century Calcutta.

But Bengali behavior was not generally emulated by students from other regions. Autobiographical accounts indicate that first-generation students elsewhere in India were liable to express their affinity for modern ideas and values through forms of behavior which were less openly defiant. When K.P. Menon, for example, attempted to express his new convictions that superstition and idolatry were wrong, his parents berated him. "That was the end," he recalls, "of my youthful crusade against superstitions. Thereafter I was content to follow them when it was convenient for me to do so, even though I did not believe in them. . . . "[16]

Outside Bengal, unorthodox behavior was likely to be carried out in secret, or, if forced into the open, to be accompanied by mild actions and a self-abnegating meekness as first-generation students attempted to ameliorate the demands of newly acquired principles and the requirements of older traditional norms. D.C. Pavate, returning to west India from an education in England, had no wish to disturb his family's peace with the announcement that he had acquired unorthodox eating habits while abroad.[17] R.P. Paranjpye refused to perform any *prayascitta* ("penance") when he returned to Poona from Cambridge — "as I did not think I had committed any sin" — but, for the remainder of his life, when he visited his familial village, Paranjpye ate apart from the others, a gesture of conciliation to more orthodox sensibilities.[18] Paranjpye's cousin, Dhonde Karve, was banned from his parents' village because he had married a widow. When, ten years later, the villagers became reconciled to his marriage, Karve was sure they accepted it only because of the attitude of diffidence he had adopted from the start.[19]

Yet whether the response to orthodoxy was open rebellion, superficial acquiescence, diffidence, or circumspection, the situation faced by first-generation students of all regions was essentially the same. Two pathways stretched before them — two cultures, two separate ways of life. Even if they did not always make an absolute choice between the two, even if sometimes they chose (as many first-generation students, including Bengalis, did) to both acculturate and accommodate, still the choices were at least apparent to them.

A consciousness of clear alternatives and a preference for Western ways is apparent also in descriptions of fathers by their second-generation sons. Any reader of the nineteenth-century textbooks of the Raj would recognize the reformist ideas and beliefs attributed to these parents, for they are the qualities defined there as the hallmarks of a modern and acculturated Indian. Fathers are frequently identified by their sons as religious reformers; they are men concerned with education, specifically the education of their sons, and they are invariably convinced of the necessity and desirability of physical exercise for the maintenance of health and well-being. One father "prided himself upon being a social rebel who laughed at stuffy traditions."[20] A more famous father, Motilal Nehru, was attracted to Western dress and ways during his college years; his son recalls his father's regular tennis parties and the swimming pool his father had built in the family home.[21] A third author's father "saw to it that I developed a good physique and took regular exercise both at home and in school . . . [he] tried to give us an all-round training and education in order to equip us well for life."[22]

P.C. Tandon's father was a West Punjab Khatri who was an engineer for the government of India. He became a member of the Arya Samaj during his working life. (His son observes that his thinking was already "somewhat unorthodox."[23]) But the father's real dedication was his devotion to work.

> He continually exhorted us to work and looked upon play as an exercise which you needed at regular intervals in order to work even harder.[24]

This father especially admired the British for their "many virtues, the conscientiousness, sense of responsibility, industry and integrity. . . . "[25] In his enthusiasm for acculturation, the father even managed to persuade his wife into the clothing of a European lady — at least for the duration of one solitary photograph. There her son sees her "incredibly" dressed in a "European blouse, long skirt and shoes and with her head uncovered. . . . "[26]

First-generation autobiographers and the fathers described in second-generation memoirs are both notable for the certainty of their opinions and the absence of self-doubts. Tandon, for example, writes of his father, "There was no contradiction or ambivalence in his makeup, he was all of a piece and lived up to what he preached."[27] Tandon's father had by no means abandoned traditional habits entirely — his consistency was to be found mainly in his lack of ambivalence. This absence of self-doubt is characteristic of a number of first-generation students. Ideas formed on exposure to foreign values may change with later experiences — this happened to both Gandhi and Bipin Chandra Pal. There may be, as in the writings of R.P. Paranjpye or Dhonde Karve, grief over personal problems or sorrow for the ties broken by the acceptance of modern ideas and identifications. There may even be a certain amusement, as with K.P. Menon, at the restrictions imposed by orthodox society on the expression of new beliefs. Nevertheless, there remains in most of the first generation an overwhelming certainty of the value of Western ideas and practices and an assertion of one's preference for them. The old ways must give place to the new. The new ways could be adopted by those who had come to understand them and — in the future — even more fully by their children.

That acceptance extended even to the stratification within the civil service in India, a stratification which clearly subordinated the Indian to the Englishman. "At the time my father began his career," Tandon writes, "the service rules, like the Indian caste system, were clearly defined, well understood and fully accepted. You accepted them as the natural order of things."[28] Those who were the first in their families to obtain Western education did, in many cases, accept their positions within the British bureaucracy as necessarily that of trainees and subordinates to the British who, after all, were by nature and culture more perfect in their ideas and behavior.

The negative image of India and Indians presented in the English-language schoolbooks was not felt so keenly by first-generation fathers. The textbooks were far from flattering in their characterizations of India and her peoples; for many boys, in later years, to appear weak, sickly, unenergetic or unprincipled was to demonstrate one's failure to overcome the "Indian" aspects of one's background. The textbooks had a positive message, however, and that lay in their exhortation to convert, to acculturate, to become "English in taste, in opinions, in morals and in intellect."[29] It was an invitation which first-generation students were likely to accept.

Those students were to become Western along the lines and according to the suggestions laid down throughout their education. Their main struggle was primarily with the orthodox and traditional society from which they had come. The knowledge that adaptation to Western values and success in the hierarchies of British India would enhance a family's position may have, ironically, helped sustain boys through bitter family quarrels over orthodox behavior and customs. Their family's status contributed to their own sense of well-being — their own accomplishments would contribute to the family's status.[30] The basic symbiosis of Indian family life would also allow students to comfort themselves with the knowledge of their family's traditional standing even as they were rejecting its customs and orthodoxy for the newer Western values.

For a first-generation student, acculturation was only the beginning of a process which, if not he, then his children, raised according to these new precepts and beliefs, would complete. That his own education was in some ways imperfect and his acculturation somewhat faulty, that a certain accommodation with orthodox society was necessary, that British superiors treated him with condescension or contempt — all this did not pass unnoticed, but seems not to have threatened his emerging self-image. His new identification was that of a member of the Educated Elite. The Western-educated Indian was a Renaissance man, a Reformer, a member of Young Bengal — one of those who had come out of the old world of tradition and superstition into the sunlight of the new.

This security of self-image and certainty of purpose was denied, however, to the children of these first-generation students. The sons, the second generation within a family to be English-educated, had to respond to the double directives of traditional culture and British education. But they also had to contend with the image of what they were to be and what they absolutely must not become as these filtered down to them through the edicts and advice of their Western-educated fathers. Their environments — their households, villages, and regions — constantly confirmed their own innate, immutable Indian-ness. The directives and examples of their fathers, on the other hand, repeatedly called that identity into question.

The life of Aurobindo Ghose offers an extreme case of the way in which parental directives could be internally inconsistent. His Western-educated father sent the seven-year-old boy and two older brothers to England. There they were placed with "an English clergyman and his wife with strict instructions that they should not be allowed to make the acquaintance of any Indian or undergo any Indian influence."[31] Indian influences persisted, however, through the agency of the father himself. According to his son, he frequently sent the boys letters denouncing the British government in India and "sending the *Bengalee* newspaper with passages marked relating cases of maltreatment of Indians by Englishmen."[32] By the age of eleven, Aurobindo was firmly convinced that a "period of general upheaval and great revolutionary change was coming in the world."[33]

Even when a father was more consistent in his design for a son's future, others in the family might raise contradictory loyalties and emotions in a child. Surendranath Banerjea's father was one of those "whose culture had dispelled from his mind the orthodox ideas fostered by his domestic environment."[34] But his paternal grandfather was an orthodox Hindu of Kulin Brahmin descent. The two were in constant conflict; as a boy, Banerjea recalls, their antagonism flared over the issue of the remarriage of a young widow — "my grandfather was violently opposed ... my father was as eager in its support."[35] Banerjea could never pass her house "without the liveliest emotions" and a host of confused loyalties and conflicting identifications grew out of this environment.

Parental directives combined with childhood observations could carry more meaning than parents might wish, and second-generation children sometimes learned more than was intended from the behavior of their fathers. Health and exercise, Surendranath Banerjea assures us, were believed by his father to be the basis of a sound life. Yet Banerjea's father was reputedly well-known to be an alcoholic.³⁶ P.C. Tandon's father continually emphasized the need for hard and continuous work. But his children were acutely aware that the British, for whom he worked so hard, would keep him "always on test."³⁷ Tandon and his siblings saw their father as an "austere and colourless person."

> Father who never relaxed from work, explained it to us by saying that the Englishmen could afford to relax because if things went wrong they managed to explain it to each other. . . . But when an Indian made a mistake the reaction, if an understanding one, was that the job, perhaps, was too difficult for him. . . . "³⁹

Sent to England for a course of study, Tandon remained abroad for over eight years, a period of time, he recalls, in which he devoted himself "to every phase of university life except work."³⁹

Where first-generation students tended to accept their subordinate status within the British Raj, the second generation displayed much more ambivalence towards their role as Westernized Indians and could show an extraordinary sensitivity to issues of status and position. Subhas Bose links the abandonment of his self-definition as a man of traditional religious philosophy with his growing consciousness of the arrogant and superior behavior of Englishmen in Calcutta. "It was quite impossible to persuade myself," he writes, "that to be insulted by a foreigner was an illusion that could be ignored."⁴⁰ M.R. Jayakar believed that his father dropped dead from "the strong resentment caused by the disrespectful behavior of his British superior."⁴¹ Autobiographies overflow with stories of protests, memoranda, and resignations filed by the Western-educated over treatment they perceived as insulting. Dhonde Karve records that his eldest son left a government job over just such an injury.⁴²

Ambivalence, self-doubt and defensiveness in second-generation autobiographies are most noticeable in discussions of those matters established (by fathers and schools) as indispensable for a Westernized Indian — that is, the ability to work hard, be successful, and maintain health and strength. Failure of any sort was felt with great intensity. Nirad Chaudhuri explicitly contrasts his life of failure with that of his "pioneering" father. Opposite the strength and conviction of that man, Chaudhuri places his own physical weakness, lack of vitality, and failure of will. He, who had heard his father say "a score of times that a man was nothing if he was not self-willed," found himself in early adulthood unable to carry out the elaborate plans he felt compelled to make.⁴³ He drew up agendas for his studies, but "never commanded the will power to carry out my own deliberate projects."⁴⁴ Failing his first attempt to pass the master's examination, he refused to sit for it a second time. Given a job through the help of friends, he was unable to work. In the grip of a total paralysis of will, his sufferings intensified to the point where he thought continually of death. It was as if, he writes,

> the spirit of a man lying dead on the wayside had taken perch on a withered branch nearby and was crying bitterly as he contemplated the inert body for which it still felt a passionate and agonizing love. . . . [45]

A severe identity crisis marked and prolonged Chaudhuri's passage into adulthood. The confusions that characterized this crisis were shared in differing degrees by other second-generation authors and may be accounted for, in part, by their unique positions both within their families and in relation to their fathers. In contrast to other generations of Indian families, the second Western-educated generation had to rely on an identification with their fathers, and only with their fathers, for their future status, security, and for their basic sense of self-esteem. The intensity of this identification was previously unknown in Indian family life. That "familial" orientation which, one psychologist has suggested, provides the basic context for Indian emotional and psychological life, bound family members into an intense symbiotic interdependence.[46] But, in contrast to preceding generations, the second Western-educated generation of a family could fulfill their family obligations only by adopting and emulating the Western heritage presented to them by their fathers. To reject that identification meant a return (if only in imagination) to indigenous definitions of caste and village, definitions that were rapidly losing their ability to command wealth, power, or social prestige. Only through identification with their Western-educated fathers could sons claim an entree to the Westernized world of the Raj.

Family ambitions encouraged this identification as insistently as older loyalties, lifeways, and the ambiguous inconsistencies of paternal directives challenged it. Moreover, some aspects of such an identification brought additional fears, anger, and hostility. Boys saw the condescension meted out to their parents by the foreign world they were expected to enter and the British officials they were encouraged to emulate. They knew more clearly than their fathers the limitations on their ability to become as fully British as their fathers wanted; they wished, on occasion, for the continuation of a more traditional protection and intervention in their lives than was acceptable within the Western definition of paternal responsibility. Moreover, the intensity of a son's identification with his father meant that a son's self-worth fluctuated with his father's; when a father was demeaned and his status diminished, his son also was made smaller. One aspect of the dilemma of the second generation was this: to be the son of a Western-educated father within Indian society was to have the status of a *sahib*, to be a Western and a modern man. But to be that father's son within British India was to be forever stigmatized as an Indian, a small, weak, unprincipled man, belittled and despised by the officials, the institutions and the teachers of the very culture the father was urging him to adopt. Ambivalence towards one's role as a Westernized Indian, conflicting loyalties and identifications from one's early years, a childhood dotted with double directives — be English, be Indian — these were the legacies of the second generation. Severe confusion and a paralysis of will often seized young men troubled by these conflicts at a time when they had to select adult roles and occupations from among the contradictory offerings of their early years.

Some autobiographies, particularly from Bengal where regional culture encouraged the publication of grievances, reveal the intensity of the identity confusion that was faced by many second-generation students. We have traced this confusion through three autobiographies, the works of Banerjea, Bose, and Chaudhuri. While never as fully articulated as in these three accounts, issues of identity surface also in the books of other authors. K.G. Ghose, Nripendra Banerji, P.C. Tandon, Bhagat Singh and others allow us to see, in varying degrees, the problems and confusions they faced in school careers and adult life. Krishnan Sondhi states somewhat self-consciously in his autobiography that "identity" was the continuing and central problem in his adult life. The South Indian author Y.G. Bonnell recalls his disastrous school career and its dramatic end in a furious quarrel with school authorities. In *The Book "I"* Bonnell capitalizes and puts into dark type all personal pronouns. *"I,"* Bonnell writes in explanation,

> is an autobiography of Me, Y.G. Bonnell, P.B. mostly taken from My diaries faithfully recorded... *I* write the book *I* and *I* therefore is all important. To indicate the importance of it, the singular first personal pronoun *I* and its cognate forms *Me, My Mine* etc. will be printed in thick antique type throughout the book....[47]

Through physical format, then, as well as through content, Bonnell's book reveals its author's deep concern with issues of identity.

*   *   *

Autobiographies show us two separate psychological responses to the English educational system. Which pattern appears, we have suggested, depends on whether an individual is in the first or the second generation of a family to enter the English-language schools. Was this process completely ahistorical? Was there no relation between the political and social developments of these centuries and the psychological development of autobiographers?

The psychological responses characteristic of first- and second-generation students appear and reappear during the nineteenth and early twentieth centuries without apparent connection to historical events. Surendranath Banerjea, born in 1848, faced a crisis at the end of the first twenty years of his life markedly similar in its confusions and conflicts to that of Nirad Chaudhuri, a man born some fifty years later. Lal Behari Day journeyed to Calcutta from the *mofussil* in the early nineteenth century, entered the English-language school system, and soon converted to Christianity. Forty years later two other *mofussil* boys, Sitanatha Tattvabhushan and Bipin Chandra Pal, also traveled to Calcutta for the purpose of education and soon after repudiated the orthodox traditions of their village homes — this time, however, not for the Christian religion but for the reformed Hinduism of the Brahmo Samaj. One may find the ambivalence and confusion of a second-generation student as early as the 1820s — reflected in the autobiography of Khetter Chunder Ghose — or as late as the twentieth century, discreetly hinted at in Prakash Tandon's *Punjabi Century*. First-generation responses appear over a similar time span. First-generation challenges to orthodoxy and enthusiasm for Western values and ideas occur in stories about men who were boys during the earliest years of the nineteenth century. (Surendranath Banerjea tells these stories about his own father.) The same pattern of responses reappears in the autobiographies of men born at almost any point during the succeeding years of the nineteenth and early twentieth century.

The most famous example of how late in this historical period first-generation responses appear is that of an autobiographer not strictly within the province of this study. M.K. Gandhi wrote his *Autobiography: The Story of My Experiments with Truth* originally in Gujarati and published it in weekly installments in a Gujarati magazine. Gandhi describes himself there as many others since have described him; an Indian who has rejected Westernization and returned to the traditions and lifeways of indigenous society. By his dress, a simple loin cloth; his meals of fruit, milk and nuts; his devotion to *ahimsa* (nonviolence discovered in traditional texts and redefined); and his vow of *brahmacarya* (a celibate committed to search for understanding of and union with the ultimate religious force) — through all these acts and commitments, Gandhi, in the middle years of his life, declared his return to the identity of an Indian — indeed, apparently to that of the most traditional Indian he could become.

But in the terms of this study, Gandhi was a first-generation Indian. His childhood and youth were spent within a primarily traditional home and he became in his youth the most fervent admirer and imitator of the values and customs of the West. His life, viewed somewhat apart from the didactic emphasis of the *Autobiography*, repeats many first-generation themes. The autobiography discusses, in turn, Gandhi's eating of meat, his extracaste friendships, and his adoption of Western clothing and ideology. The urge for cultural conversion which had seized many first-generation students also seized him. Newfound enthusiasm (and his family's economic ambitions) led him, as many others, to journey abroad and study for the Bar in London and the proposed journey precipitated first a conflict, then a split between Gandhi and the leaders of his caste's community. On his return from England, Gandhi remained only briefly in India before leaving once again for residence and employment in South Africa. Abroad, in an exile that lasted twenty years, removed from local family and community pressures, Gandhi's interest in Westernization and Indian social and religious reform yielded to new concerns. In South Africa Gandhi began to reconsider his identity as an Indian — and to reevaluate relations between Indians and the British.

But even after his rediscovery and reassertion of a more traditional identification, Gandhi's early education left him with a permanent residue of Western ideas and values. Among these were a lifelong commitment to extracaste associations, a tendency to insist that he and his followers perform their own manual labor, and a clocklike devotion to punctuality. These lasting commitments are obscured within the *Autobiography*. In its didactic framework, Gandhi's exposure to the West appears only as a series of "experiments," experiments with truth. Gradually and inexorably, these tests turn the experimenter away from the false promises of foreign ways and back to the truths of his own culture, its food, clothing, and religion. To some extent, the autobiography's format mirrors Gandhi's actual experience. But, in addition, the book's episodes are deliberately constructed to awaken similar recollections and touch on areas of continuing uncertainty in the lives of other Western-educated Indians. Nehru believed that Gandhi's life and example were the catalysts for his own resolution of a lifetime's conflicts and fears. Gandhi's unique ability to provoke these crises and provide their resolution was certainly one reason for his extraordinary appeal. The autobiography is a testimony to the altered interests of his life; it is also a mark of his talent as an author and a measure of his genius as a political organizer.

Gandhi was able to take up and put down the paraphernalia of Westernization because he was gifted with distinct and unusual genius. But his ability also stemmed from the fact that he was the first in his family to be exposed to the ideas and values of the English educational system. His autobiography repeats many items often heard in the cultural litany associated with sons' memories of first-generation fathers. His concern for physical exercise, his preoccupation with health, his initial desire to be accepted in the role of a British *sahib* (in London he wore three-piece suits and took dancing lessons), even his fabled passion for "Truth" — these are all virtues included as part of the catalog of first-generation virtues.

In their own autobiographies, first-generation fathers rarely tell us what directives and lessons they attempted to teach their sons. Involvement with one's children is considered tangential to autobiographical recollection. But to hear Gandhi's voice in the weekly messages of his autobiography, to note the lessons he emphasizes, the morals he reinforces, is to hear, from the parent himself, a message already familiar from the memories of many sons. To see the effects these messages had on the life of Gandhi's own sons is to see writ tragically large the conflicts of many who were the children of men with similar convictions.

Gandhi's eldest son, Harilal, ended his life as a Muslim convert and an alcoholic. His final identity, often noted for its vengeful contradiction of his father's carefully held beliefs, may also convey something of the desperate confusion in the life of that second-generation son. Harilal Gandhi was unusual in both the extremity and the public display of his chosen identity, but the conflicts he faced were shared by many in the nineteenth and twentieth centuries. Numerous studies have indicated how critical issues of identity, self-definition, and relations between Indian culture and the West were to Western-educated Indians.[48] To draw a distinction between the problems faced by those who were the first in their families to have this experience and the problems of those who were their children is only to elaborate on what was a serious and ongoing problem for all.

Gandhi's early ideas developed in the context of his family environment, without much relation to the historical period of his birth; his later life and *Autobiography* show us the connections that did bind him to the period in which he lived. Autobiographies and life stories, appearing in other contexts, indicate how complex this relationship was for all Indians growing up in British India. In the early years of the nineteenth century, in Bengal and perhaps Bombay, Western-educated students did undergo a true generational experience. The Bengali students at Hindu College in its earliest years were irrevocably altered by their experience there. They shared an experience which bound them together as a group, setting them apart equally from those who came before and from those who would come after. They were a *generation* in the true historical meaning of the term.[49]

As the educational system widened its impact in the middle years of the nineteenth century, this momentary generational simplicity vanished. Boys entered educational institutions from a variety of family backgrounds and with an increasing diversity of prior exposure to Western ideas and images. Those who had been the first in families, villages, and districts to enter the English schools had grown up in circumstances of particular isolation. But later in the century, more shared the same experience, and even a boy home only for summer vacations — as Dhonde Karve was in the Konkan — might find others who understood his experiences and shared his new interests. The reform associations, clubs, and societies of Western-educated Indians which flourished throughout the later years of the nineteenth century established an institutional context for their members' Western identities — a need of special importance, we should note, in a society organized, as India was, primarily along caste and community lines.

Organizations and occupations brought individuals in varying stages of acculturation into contact with each other during the late nineteenth and early twentieth centuries. These years show the growth within the English-educated community in India of a collective consciousness of the meaning and power of British rule. Family background — the presence or absence of Western-educated elders during childhood — was the first determinant of a boy's response to Western education. But in later life his responses would be modified by contacts with other Indians, the British, or by exposure to the collective assessment of the British current in the Western-educated Indian community. The more simple enthusiasms of the very first in the culture to become Western educated were lost to later first-generation students. They had to come to terms not only with differences between orthodox demands and English values, but also with the more sophisticated evaluations of British ideas and British rule presented to them by other Western-educated Indians. One of the continually complicating factors of this historical period is the interplay between the psychological development of individuals and the growing collective consciousness of Western-educated Indians.

Throughout the nineteenth and twentieth centuries the process of individual acculturation took place both outside of and alongside the historical chronology of the period. Even as late as the twentieth century, individuals could emerge from the *mofussil*, still in the early stages of first-generation enthusiasm for Western ideas and values, only to be confronted, in the administrative centers of the Raj, by a world into which a deeper, more ambivalent understanding of British rule had been infused. This was the fate of Bipin Chandra Pal — in his youth "very partial" to English ways, in his old age a nationalist no longer able to understand the enthusiasms of his younger days. Pal had moved from a childhood in the East Bengal *mofussil* to college in Calcutta. In the capital city of the Raj he encountered a collective interpretation of British rule more sophisticated and less sympathetic than his own. Ultimately it reshaped his life and political ideology, leaving him to wonder, as an old man, about the convictions of his earlier years. Similarly, Gandhi, as a youth in England, had been eager to acculturate, his enthusiasm for British habits tempered only by a determined loyalty to his mother. Later in his life, removal from his region and exposure to a more brutal side of British rule precipitated a rearrangement of his priorities and a rethinking of his commitment to acculturation.

It was in Gandhi and the Gandhian movement of the twentieth century that the process of individual acculturation and the growing collective consciousness of the Western-educated community reached a mutual catharsis. If the message of Gandhi's ideology had disastrous consequences for the lives of his own children, it had, at least, a more therapeutic effect upon the Western-educated community at large. Gandhi's political behavior towards the British — his courage, his principled positions, his insistence on truth and nonviolence — brilliantly asserted all those virtues which the British, officials and educators alike, insisted were lacking in Indians. His political dramas repeatedly reversed the negative stereotypes of Indians. Again and again, Gandhi's tactics revealed that it was the British who possessed those very weaknesses — lack of principle, truthfulness, and integrity — that they claimed to despise in Indians and had taught Indians to despise in themselves. It was the British who lied — promising self-government and yet refusing to grant it. It was the British who were cowardly — setting troops with clubs to beat down nonviolent protestors. It was the British who were unprincipled in their dealings with Indians — speaking of liberty, freedom, and integrity and yet using their laws to imprison those, such as Gandhi, who honestly and forthrightly acted on principled opposition to their rule. The fact that those revelations came through the acts of a man whose nakedness, both physical and spiritual, showed an unashamed identity with all that was Indian added immeasurably to their effect.

Gandhi's campaigns were the fruit, not only of his life and experience, but of the way that life intertwined with the growing collective consciousness of the Western-educated community. The response to his tactics and appeals may indicate how fully they embodied perceptions that were just breaking into people's consciousness. Not all the Western-educated responded to his call. But for many, and, it would seem — given the strength of the Congress organization among the Western-educated — for a large part of that community, Gandhi's message and personal example provided a resolution to the conflicts of a lifetime. Nehru, a member of the second generation, was one of those for whom Gandhi's appeal had profound meaning. It was as if, he wrote, in a much quoted passage,

> an expert in psychoanalytic method had probed deep into the patient's past, found out the origins of his complexes, exposed them to his view and thus rid him of that burden.[50]

Conclusion

A FOREIGN CULTURE has its most serious and long-lasting impact, not on the first generation exposed to its lessons, but only with the internalization of its values and directives during the childhoods of the second. The experience of childhood and education under the Raj was shaped, in part, by the particular moment in the nineteenth or twentieth century when a child was born, but even more crucially by the ideas, culture, and values already accepted by the family into which he was born. The first generation, the first in their families to be exposed to the English-language schools, could take up the ideas and values of that education in much the same way as they did the foreign clothing of the Raj. These Indians noticed, perhaps, a certain awkwardness of fit, but were not troubled — possibly not even aware — that their clothing changed little more than their outward appearance. Their problems were those of the convert. They struggled against the wishes of those who wanted them to remain with the old ways; they made accommodations (or chose not to, at some personal risk) between what they believed and what they did. By and large, they were not aware of the deeper levels on which their newly acquired ideas conflicted with their orthodox traditions.

This is not to underestimate the power of orthodox society in India to punish deviations nor to imply that the quarrels and rebellions of first-generation students caused them no fear, tension, or grief. The regrets of a Bipin Chandra Pal, the altered life of a Dhonde Karve, the suicide of a couple in Bombay — all point to the potential pain and hazard of acculturation. Families sent their sons off to institutions offering Western education only to react with horror and outrage to the changes education brought. But however frightening those struggles, at least the dimensions of the problem were clear. The conflicts of the first generation were on the surface. Whether individuals chose rebellion or accommodation, they understood both the meaning of their choice and, usually, its potential cost.

The same statement could not be made about the problems faced by the second generation. For this group, children who grew up in families with a Western-educated father, the problems of negotiating both the traditional world and the world of the British Raj had become considerably confused. British values and stereotypes were being introduced into Indian family life in their generation. Children growing up in Westernized homes were presented with multiple and contradictory images of what they could or should become as adults. They were taught certain Western values by their fathers, yet they recognized that in India the British representatives of these values would not allow an Indian to claim them as his own. They were presented with images of what they were to become in their future lives, only to be told, in other ways, that it would never be possible for them to make those images real. At home as well as in school the most negative stereotype of what it meant to be an Indian was pressed upon them. Yet the world in which they lived and the people who surrounded them were in almost all ways — physical and psychical — obviously Indian. It is not surprising that some of these children faced difficulties in their adolescent years.

The point of this study, however, is not to argue categorically that all children of first-generation Western-educated families experienced identity crises. The evidence of the autobiographies would not support so unqualified a statement. And Erikson's conceptual framework, placing, as we have said, an emphasis on the normalcy of some adolescent identity confusion and the individuality of "crises" where they do occur, is not entirely congruent with the pattern of psychological responses found among second-generation autobiographers. Nevertheless, the concept of identity and Erikson's description of the pathography of identity confusion are essential for understanding the crises that did disrupt the lives of many authors. For it is clear that the values of British education and the negative image of what it meant to be an Indian, when presented to growing boys through both the educational system and the agency of their families, created confusion and intense ambivalence — and sometimes raised unanswerable questions about future roles and responsibilities. How were these children to become adults in British India — and what, as adults in that society, would they be able or, indeed, allowed to do?

"I am," wrote one sophisticated autobiographer, "an Indian who is trying to be a man."[1] The intensity of Indian family life gave added potency to a son's identification with his male elders, and especially with his father. Second-generation sons willingly incorporated the foreign values and ideas of these fathers into their own self-images. But even while identifying — and later publicly acclaiming — what was Western in their parents, sons could not possibly avoid seeing what was Indian. Whether they admitted this recognition or not, they had to remember, imitate, and be loyal not only to the Western-educated man who was their father, but to the Indian as well. Where first-generation fathers suffered the indignity of ridicule for their imperfect attempts to become Anglicized, second-generation sons suffered the internal torments of those who felt always, as an inalienable part of themselves, qualities and characteristics despised and stigmatized by British culture.

Yet the autobiographers frequently seemed to lose all memory of the foreign origins of even their most searing self-criticisms. For in the process of integrating education and family background — indeed, in the process of growing up in British India — the second Western-educated generation began to lose a clear sense of the distinction between the two cultural traditions to which they were heir. No longer completely certain what was Western, what Indian, in either background or self, individuals came to doubt the appropriateness of even their most spontaneous responses. They had lost the unity of ideology, behavior, and custom which is, for better or for worse, part of a life fully situated within a parent culture.

The experience of acculturation was not unique to India. As Erikson has suggested, similar problems are shared by other Third World countries, by subcultures such as blacks in the United States, and by immigrants everywhere. The total surrendering of older ethnic identities may allow immigrants to slip unnoticed into the culture and ethos of their adopted land. But total accommodation may be neither possible nor desirable for permanent minorities — nor is escape from the identity imposed by the dominant majority easily accomplished. In Third World cultures, however, where conditions of subordination existed because of foreign domination, a partial solution to these intolerable psychological pressures was the expulsion of the rulers.

During the nineteenth and twentieth centuries, the Western-educated community in India moved slowly but inexorably towards a recognition of the need for an end to British rule. Given the dependence of the English-educated on the continued presence of the Raj for employment, status, and even the legitimacy of their leadership, it is not surprising that movement was slow. Independence, however desirable psychologically, conflicted sharply with their economic interests. But there was, ultimately, no other escape possible from the negative identity projected through the agencies of the Raj and internalized during childhood. No action, no thought, no wish, no idea took form in the lives of the English-educated that did not owe some portion of its existence to the complex pattern of cultural accusations, defences, and counteraccusations with which they had grown up. For India, as for other Third World countries, independence was the only possible solution to the psychological conflicts of its Western-educated community.

The necessity of this solution was clearly recognized by Mohandas

Gandhi and expressed in the movement he led in the twentieth century. Gandhi was the first Western-educated generation of his family. His background had been traditional; his understanding of Western culture and values, the product of schools and schoolbooks. His analysis of British power was the fruit of adult life and experiences uncomplicated by identification with a Westernized father or the internalization of foreign values in childhood. He could — as did others similarly situated — value the ideas of the West and incorporate those values into his ideology. But his exposure to Western culture had not disturbed the core of his being. That "inner voice" to which Gandhi listened so intently was not primarily that of an English-educated Indian. Listening, he could ask for separation from the British, for independence for his country.

By the twentieth century, it had become apparent that independence would not threaten the hegemony of the Western-educated in India. But psychological ties still bound many Indians to the culture of the Raj and made even the thought of severance from the empire painful to them. Surendranath Banerjea — a man of the second generation, one in whom the Indian and the foreign were inextricably intertwined — wrote that separation from England would cut India off from "the sap that feeds humanity"; Indians would be left

> to flow down the stream of life, unfed, unsupported by the culture, the art and civilization of the rest of mankind, rejoicing in our isolation, taking pride in our aloofness. To me the thought is intolerable.[2]

To this Gandhi could have responded with unequivocal directness. "If India copies England," he had written in the course of an essay on India's technological needs, "it is my firm conviction that she will be ruined."[3]

*   *   *

In Bangalore, an elderly Indian gentleman from a once traditional family was asked about his education. After he had been in Western schools for some time, were there traditions he no longer believed in? Did he find his way of life had changed? "Actually, when we changed," he answered slowly, "we maintained our affinity for our culture and our love for our family, but our thinking was different. Yes, our thinking was different but it was all an unconscious stream coming slowly. Because we had our own culture and our family traditions, but gradually they were suppressed by the Western culture." "You see, it was an unconscious change," he said, "because we don't know when I changed or how I changed. But the change has been enormous and that's the sum total at the end."[4]

APPENDIX

I

The Sources and Their Limitations

IN A STUDY SUCH AS THIS, based on a group of writings that share a common form, there is a tendency to assume that what is said about one is true for all. As some characteristics of each book are common to most, the assumption has a partial validity. But as individual personalities, location, and circumstances also determine the context of these works, the outlines of the homogeneity of these autobiographies and their authors must be defined.

The study is based primarily on one hundred and two works written in English by Indians in the nineteenth and twentieth centuries. Most are book length; some, short articles; and some, only fragments of perceptions and impressions. They range from life story to diary to travelogue to journal. The intention behind so diverse a collection was both to reproduce a sampling of autobiographical writings and to establish the outer limits of the form as it appears in India. Out of one hundred and two sources, then, eighty-nine are memoirs or autobiographies, seven are diaries, five are travel books, and one is a work of fiction.

Autobiographies written in English by Muslims have been excluded from this study. Whatever cultural and philosophical differences originally existed between Hindus and Muslims have been exacerbated by the events of the past thirty years. It was thought that these tensions would inevitably dominate any study seeking to encompass the writings of both groups. Most of the autobiographers whose books have been used in this study are Hindus. Three, however, are Parsis; three are Christians; and one is a Sikh. In referring to non-Hindu authors, their communal identities have generally been given.

The writings represent most geographic regions of the subcontinent, and a number of communities and caste groups. Bengal is most conspicuous among the provinces represented — almost one-third of the works were written by Bengalis. Of the other provincial areas, Bombay and

Madras are about equally represented; there are a few works from the
northwestern sections of the country, the North West Provinces, Oudh and
the Punjab, and a scattering from areas like Rajputana, Sind, and Gujarat.
Almost all of the writers, with one or two notable exceptions, are or
describe themselves as from relatively high-caste families. Nor is there any
clear domination of profession or occupation among the group, although
lawyers are easily the most numerous. Most work in occupations related to
or dependent on British power and rule. No one (except for one
untouchable) recalls doing manual or day labor. Many from village areas
appear to come from dominant landowning families there, and, in urban
areas, the poorest backgrounds seem to be those of small shopkeepers.

Indian autobiographical materials, especially those of less prominent
figures, are fugitive and often quite private pieces of writing. A number of
authors specifically request that their works not be published until after
their death. The same tendency may be seen in the fact that not only are
most autobiographies written only towards the end of the author's
life — not unusual for the genre in any setting — but many such books
were kept for long periods by the family of the author, which for a variety
of reasons postponed or attempted to avoid altogether further publication
of these works. One piece (*The Life of V. Soob Row, Translator and
Interpreter of the Late Sudr Court*) seems to have been published only in
an attempt to influence a property struggle among the author's heirs.
Another appears some thirty years after the author's death, its publication
prompted either by the bad conscience of a daughter who had neglected
her father's wishes, or perhaps by the better finances of the family at this
later time (*Autobiography of Sir C. Sankaran Nair*).

Self-publication is more the rule than the exception. The result is a
variety of books, many of which would never have appeared had it been
necessary to justify their publication in terms of potential sales or of their
authors' reputations. This results, however, in the appearance of extremely
small editions (as few as fifty copies on occasion) with little fanfare and
virtually no circulation. The survival of such writings is problematic. In this
study, well over 90 percent of the materials used were written in the
twentieth century, and the largest share of these works have been
published or republished within the last twenty-five years. While there has
been some increase in publication of autobiographies over the last two
centuries and recently, even some increase in the interest such works
provoke, still the works published and extant today probably represent
only a small proportion of the number of autobiographies actually written
during this time. How small a proportion, and how representative it is, will
only be revealed as materials continue to be turned up under the probings
of regional studies and biographical projects (see Appendix II).

These one hundred and two autobiographies give a view of a specific strata of Indian society, and one profoundly influenced by the Western system of education. While almost half of these works have been written and published since 1947, only twelve out of the eighty authors whose dates of birth could be determined were born within the twentieth century. Of the others, almost all were born between the years of 1850 and 1900; their works as a group reflect the experiences of Indians whose years of childhood and schooling were within the span of seventy years from 1850 to 1920. Authors were influenced by events which took place in their adult years, but it is helpful to realize the degree to which the experiences that shaped their early lives share a common time frame.

In addition, the writers have in common an extremely high level of education. Although raised in a period when only a fraction of the Indian population had been exposed to English-language education, over half of them had a bachelor's degree and over a third had been educated beyond the B.A., winning degrees which ranged from M.A.s to law degrees to Ph.D.s. Some had studied abroad; a few had succeeded in passing the examination for the Indian Civil Service. Only rarely does an autobiography move away from the world of formal education into that of people whose connections to the system of English-language education was more tangential and whose lives and careers were correspondingly more haphazard and less structured by the timing and requirements of that educational and occupational system.

The relative consistency of educational background in the majority of books is echoed in certain life patterns and problems which the writings reveal. The early experience of many an author was shaped by the necessity of locating and attending English-language schools, by examinations and other tensions of school life, by financial struggles, and, later on, by the effort to find and keep employment. When Indians came to define themselves, as they did in the late nineteenth and early twentieth centuries, in opposition and in contradistinction to the British and the West, they did so, in part, as an all-India group, one whose educational experience and early growth had been shaped by similar pressures.

In an early study of the influence of English education on Indians, Bruce McCully compiled some figures on the numbers of the Western-educated in India in the late 1880s.[1] While many of our authors were educated in later times, when the numbers being educated had considerably grown, McCully's figures offer some interesting comparisons. By the late 1880s, for instance, out of the total population of India, estimated at about one hundred and ninety-five million, perhaps fifty-five thousand had been exposed to English education, having attained at least the level of the Matriculation Examination. The number who had been granted the B.A. degree or higher was much smaller, about six thousand in all, only one-tenth of the total number of the Western-educated. By the 1920s, the number of Western-educated had increased, as had the number holding the bachelor's degree, in both absolute and percentage terms. Still, in comparison to these earlier figures, over half of the authors of these autobiographies were part of that inner circle of Western-educated Indians, that group which McCully had considered earlier in the nineteenth century to be only an "imperceptible proportion" of the total population.[2]

One might expect the backgrounds of these educated autobiographers to reflect the greater availability of educational possibilities in urban areas. Particularly in the administrative and university centers of the provinces — Calcutta, Bombay, Madras, and, later, Lahore — the level of literacy was generally higher than in the *mofussil* and the concentration of schools and colleges also greater.[3] The manner in which, according to authors, many *mofussil* children physically pursued English education from village to village within their provinces, traveling great distances to find schools which carried the desired programs, testifies to the greater difficulty in obtaining education in outlying areas. Yet among those who tell us where they came from, only sixteen authors grew up in the great administrative centers of the Raj, while thirty-five came from the smaller towns and villages of the outlying regions. (A few others were raised outside of India entirely or were the children of government officials who frequently transferred from region to region.)

This distribution may not be unusual. The nineteenth century was a period when many students, as shown both by our authors' lives and by educational statistics, traveled to provincial centers such as Calcutta for education and then traveled out again for jobs in the *mofussil*.[4] At least one regional study — of Fergusson College in Bombay — has revealed a similarly high proportion of *mofussil* students at that college.[5] Still, if not exceptional, the combination of relatively rural backgrounds with exceptionally high levels of education is interesting. When a third factor is added — the low level of familiarity with Western education in the families of these writers — the group profile becomes even more intriguing.

When one looks at the autobiographies to discover how far back a familiarity with Western education exists in the families of authors, an interesting pattern emerges. Out of the total of sixty-eight authors for whom such information can be developed from internal evidence, only in seven cases can we trace the appearance of Western education in the family beyond the father of the author. (Only in one case, that of the Tagore family in Bengal, can the involvement with Western education clearly be traced to the fourth generation, that is, back to Dwarkanath Tagore, the great-grandfather of the most recent Tagore autobiographer.)

In twenty-four other cases we can find some level of Western education definitely present in the parental generation — in most of these it is the father who is literate in English and has been educated in the Western system. At least twenty-eight writers were the first in their families (of the first generation, that is, if not always the very first person) to have obtained English education.

The authors then, are distinguished by three interrelated features: their high degree of education; the lack or low level of previous familiarity with Western education in many of their families; and the *mofussil* background of their childhood homes. Those qualities identify them as a distinct group, setting them apart from other Western-educated peers, and this distinctiveness may be related to their decision to describe their lives in autobiographies written in the English language. Many authors had moved in only one or two generations, from the traditional culture of small villages to higher education and vastly more profitable occupations in the larger cities of the Raj. It may have been the sharpness of this contrast that prompted authors to write their life histories, both as a means of expressing and as a coming to grips with the nature of the changes in their worlds.

This impulse is somewhat closer to the surface of everyday life than the more introspective impulse, rooted in a culture's assumptions and values, that has been described as the fundamental motivation for autobiographical writing in the West.[6] It was only during the nineteenth and twentieth centuries that Indians, as a result of English-language education, discovered the Western autobiographical form. The impetus to use the form, then, grew out of their educational training and also from the relationship that Western culture and values were coming to have to their own lives.

APPENDIX
II

The Selection of the Sources

THE SOURCES USED FOR THIS STUDY are a representative selection chosen from the autobiographical literature found in bibliographical listings and major research libraries in the United States, England, and India. Nevertheless, the materials unearthed have some inherent limitations. Many life histories, one suspects, were never printed and remain in the hands of families. Even restricting ourselves to printed material, problems remain. No existing bibliography in this area was complete; that is, no one bibliography contained all known autobiographies. It was to determine the relationship between the autobiographies available in libraries and the total number presently extant or once printed, that the *Catalogue of Books* was sampled.

The *Catalogue* was begun in India in 1867 in response to a law requiring the registration of all materials published in India regardless of language or size. Lists were printed quarterly, and works were listed in topical classifications. Autobiographies in all languages were included within the more general category of biography. Occasionally, depending on the energies of the particular official, annotations or short descriptions of contents were added. These bound lists were sampled for five provinces: Bengal, Bombay, Madras, the United Provinces, and the Punjab. The sampling was done at five-year intervals from the date of the *Catalogue's* inception through 1947, the last year in which the *Catalogue* survived in anything like its original form.

The *Catalogue* is not complete. It does not include works published outside of India and, of course, tells us nothing about the number of autobiographies which might have been written, but not published, during that period. As a general indication of the number of books published, however, it has some use. For the seventeen years surveyed, a total of eighty-two autobiographies were found. Seventeen of these works were in English. Among the various provincial regions, Bengal was clearly dominant, producing forty-three autobiographies, ten of which were in English. Other provinces showed considerably less activity. Thirteen autobiographies were published in Bombay, three of these in English; seven were published in Madras, three in English; in the United Provinces also seven autobiographies were published in these years, two in the English language; and in the Punjab, eight were published but none of these were written in English.

The *Catalogue* figures reflect some increase in autobiographical publication from the mid-nineteenth century to the 1940s. Well over 90 percent of the works located were published after 1900; almost 75 percent were printed after 1920. Here again, Bengal was notable both for the numbers of autobiographies and for the earlier dates at which they appeared.

Multiplying these figures by five, we can estimate that perhaps four hundred autobiographies were published during the late nineteenth and early twentieth centuries and somewhere between eighty and eight-five of these works might be expected to be in English. Thirty of the sources used for this study were written during the years covered by the *Catalogue*; these books represent, then, perhaps one-third of the English autobiographies produced during this time. Given the greater availability of bibliographical materials for the period after 1947, the remainder of our sources, most of which were published after that date, may represent a somewhat greater percentage of the total number available. Finally, we might note that the distribution of autobiographies used for this study, both by province and in time, is roughly the equivalent of that found in this sampling. In both cases, works by Bengalis dominate the whole. In both, the majority of the writings are from the twentieth century.

Notes

Introduction

1. Interview with Vimala Appasamy, April, 1977.
2. Interview with D.C. Pavate, April, 1977.
3. Ibid.
4. Letter from R.P. Paranjpye, Fergusson College, Poona, March 10, 1905 (Manuscript collection, Nehru Memorial Museum and Library, New Delhi).
5. Ibid., March 16, 1905.
6. Thomas Babington Macaulay, "Minute on Education," in *Sources of Indian Tradition*, edited by Wm. Theo. de Bary et. al. (New York: Columbia University Press, 1958), p. 601.
7. *Bombay University Calendar*, 1900–1901, p. 48.
8. *Punjab University College Calendar*, 1874, p. 195; *Madras University Calendar*, 1866, p. 84.
9. Some examples of other questions were: from Calcutta, 1861, for the Matriculation Examination, "Who was the founder of the Mahratta dynasty? Give a brief account of his career." *Calcutta University Calendar*, 1861, p. 32: from Bombay, 1900, for the B.A. exam, a question which left more room for interpretation, "Discuss the statement that it was the annexation of Lord Dalhousie which lead to the Indian Mutiny." *Bombay University Calendar*, 1900, p. 164.
10. In the 1880s the Hunter Commission, appointed to investigate the workings of the educational system throughout India, routinely asked in each province whether education was too directed and limited by governmental restrictions. Numerous missionary witnesses said that it was. One missionary from Bombay complained that "the stereotyped course of instruction which prevails in government schools and which practically compel aided schools to adopt the same or to relinquish their grants cannot fail to have an injurious effect upon education." India, Education Commission (Hunter Commission), *Report* (1883); Appendices, Provincial Reports: Bengal, Bombay, Madras, Northwest Provinces and Oudh, Punjab (1884), p. 121; Appendix, Bombay, p. 489.

11. A.C. Miller, *Seven Letters to Indian Schoolboys*, 2nd ed. (Bombay: Humphrey Milford, 1917), preface.
12. Ibid, p. 89.
13. See for example Henry Morris, *The History of India*, 5th ed. (Madras: n.p., 1864), a text widely used in Bombay and Madras; or John Marshman, *The History of India*, 2 vols. (London: Longmans, Green, Reader and Dryer, 1867), a classic for Bengal.
14. Henry Morris, *The History of India*, p. 7.
15. Ibid.
16. Miller, *Seven Letters*, p. 3.
17. Edmund Marsden, *History of India for Middle Schools* (London: Macmillan, 1900), p. 13.
18. E.W. Thompson, *A History of India for High Schools and Colleges*, 1st ed. (Madras: Christian Literature Society, 1908), p. 5.
19. Marsden, *History of India*, p. 16.
20. Ibid., p. 227.
21. Thompson, *A History of India*, p. 4.
22. Marsden, *History of India*, p. 16.
23. Morris, *The History of India*, p. 5.
24. Thompson, *A History of India*, p. 392.
25. Ibid., p. 393.
26. Morris, *The History of India*, p. 213.
27. Erik H. Erikson, *Identity: Youth and Crisis* (New York: W.W. Norton, 1968), pp. 295–321.
28. Ibid., p. 303.
29. Photograph of R.P. Paranjpye in the collection of Shr. Shakuntala Paranjpye, Poona.

Chapter 1

1. M.R. Jayakar, *The Story of My Life*, 2 vols. (Bombay: Asia Publishing House, 1959).
2. Sudhir Kakar, *The Inner World: A Psycho-analytic Study of Childhood and Society in India* (Delhi: Oxford University Press, 1978), p. 79.
3. Quoted in Kakar, *The Inner World*, p. 127.
4. S.C. Talukdar, *Random Recollections* (Calcutta: by the author, 1938), p. 13.
5. Mehendra Pratap (Singh), *My Life Story of Fifty-five Years* (Dehradun: by the author, 1947), pp. 2–3.
6. Ravi Shankar, *My Music, My Life* (Delhi: Vikas Publications, 1968), p. 60.
7. Bipin Chandra Pal, *Memories of My Life and Times*, reprint (Calcutta: Bipin Chandra Pal Institute, 1973), p. 8.
8. G. Morris Carstairs, *The Twice-Born: A Study of a Community of High Caste Hindus* (Bloomington, Ind.: Indiana Unviersity Press, 1967), p. 150.
9. Kakar, *The Inner World*, p. 127.

10. Talukdar, *Random Recollections*, p. 27.
11. Y.G. Bonnell, *The Book 'I': The Autobiography of Y.G. Bonnell*, 2 vols. (Madras: by the author, 1930–1938), 1:1–2.
12. D.S. Sarma, *From Literature to Religion: An Autobiography* (Bombay: Bharatiya Vidya Bhavan, 1964), p. 22.
13. Pradip Bose, *Growing Up in India* (Calcutta: Minerva Associates, 1972), p. 41.
14. Kakar, *The Inner World*, p. 128; Carstairs, *The Twice-Born*, p.53; Erik Erikson, *Gandhi's Truth: On the Origins of Militant Non-Violence* (New York: W.W. Norton, 1969), p. 42. Psychoanalyst Alan Roland suggests that as a result of childhood training Indians develop a more "familial" self, and a more "symbiotic" mode of relating to others: "The early development of the self along these lines becomes totally consonant with a social structure and roles in which the individual remains far more involved and embedded within close, well-defined, hierarchical family relationships and roles throughout life than in the modern, industrialized, urban West." Alan Roland, "Psychoanalytic Perspectives on Personality Development in India," forthcoming, pp. 11–12.
15. Erikson, *Gandhi's Truth*, p. 42.
16. R.P. Paranjpye, *84 Not-Out* (Delhi: National Book Trust, 1961), p. 6.
17. Bose, *Growing Up*, p. 9.
18. Leigh Minturn and John T. Hitchcock, *The Rajputs of Khalapur, India*, Six Cultures Series, no. 3 (New York: John Wiley and Sons, 1966), p. 123.
19. Talukdar, *Random Recollections*, p. 13.
20. Subhas Chandra Bose, *An Indian Pilgrim: an Unfinished Autobiography and Collected Letters 1897–1921*, edited and translated by Sisir Kumar Bose (Calcutta: Asia Publishing House, 1965), p. 13.
21. Bhagat Lakshman Singh, *Autobiography*, edited by Ganda Singh (Calcutta: Sikh Cultural Center, 1965), p. 11.
22. Ruth Benedict, *The Chrysanthemum and the Sword: Patterns of Japanese Culture* (New York: Meridian Books, 1967), pp. 253–254.
23. Carstairs emphasizes that an additional factor in this relationship was the potential competition between the father and his eldest son and heir. Carstairs, *The Twice-Born*, p. 113.
24. Nripendra Chandra Banerji, *At the Crossroads: An Autobiography* (Calcutta: A. Mukherjee, 1950), p. 27.
25. Jawaharlal Nehru, *An Autobiography* (London: John Lane, The Bodley Head, 1936), pp. 7–8.
26. Talukdar, *Random Recollections*, p. 17.
27. Sarma, *From Literature*, p. 7.
28. D.K. Karve, *Looking Back* (Poona: B.D. Karve, 1936), pp. 32–33.
29. Kakar, *The Inner World*, p. 83.
30. Savitri Devi Nanda, *The City of Two Gateways* (London: George Allen and Unwin, 1950), p. 233.
31. Lal Behari Day, *Recollections of My School-Days*, edited by Mahadevprasad Saha (Calcutta: Editions Indian, 1969), p. 463.
32. Nanda, *The City*, p. 197.

33. Talukdar, *Random Recollections*, p. 12.
34. Sitanatha Tattvabhushan, *Autobiography* (Calcutta: by the author, 1943), pp. 26 – 28, 30.
35. Quoted in Kakar, *The Inner World*, p. 93.
36. Carstairs, *The Twice-Born*, pp. 66, 72 – 73.
37. Kakar, *The Inner World*, p. 95.
38. Ibid., p. 91.
39. Ibid., p. 93.
40. Krishna Nehru Hutheesing, *With No Regrets* (New York: John Day, 1945), pp. 23 – 24.
41. S. Muthulakshmi Reddi, *Autobiography of Dr. S. Muthulakshmi Reddi* (Madras: by the author, 1964), pp. 15 – 17.
42. Paranjpye, *84 Not-Out*, p. 12.
43. Bose, *An Indian Pilgrim*, pp. 2 – 3.
44. Pal, *Memories*, p. 10.
45. Ibid.
46. Nirad C. Chaudhuri, *The Autobiography of an Unknown Indian*, reprint (Berkeley: University of California Press, 1968), p. 164.
47. Ibid.
48. Ibid., p. 157.
49. Ibid., pp. 162 – 163.
50. D.C. Pavate, *Memoirs of an Educational Administrator* (New Delhi: Prentice Hall of India, 1964), p. 1.
51. Ibid., pp. 1 – 2.
52. Tattvabhushan, *Autobiography*, p. 14 – 15.
53. Interview with D.C. Pavate, April, 1977.
54. Tattvabhushan, *Autobiography*, p. 18.
55. Gulab Singh, *Thorns and Thistles: An Autobiography of a Revolutionary*. (Bombay: The National Information Publications, 1948), p. 50.
56. Sunity Devi, *The Autobiography of an Indian Princess* (London: John Murray, 1921), p. 10.
57. Dhan Gopal Mukherji, *Caste and Outcast* (New York: Dutton, 1923), p. 23.
58. Carstairs, *The Twice-Born*, p. 68.
59. Prafulla Chandra Ray, *Life and Experiences of a Bengali Chemist*, reprint (Calcutta: Orient Book, 1958), p. 23.
60. Day, *Recollections*, p. 451.
61. Carstairs, *The Twice-Born*, p. 68.
62. Amar Singh, Manuscript of Diary, edited by Lloyd Rudolph and Susanne Rudolph, Chicago, 1974 (Typewritten), p. 83.
63. Ibid.
64. Bonnell, *The Book 'I'*, 1:24.
65. S.V. Ramamurthi, *Looking Across Fifty Years* (Bombay: Popular Prakashan, 1964), pp. 1 – 2.
66. Ray, *Life,* p. 128.
67. Ibid., p. 23.

68. Ibid.
69. Nanda, *The City*, p. 145.
70. Rabindranath Tagore, *My Reminiscences*, translated from the Bengali (London: Macmillan, 1917), p. 7.
71. Ibid., p. 96.
72. Day, *Recollections*, p. 495.
73. Morarji Desai, *The Story of My Life*, 2 vols (Delhi: Macmillan of India, 1974), 1:7.
74. Kakar, *The Inner World*, p. 131.
75. Chaudhuri, *The Autobiography*, p. 139.
76. Ibid.
77. The "narcissism" of the child and his identification with the reputation of his family is discussed in Roland, "Psychoanalytic Perspectives," pp. 11–20.
78. Tattvabhushan, *Autobiography*, pp. 16, 122–123, 46. Although the author mentions some more complementary qualities, saying for instance that the "biggest landlords sought his help and advice" (p. 16) on balance the negative references are more pervasive and consistent.
79. Surendranath Banerjea, *A Nation in the Making*, reprint (London: Oxford University Press, 1963), p. 7.
80. Ibid., p. 87.
81. Kylas Chunder Bose, *A Brief Memoir of Baboo Durga Churn Banerjee* (Calcutta: by the author, 1871), p. 22.
82. Meharcand Mahajan, *Looking Back* (Bombay: Asia Publishing House, 1963), pp. 1–3.
83. Mahajan, *Looking Back*, p. 7.
84. Paranjpye, *84 Not-Out*, p. 171.
85. Ibid., p. 7.
86. Mohandas K. Gandhi, *An Autobiography: The Story of My Experiments with Truth*, translated by Mahadev Desai (Boston: Beacon Press, 1957), p. 30.
87. Day, *Recollections*, p. 495.
88. Ibid.
89. Ibid.
90. Ibid., pp. 495–496.
91. Kakar, *The Inner World*, p. 133.
92. Ibid., p. 132.
93. Roland, "Psychoanalytic Perspectives", pp. 25–28, 30–31.
94. Ibid.
95. Kakar, *The Inner World*, p. 119.
96. Carstairs, *The Twice-Born*, p. 57.
97. Lloyd Rudolph and Susanne Rudolph, *The Modernity of Tradition* (Chicago: University of Chicago Press, 1967), pp. 183–192.
98. Minturn and Hitchcock, *The Rajputs*, p. 124.
99. Bonnell, *The Book 'I'*, 1:87.
100. Mahajan, *Looking Back*, p. 16.
101. Tattvabhushan, *Autobiography*, p. 35.

102. Ibid.
103. Aileen Ross, *The Hindu Family in Its Urban Setting* (Toronto: University of Toronto Press, 1961), p. 127.
104. Singh, *Autobiography*, pp. 13 – 14.
105. Kakar, *The Inner World*, p. 119.
106. Desai, *My Life Story*, 1:6 – 7.
107. Shudha Mazumdar, *A Pattern of Life*, edited by Geraldine H. Forbes (New Delhi: Manohar Book Service, 1977), p. 100.
108. Christine Dobbin, *Urban Leadership in Western India: Politics and Communities in Bombay City: 1840 – 1885* (London: Oxford University Press, 1972), pp. 70 – 71.
109. Told in Banerjea, *A Nation in Making*, pp. 285 – 286.
110. Debendranath Tagore, *The Autobiography of Maharshi Devendranath Tagore*, translated by S. Tagore and Indira Devi (London: Macmillan, 1914), p. 104.
111. Ibid.
112. Ghose's wife was the daughter of a member of the Brahmo Samaj and this may have caused her to be blamed for her son-in-law's behavior. Khetter Chunder Ghose, *Truth Stranger than Fiction* (Calcutta; N.G. Goswamy, 1896), p. 47.
113. Ibid.
114. Ibid., pp. 8 – 9.
115. Ibid.
116. Jogesh Chandra Chatterji, *In Search of Freedom* (Calcutta: Paresh Chandra Chatterjee, 1967), pp. 196 – 197.
117. Ibid.
118. See Leonard Gordon, "Bengal's Gandhi: A Study in Modern Indian Regionalism, Politics and Thought," in *Bengal Regional Identity*, edited by David Kopf, Occasional Paper, South Asia Series (East Lansing: Michigan State University, 1969), pp. 87 – 89. Nirad Chaudhuri, commenting on Subhas Bose's attitude towards Gandhi, states that for centuries Bengali gentlemen had had contempt for "the beggarly or cringing Vaishnavite," Nirad C. Chaudhuri, "Subhas Chandra Bose — His Legacy and Legend," *Pacific Affairs* 26 (December, 1953): 354 – 355.
119. This is the indirectly stated but constant refrain of much of the second volume of M.R. Jayakar's autobiography.

Chapter 2

1. R.P. Paranjpye, *84 Not-Out* (Delhi: National Book Trust, 1961), pp. 19 – 20.
2. Mahendra Pratap (Singh), *My Life Story of Fifty-five Years* (Dehradun: by the author, 1947), p. 25.
3. A.S. Pancapakesa Ayyar, *Twenty-five Years a Civilian* (Madras: V. Ramaswamy Sastrulu, 1962), p. 108.
4. M.R. Jayakar, *The Story of My Life*, 2 vols. (Bombay: Asia Publishing House, 1959), 1:13.

5. S.N. Banerjea, Assistant Magistrate of Sylhet to H. Sutherland, the Magistrate of Sylhet, 7 June 1873, "The Official Conduct of S.N. Banerjea, Assistant Magistrate of Sylhet," Government of India, *Proceedings Home Department (Public)*, September, 1873, p. 2118.

6. A.C. Miller, *Seven Letters to Indian Schoolboys*, 2nd ed. (Bombay: Humphrey Milford, 1917), p. 13.

7. T. Vedadrisadasan, Journal in English of a student at Elphinstone College, Bombay, for the period June–October 1839, preceded by a short autobiography, London, School of Oriental and African Studies, Manuscript, p. 72.

8. Ibid., p. 77.

9. India, Education Commission (Hunter Commission), *Report* (1883); Appendices, Provincial Reports: Bengal, Bombay, Madras, Northwest Provinces and Oudh, Punjab (1884), p. 88. Hereafter cited as *Hunter Commission*.

10. M.P. Trivedi, *My Struggles in Life* (Bombay: by the author, 1937), pp. 4–5.

11. Sacchidananda Sinha, "I am Admitted to School," in *Indian Autobiographies*, edited by S.P. Saksena (Calcutta: Oxford University Press, 1949), pp. 69–71.

12. Ibid.

13. Vedadrisadasan, Journal, p. 4.

14. Ellen McDonald and Craig M. Stark, *English Education, Nationalist Politics and Elite Groups in Maharashtra, 1885–1915*, Occasional Papers of the Center for South and Southeast Asia Studies, no. 5 (Berkeley: University of California Press, 1969), pp. 20, 40.

15. D.S. Sarma, *From Literature to Religion: An Autobiography* (Bombay: Bharatiya Vidya Bhavan, 1964), p. 19.

16. Rajendra Prasad, *Autobiography* (Bombay: Asia Publishing House, 1957), pp. 7–9.

17. Lal Behari Day, *Recollections of My School-Days*, edited by Mahadevprasad Saha (Calcutta: Editions Indian, 1969), p. 454.

18. Debendranath Tagore, *The Autobiography of Maharshi Devendranath Tagore*, translated by S. Tagore and Indira Devi (London: Macmillan, 1914), pp. 25–26.

19. Trivedi, *My Struggles*, p. 5.

20. Ibid., pp. 7–8.

21. Day, *Recollections*, p. 464.

22. Sitanatha Tattvabhushan, *Autobiography* (Calcutta: by the author, 1943), pp. 23, 33.

23. Meharcand Mahajan, *Looking Back* (Bombay: Asia Publishing House, 1963), pp. 5–9.

24. Prasad, *Autobiography*, pp. 15–26.

25. Nirad C. Chaudhuri, *The Autobiography of an Unknown Indian*, reprint (Berkeley: University of California Press, 1968), pp. 3–97.

26. Morarji Desai, *The Story of My Life*, 2 vols. (Delhi: Macmillan of India, 1974), 1:7.

27. Ayyar, *Twenty-five Years*, p. 316.

28. Pradip Bose, *Growing Up in India* (Calcutta: Minerva Associates, 1972), p. 123.
29. S.C. Talukdar, *Random Recollections* (Calcutta: by the author, 1938), p. 17.
30. Rajendra Prasad, *Atmakatha* (New Delhi: Sasta Sahitya Mandal, 1965), p. 48.
31. Jogesh Chandra Chatterji, *In Search of Freedom* (Calcutta: Paresh Chandra Chatterjee, 1967), p. 11.
32. Sinha, "I am Admitted to School," p. 75.
33. Prasad, *Autobiography*, pp. 16 – 18.
34. *Hunter Commission*, Bengal Appendix, p. 118; Madras Appendix, p. 139.
35. *Hunter Commission*, Madras Appendix, p. 139.
36. See for example Peary Chand Mittra, *A Biographical Sketch of David Hare* (Calcutta: W. Newman, 1877), p. 45.
37. Day, *Recollections*, pp. 490 – 491.
38. Subhas Chandra Bose, *An Indian Pilgrim: an Unfinished Autobiography and Collected Letters 1897 – 1921*, edited and translated by Sisir Kumar Bose (Calcutta: Asia Publishing House, 1965), p. 38.
39. Mittra, *A Biographical Sketch*, pp. 24 – 25.
40. Day, *Recollections*, pp. 498 – 499.
41. Surendranath Banerjea, *A Nation in the Making*, reprint (London: Oxford University Press, 1963), p. 1; Mittra, *A Biographical Sketch*, p. 19.
42. K.P. Menon, *Many Worlds: An Autobiography* (London: Bombay: Perl Publishing Co., 1971), p. 21.
43. Ibid.
44. D.K. Karve, *Looking Back* (Poona: B.D. Karve, 1936), p. 46.
45. Ibid.
46. Ibid., p. 57.
47. G. Morris Carstairs, *The Twice-Born: A Study of a Community of High Caste Hindus* (Bloomington, Ind.: Indiana University Press, 1967), p. 150.
48. Talukdar, *Random Recollections*, p. 58.
49. Ibid.
50. Nripendra Chandra Banerji, *At the Crossroads: An Autobiography* (Calcutta: A. Mukherjee, 1950), p. 60.
51. Mohandas K. Gandhi, *An Autobiography: The Story of My Experiments with Truth*, translated by Mahadev Desai (Boston: Beacon Press, 1957), pp. 13 – 14.
52. Interview with D.C. Pavate, April, 1977.
53. Dosabhoy Framjee, *The Parsees, Their History, Manners, Customs and Religion* (London: Smith, Elder, 1858), p. 216.
54. R.C. Dutt, *Three Years in Europe, 1868 – 1871*, 3rd ed. (Calcutta: S.K. Lahiri, 1890), p. 20.
55. Prasad, *Autobiography*, p. 6.
56. Desai, *The Story*, 1:22 – 23.
57. Chaudhuri, *The Autobiography*, p. 353.
58. Y.G. Bonnell, *The Book 'I': The Autobiography of Y.G. Bonnell*, 2 vols. (Madras: by the author, 1930 – 1938), 1:110.
59. K.N. Katju, *The Days I Remember* (Calcutta: New Age Publications, 1961), pp. 41 – 42.

60. Desai, *The Story*, 1:22–23.
61. Bonnell, *The Book* T, 1:111.

Chapter 3

1. Erik H. Erikson, *Identity: Youth and Crisis* (New York: W.W. Norton, 1968), p. 212.
2. Ibid.
3. Ibid., p. 174.
4. Christine Dobbin, *Urban Leadership in Western India* (London: Oxford University Press, 1972), p. 75.
5. D.K. Karve, *Looking Back* (Poona: B.D. Karve, 1936), p. 53.
6. Ibid., p. 33.
7. Ibid., p. 37.
8. Ibid.., pp. 37–38.
9. Ibid.
10. Ibid.
11. Ibid.
12. Ibid.
13. Ibid., p. 46.
14. Ibid.
15. Ibid.
16. Iravati Karve, "Grandfather," in *The New Brahmans*, edited and translated by D.D. Karve (Berkeley: University of California Press, 1963), pp. 88–89.
17. R.P. Paranjpye, *84 Not-Out* (Delhi: National Book Trust, 1961), p. 14.
18. Karve, *Looking Back*, p. 27.
19. Ibid., pp. 29–30.
20. Ibid., p. 47.
21. Ibid., p. 46.
22. Ibid., pp. 48–49.
23. Ibid.
24. Anandibai, "Autobiography," in *The New Brahmans*, edited and translated by D.D. Karve (Berkeley: University of California Press, 1963), p. 79.
25. Karve, *Looking Back*, p. 51.
26. Ibid., p. 52.
27. Anandibai, "Autobiography," p. 78.
28. Ibid., p. 72.
29. Karve, *Looking Back*, p. 171.
30. Interview with D.D. Karve, July, 1978.
31. Karve, *Looking Back*, p. 57.
32. Sitanatha Tattvabhushan, *Autobiography* (Calcutta: by the author, 1943), p. 31.
33. Ibid.
34. Ibid., p. 40.
35. Ibid.

36. Ibid., p. 30.

37. Ibid.

38. Ibid.

39. Ibid., p. 43.

40. Ibid., p. 46.

41. Ibid., p. 115.

42. Pradip Bose, *Growing Up in India* (Calcutta: Minerva Associates, 1972), p. 162.

43. Y.G. Bonnell, *The Book 'I': The Autobiography of Y.G. Bonnell*, 2 vols. (Madras: by the author, 1930–1938), 1:124.

44. India, Education Commission (Hunter Commission), *Report* (1883); Appendices, Provincial Reports: Bengal, Bombay, Madras, Northwest Provinces and Oudh, Punjab (1884), p. 127.

45. Ibid.

46. Mohandas K. Gandhi, *An Autobiography: The Story of My Experiments with Truth*, translated by Mahadev Desai (Boston: Beacon Press, 1957), p. 15.

47. Subhas Chandra Bose, *An Indian Pilgrim: An Unfinished Autobiography and Collected Letters 1897–1921*, edited and translated by Sisir Kumar Bose (Calcutta: Asia Publishing House, 1965), pp. 27–28.

48. Srimannarayan, *Memoirs: Window on Gandhi and Nehru* (Bombay: Popular Prakashan, 1971), p. 118.

49. Nirad C. Chaudhuri, *The Autobiography of an Unknown Indian*, reprint (Berkeley: University of California Press, 1968), p. 154.

50. Nagendranath Gupta, *Reflections and Reminiscences* (Bombay: Hind Kitab, 1947), p. 22.

51. Prafulla Chandra Ray, *Life and Experiences of a Bengali Chemist*, reprint (Calcutta: Orient Book, 1958), p. 5.

52. Ibid., p. 6.

53. Ray's father identified strongly with the West, or so his son reports, but Muslim culture also seems to have had its share in shaping the father's character. Ibid., pp. 7, 20.

54. Ibid., p. 23.

55. Ibid., p. 20.

56. Ibid.

57. Ibid., p. 34.

58. Ibid., p. 20.

59. Ibid., p. 26.

60. Ibid.

61. Ibid., p. 18.

62. Ibid., pp. 30–31.

63. Ibid., p. 35. "I was very pleased," another author recalls, remembering her first prize day, "until I found that all other children had prizes too. It was disappointing." Savitri Devi Nanda, *The City of Two Gateways* (London: George Allen and Unwin, 1950), p. 74.

64. Ray, *Life and Experiences*, p. 35.
65. When R.P. Paranjpye enrolled in the B.S. course at Fergusson College in the 1890s it had only one other student. Paranjpye, *84 Not-Out*, p. 20.
66. Ray, *Life and Experiences*, p. 55.
67. Ibid., p. 60.
68. Ibid.
69. Ibid.
70. Ibid., pp. 127–128.
71. Ibid., p. 63.
72. Ibid., p. 19.
73. Ibid., p. 27.
74. Ibid., pp. 37–38.
75. Ibid., p. 92.
76. Ibid., pp. 82–83.
77. Ibid., p. 105.
78. Ibid., pp. 30–31.
79. Ibid., p. 53.

Chapter 4

1. Surendranath Banerjea, *A Nation in the Making*, reprint (Bombay: Oxford University Press, 1963), p. 30.
2. The records for Banerjea's dismissal from the ICS are: "The Official Conduct of S.N. Banerjea, Assistant Magistrate of Sylhet," Government of India, *Proceedings Home Department (Public)*, September 1873, pp. 2089–2149; "Case of S.N. Banerjea, Late Assistant Magistrate of Sylhet," Government of India, *Proceedings Home Department (Public)*, May 1874, pp. 367–417; Surendranath Banerjea, comp., *In Re Surendranath Banerjea: An Exposition* (Calcutta: by the author, 1873).
3. Banerjea, *A Nation*, p. 1.
4. Ibid., p. 2.
5. Ibid.
6. Ibid., p. 1.
7. Ibid.
8. Ibid., p. 2.
9. Ibid.
10. Ibid., p. 23.
11. Ibid., p. 147.
12. Bipin Chandra Pal, *Memories of My Life and Times*, reprint (Calcutta: Bipin Chandra Pal Institute, 1973), pp. 121–122.
13. Banerjea, *A Nation*, p. 4.
14. R.C. Dutt was one of the two others to travel with Banerjea to London in 1868. Dutt, who passed the ICS. examination and was appointed to the service,

wrote in a later reminiscence: "The great undertaking on which we had staked everything in life had succeeded. The future of our life was determined." R.C. Dutt, *Three Years in Europe, 1868–1871*, 3rd ed. (Calcutta: S.K. Lahiri, 1890), p. 20.

15. Banerjea, *A Nation*, p. 30.
16. Ibid., p. 31.
17. Ibid.
18. Ibid.
19. Ibid., Appendix.
20. Banerjea, *In Re Surendranath*, p.s.
21. Judge F.C. Glover, Minute by the High Court Judges, June 27, 1873 in "The Official Conduct of S.N. Banerjea," *Proceedings*, p. 2100.
22. Banerjea, *A Nation*, p. 31.
23. Erik H. Erikson, *Gandhi's Truth: On the Origins of Militant Non-violence* (New York: W.W. Norton, 1969), pp. 47, 169.
24. Banerjea, *A Nation*, p. 64.
25. Ibid., p. 8.
26. Ibid., p. 218.
27. Ibid., p. 365.
28. Ibid., p. 148.
29. Ibid., p. 121.
30. Ibid., pp. 349–350.
31. Ibid., p. 328.
32. Ibid., p. 109.
33. Ibid., p. 95.
34. Ibid., p. 109.
35. Ibid.
36. Ibid., p. 112.
37. Ibid.
38. Ibid.
39. Ibid., p. 4.
40. Ibid., p. 338.
41. Ibid., p. 339.
42. Ibid., p. 71.
43. Ibid., pp. 289–290.
44. Ibid., p. 312.
45. Ibid., p. 193.
46. Ibid., pp. 285–286.

Chapter 5

1. Subhas Chandra Bose, *An Indian Pilgrim: An Unfinished Autobiography and Collected Letters 1897–1921*, edited and translated by Sisir Kumar Bose (Calcutta: Asia Publishing House, 1965), p. 97.

2. Ibid., pp. 99 – 100.
3. Ibid., p. 95.
4. Ibid., p. 2.
5. Ibid., pp. 1, 3.
6. Ibid.
7. Ibid., p. 2.
8. Ibid., p. 17.
9. Ibid., p. 10.
10. Ibid., p. 16.
11. Ibid., p. 9.
12. Ibid., p. 3.
13. This was the Protestant European School run by the Baptist Mission in Cuttack. Bose describes it as a "missionary school meant primarily for Europeans and Anglo-Indian boys and girls with a limited number of seats (about 15 percent) for Indians." The "majority" of the teachers and pupils, he notes later, were Anglo-Indians. Ibid., pp. 19 – 20.
14. Ibid., p. 24.
15. Ibid.
16. Ibid., p. 28.
17. Ibid., p. 25.
18. Santha Rama Rau describes her brief attendance at a similar institution. The children were all given English names and during examinations the Indians were placed in the back of the room seated apart from one another to prevent cheating. Santha Rama Rau, *Gifts of Passage* (New York: Harper, 1961), chap. 1 passim.
19. Bose, *an Indian Pilgrim*, p. 24.
20. Ibid., p. 26.
21. Erik H. Erikson, *Identity: Youth and Crisis* (New York: W.W. Norton, 1968), pp. 172 – 173.
22. Ibid., p. 174.
23. Ibid., pp. 166 – 167.
24. Bose, *An Indian Pilgrim*, pp. 31 – 32.
25. Ibid., p. 38. Leonard Gordon has suggested that throughout his life Bose alternated between seeing himself as a "good boy" and a rebel. Leonard A. Gordon, *Bengal: The Nationalist Movement, 1876 – 1940* (New York: Columbia University Press, 1974), p. 225.
26. Bose, *An Indian Pilgrim*, p. 44.
27. Ibid., p. 35.
28. Gordon, *Bengal*, p. 236.
29. Bose, *An Indian Pilgrim*, p. 32.
30. Erikson, *Identity*, pp. 187 – 188, 232 – 260.
31. Bose, *An Indian Pilgrim*, p. 36.
32. Ibid., p. 35.
33. Ibid.

34. Ibid., p. 36.

35. Ibid., pp. 38–39.

36. Ibid., p. 35.

37. Ibid., p. 46.

38. Gordon, *Bengal*, p. 226.

39. Bose, *An Indian Pilgrim*, p. 44.

40. Ibid., p. 60.

41. Ibid., p. 139. Letters translated from Bengali and appended to this edition of Bose's autobiography complement the autobiography's version of this story.

42. Ibid., pp. 62–63.

43. Ibid., p. 139.

44. Ibid.

45. Ibid.

46. Ibid., p. 66.

47. Ibid.

48. Ibid., p. 67.

49. Ibid., p. 68.

50. Ibid., p. 69.

51. Ibid., p. 70.

52. Gordon, *Bengal*, p. 228.

53. Bose, *An Indian Pilgrim*, p. 70.

54. Ibid.

55. Ibid., p. 35.

56. Erikson, *Identity*, p. 255.

57. Bose, *An Indian Pilgrim*, pp. 70–71.

58. Ibid., p. 71.

59. Ibid., p. 70.

60. Ibid., p. 73. Bose contends there was no family disapproval: "There was no change whatsoever in the attitude of my parents and strange to say, my father never put one question to me about the events in College or my part therein." (Ibid., p. 72.) Silence in this situation was probably something less than sympathetic approval.

61. Ibid., p. 77.

62. Ibid., p. 79.

63. Ibid., pp. 82–83.

64. Ibid., p. 97.

65. Ibid.

66. Ibid., p. 99.

Chapter 6

1. Nirad C. Chaudhuri, *The Autobiography of an Unknown Indian*, reprint (Berkeley: University of California Press, 1968), p. 1.

2. Ibid., p. 457.
3. Ibid., p. 504.
4. Ibid.
5. Edmund Marsden, *History of India for Middle Schools* (London: Macmillan, 1900), p. 72.
6. Chaudhuri, *Autobiography*, p. 461.
7. Ibid., p. 75.
8. Ibid., p. 72.
9. Ibid., p. 71.
10. Ibid., p. 152.
11. Ibid., p. 71.
12. Ibid., p. 136.
13. Ibid.p. 137.
14. Ibid., pp. 23 – 25.
15. Ibid., p. 103.
16. Ibid., p. 155.
17. Ibid., p. 138.
18. Ibid., pp. 153 – 154.
19. Ibid., p. 156.
20. Ibid.
21. Ibid., p. 153.
22. Ibid.
23. Ibid., pp. 138, 127.
24. Ibid., p. 164.
25. Ibid., p. 219.
26. Ibid., p. 234.
27. Ibid., p. 223.
28. Ibid., p. 225.
29. Ibid., pp. 300 – 301.
30. Ibid., p. 308.
31. Ibid., p. 347.
32. Ibid., p. 395.
33. Ibid., p. 412.
34. Ibid., p. 315.
35. Ibid.
36. Ibid., p. 281.
37. Ibid., p. 294.
38. Ibid., p. 256.
39. Ibid., p. 257.
40. Ibid., p. 256.
41. Ibid., p. 257.
42. Ibid., p. 349.
43. Ibid.

44. Ibid., p. 324.

45. Ibid., pp. 326–327.

46. Ibid., pp. 352–353.

47. Ibid., p. 351.

48. Ibid., pp. 452–453.

49. Ibid., p. 453.

50. Ibid., p. 155.

51. Ibid., p. 453.

52. Ibid.

53. Ibid., p. 454.

54. Ibid., pp. 454–455.

55. Erik H. Erikson, *Identity: Youth and Crisis* (New York: W.W. Norton, 1968), p. 158.

56. Chaudhuri, *Autobiography*, p. 352.

57. Ibid.

58. Ibid.

59. Ibid.

60. Ibid., p. 154.

61. Ibid., pp. 454–455.

62. Ibid., p. 502.

63. Ibid., p. 4.

64. Ibid.

Chapter 7

1. Bipin Chandra Pal, *Memories of My Life and Times*, reprint (Calcutta: Bipin Chandra Pal Institute, 1973), p. 11.

2. Ibid., p. 310.

3. Ibid., p. 9.

4. Ibid., p. 10.

5. Ibid.

6. Ibid. Pal was sensitive to the implications of sexual self-indulgence implicit in the double marriage of his father. He emphasizes that the father only married the second wife (Pal's mother) on the insistence of the still living first wife. In a later passage which adds an interesting dimension to his conflicts with his father, he explains how in conversation with his father shortly before his death, he came to understand "the desolation of his heart caused by my apostasy." "This brought home to me," he writes, "that I was not the fruit of my father's sex-passion, but was in his eyes a gift of the Gods, given in response to his profound religious and spiritual longing, what is called in Sanskrit *'Tapasya.'* Ibid., p. 265.

7. Ibid., p. 252.

8. Ibid., p. 254.

9. Ibid., p. 252.

10. Ibid., p. 9.
11. Ibid., p.42.
12. Warren Gunderson, "The Self-Image and World View of the Bengali Intelligentsia as Found in the Writings of the Mid-Nineteenth Century 1830 — 1870" in *Bengal Literature and History*, edited by Edward C. Dimock Jr., Occasional Papers of the Asian Studies Center (East Lansing: Michigan State University Press, 1967), pp. 127 – 177.
13. Bhagat Lakshman Singh, *Autobiography*, edited by Ganda Singh (Calcutta: Sikh Cultural Center, 1965), p. 6.
14. D.S. Sarma, *From Literature to Religion: an Autobiography* (Bombay: Bharatiya Vidya Bhavan, 1964), pp. 98 – 99.
15. T. Vedadrisadasan, Journal in English of a student at Elphinstone College, Bombay, for the period June – October 1839, preceded by a short autobiography, London, School of Oriental and African Studies, Ms., p. 13.
16. Kumara P. Menon, *Many Worlds: An Autobiography* (Bombay: Perl Publishing, 1971), p. 21.
17. Interview with D.C. Pavate, April, 1977.
18. R.P. Paranjpye, *84 Not-Out* (Delhi: National Book Trust, 1961), p. 7.
19. D.K. Karve, *Looking Back* (Poona: B.D. Karve, 1936), p. 57.
20. Krishnalal Shridharani, *My India, My West* (London: Victor Gallancz Ltd., 1942), pp. 18 – 19.
21. Jawaharlal Nehru, *An Autobiography* (London: John Lane, the Bodley Head, 1936), pp. 3, 11 – 12.
22. Srimannarayan, *Memoirs: Window on Gandhi and Nehru* (Bombay: Popular Prakashan, 1971), p. 118.
23. Prakash Tandon, *Punjabi Century* (Berkeley: University of California Press, 1968), pp. 33 – 34.
24. Ibid., p. 35.
25. Ibid.
26. Ibid., p. 36.
27. Ibid., p. 35.
28. Ibid., p. 30.
29. Thomas Babington Macaulay, "Minute on Education," in *Sources of Indian Tradition*, edited by Wm. Theo. de Bary et. al. (New York: Columbia University Press, 1958), p. 601.
30. Alan Roland, "Psychoanalytic Perspectives on Personality Development in India," forthcoming, pp. 11 – 12.
31. Aurobindo Ghose, *Sri Aurobindo on Himself and the Mother* (Pondicherry: Sri Aurobindo Ashram, 1953), p. 9.
32. Ibid., p. 13.
33. Ibid.
34. Surendranath Banerjea, *A Nation in the Making* (Bombay: Oxford University Press, 1963), p. 1.
35. Ibid., p. 8.

36. Kylas Chunder Bose, *A Brief Memoir of Baboo Durga Churn Banerjea* (Calcutta: by the author, 1871), p. 14.
37. Tandon, *Punjabi Century*, p. 31.
38. Ibid., pp. 210–211.
39. Ibid., p. 206.
40. Subhas Chandra Bose, *An Indian Pilgrim: An Unfinished Autobiography and Collected Letters 1897–1921*, edited and translated by Sisir Kumar Bose (Calcutta: Asia Publishing House, 1965), p. 170.
41. M.R. Jayakar, *The Story of My Life*, 2 vols. (Bombay: Asia Publishing House, 1959), 1:1.
42. Karve, *Looking Back*, p. 173.
43. Nirad C. Chaudhuri, *The Autobiography of an Unknown Indian*, reprint (Berkeley: University of California Press, 1968), p. 155.
44. Ibid., p. 352.
45. Ibid., p. 455.
46. Roland, "Psychoanalytic Perspectives," p. 11–12.
47. Bonnell, *The Book 'I'*, 1:1–2.
48. This issue has been raised in various form within much scholarship on the events of nineteenth and twentieth century India. See for example: Christine Dobbin, *Urban Leadership in Western India* (London: Oxford University Press, 1972); Leonard Gordon, *Bengal: The Nationalist Movement: 1876–1940* (New York: Columbia University Press, 1974); Charles Heimsath, *Indian Nationalism and Hindu Social Reform* (Princeton: Princeton University Press, 1964); Francis Hutchins, *India's Revolution: Gandhi and the Quit India Movement* (Cambridge: Harvard University Press, 1973); Kenneth Jones, *Arya Dharma* (Berkeley: University of California Press, 1976); David Kopf, *The Brahmo Samaj and the Shaping of the Modern Indian Mind* (Princeton: Princeton University Press, 1979); Lloyd Rudolph and Susanne Rudolph, *The Modernity of Tradition* (Chicago: University of Chicago Press, 1967).
49. The appearance of this true generation in early nineteenth century Bengal may partially account for the tendency of Indian historians to periodize many separate sections of the nineteenth and twentieth centuries and sometimes all of that time into two generational cycles. Historians often explain these years in terms of a pendulum-like swing among the Western-educated from extremism to moderation or the reverse. A virtue of this dichotomy is its use of the perceptions of many Indians in this period who felt, as autobiographies illustrate, that their own experiences were absolutely distinct from the earlier generation in their families, their fathers. But a more serious weakness of these categories is their tendency to force us into describing quite different groups — early nineteenth century "extremist" students and the "extremists" of the twentieth century nationalist movement, for example — as though they were the same. Similarly, the analysis which describes nineteenth century Indians as moving from concern with social and religious reform into political activities does allow us to see the change between first-generation opposition to orthodoxy and the more diffuse concerns and conflicts of

second-generation students which these autobiographies record. The periodization breaks down, however, when applied to the renewed religious interests of late nineteenth and early twentieth century Indians. Because it ignores the psychological causes for individual interests, it may force us to label men like Vivekananda and Gandhi "traditionalists" because of their interest in Indian religion and to overlook the considerable influence that the Western educational system had on both.

50. Jawaharlal Nehru, *The Discovery of India* (New York: John Day, 1946), pp. 361–362.

Conclusion

1. Pradip Bose, *Growing Up in India* (Calcutta: Minerva Associates, 1972), p. 162.
2. Surendranath Banerjea, *A Nation in the Making*, reprint (Bombay: Oxford University Press, 1963), p. 193.
3. Mohandas K. Gandhi, "Hind Swaraj", in *Sources of Indian Tradition*, edited by Wm. Theo. de Bary et. al. (New York: Columbia University Press, 1958), p. 803.
4. Interview with D.C. Pavate, April, 1977.

Appendix I

1. Bruce Tiebout McCully, *English Education and the Origins of Indian Nationalism*, Studies in History, Economics and Public Law, no. 473 (New York: Columbia University Press, 1940), chap. 4 passim.
2. Ibid., p. 177.
3. Anil Seal, *The Emergence of Indian Nationalism: Competition and Collaboration in the Later Nineteenth Century* (Cambridge: Cambridge University Press, 1971), p. 104. Madras, according to Seal, is the exception here, with many more of the students in Madras city coming from the outlying areas than from the city itself.
4. Ibid., chapter 2 passim; Leonard Gordon, *Bengal: The Nationalist Movement: 1876–1940* (New York: Columbia University Press, 1974), p. 2.
5. Ellen McDonald and Craig M. Stark, *English Education, Nationalist Politics and Elite Groups in Maharashtra, 1885–1915*, Occasional Papers of the Center for South and Southeast Asia Studies, no. 5 (Berkeley: University of California Press, 1969), pp. 19–20.
6. Roy Pascal, *Design and Truth in Autobiography* (London: Routledge and Kegan Paul, 1960), chap. 2 passim.

Selected Bibliography

1. Bibliographies

Bengal Library. *Catalogue of Books.* Calcutta: n.p., 1867 – 1954.

Bombay. *Catalogue of Books.* Bombay: Government Central Press, 1867 – 1959.

Galanter, Marc. "An Incomplete Bibliography of the Indian Legal Profession." *Law and Society Review* 3 (December 1968), 445 – 462.

India Office Library. *Catalogue.* London: Eyre and Spottiswode, 1888. Supplement 1. London: Eyre and Spottiswode, 1895.

Kesavan, B.S., gen. ed. *The Indian National Bibliography.* 17 vols. Calcutta: Central Reference Library, 1958 – .

Kesavan, B.A., and V.V. Kulkarni. *The National Bibliography of Indian Literature 1901 – 1953.* Vol. 1: *Literature in Assamese, Bengali, English and Gujarati.* Delhi: Sahitya Akademi, 1962 – 1970.

Madras. *The Catalogue of Books.* Madras: n.p., 1867 – 1944.

North West Provinces. *Catalogue of Books.* Agra: Government Press, 1867 – 1893.

Punjab. *Catalogue of Books Registered in the Punjab.* Lahore: n.p., 1867 – 1940.

Sen, S.P., ed. *Dictionary of National Biography.* 2 vols. Calcutta: Institute of Historical Studies, 1972 – 1974.

Spencer, Dorothy. *Indian Fiction in English.* Philadelphia: University of Pennsylvania Press, 1960.

United Provinces of Agra and Oudh. *Catalogue of Books.* Allahabad: Superintendant Government Press, 1894 – 1964.

2. Official Records

Bombay City. Board of Education. *Report for the Years 1840, 1841, 1842.* Appendix no. 1: *Depository of the Elphinstone Native Education Institution.* 1842.

Bombay City. Board of Education. *Report for the Year 1843.* 1844. Appendix no. 1: *Depository of the Elphinstone Native Education Institution.* 1844.

Bombay University. *Bombay University Calendar and Examination Papers.* 1861, 1900 – 1901.

Calcutta University. *Calcutta University Calendar and Examination Papers.* 1861, 1900.

India. Education Commission (Hunter Commission). *Report.* 1883. Appendices, Provincial Reports: Bengal, Bombay, Madras, North West Provinces and Oudh, Punjab. 1884.

————. *Proceedings Home Department (Public).* "The Official Conduct of S.N. Banerjea, Assistant Magistrate of Sylhet." September, 1873. 2089–2149.

————. *Proceedings Home Department (Public).* "The Case of S.N. Banerjea, Late Assistant Magistrate of Sylhet." May, 1874. 367–417.

Madras University. *Madras University Calendar and Examination Questions.* 1866–1867, 1900–1901.

Punjab University. *Punjab University College Calendar and Examination Papers.* 1874–1875.

3. Private Papers: Nehru Memorial Museum and Library, New Delhi

Manuscript Collection. V.S. Srinivasa Sastri. 1902–1946.
Manuscript Collection. Nagendranath Gupta. 1901–1952.
Manuscript Collection. R. P. Paranjpye. 1889–1966.
Manuscript Collection. Justice Mehr Chand Mahajan. 1918–1958.
Manuscript Collection. Dr. S. Muthulakshmi Reddi. 1915–1958.
Manuscript Collection. Chimanlal Setalvad. 1899–1940.

4. Interviews

Vimala Appasamy. April, 1977.
D.C. Pavate. April, 1977.
Vikram Chand Mahajan. September, 1977.
D.D. Karve. July, 1978.
Shakuntala Paranjpye. July, 1978.
Krishna Reddi. April, 1977.

5. Autobiographies

Anand, Mulk Raj. *Apology for Heroism.* 2nd ed. Bombay: Kitab Popular, 1957.
Appasamy, A.S. *Fifty Years of a Convert.* Madras: A.J. Appasamy, 1924.
Appasamy, Mrs. E.S. "Reminiscences." *Swarna Smruti 1924–1974.* Madras: Vidyodaya, 1974.
Banerjea, Surendranath. *A Nation in the Making.* London: Oxford University Press, 1925. Reprint. Bombay: Oxford University Press, 1963.
Banerjea, Gooroo Dass. *Reminiscences, Speeches and Writings of Sir Gooroo Dass Banerjee.* pp. 110–119. Edited by U.N. Banerjee. Calcutta: n.p., 1927.
Banerji, Nripendra Chandra. *At the Crossroads: An Autobiography.* Calcutta: A. Mukherjee, 1950.

Barkataki, Satyendranath. *The Escapades of a Magistrate.* 2nd ed. Calcutta: Orient Longmans, 1964.

Basu, Baman Das. *My Sojourn in England.* Calcutta: R. Chatterjee, 1927.

Bhattacharjee, S.P. *Memoirs of the Official Career of S.P. Bhattacharjee.* Lahore: Public Advocate Press, 1894.

Bonnell, Yesadian Ghanaprakasam. *The Book 'I': The Authography of Y.G. Bonnell.* 2 vols. Madras: by the author, 1930–1938.

Bose, Bepin Krishna. *Stray Thoughts on Some Incidents in My Life.* 2nd ed. Madras: by the author, 1923.

Bose, Pradip. *Growing Up In India.* Calcutta: Minerva Associates, 1972.

Bose, Subhas Chandra. *An Indian Pilgrim: An Unfinished Autobiography and Collected Letters 1897–1921.* Edited and translated by Sisir Kumar Bose. Calcutta: Asia Publishing House, 1965.

Chatterji, Jogesh Chandra. *In Search of Freedom.* Calcutta: Paresh Chandra Chatterjee, 1967.

Chaudhuri, Nirad C. *The Autobiography of an Unknown Indian.* London: Macmillan, 1951. Reprint. Berkeley: University of California Press, 1968.

Das, Sarat Chandra. "Narrative of the Incidents of My Early Life." *The Modern Review.* 5 (January, 1908), 10–25.

Day, Lal Behari. *Recollections of My School-Days.* Edited by Mahadevprasad Saha. Calcutta: Editions Indian, 1969.

Desai, Govindji Gopalji. *Some Experiences of a Mamlatdar-Magistrate's Life.* Ahmedabad: United Printing and General Agency, 1906.

Desai, Morarji. *The Story of My Life.* 2 vols. Delhi: The MacMillan Company of India, 1974.

Devi, Sunity. *The Autobiography of an Indian Princess.* London: John Murray, 1921.

Dongerkeri, Sundararav Ramarav. *Memories of Two Universities.* Bombay: Manaktalas, 1966.

Dutt, R.C. *Three Years in Europe.* 3rd ed. Calcutta: S.K. Lahiri, 1890.

Ghose, Aurobindo. *Sri Aurobindo on Himself and the Mother.* Pondicherry: Sri Aurobindo Ashram, 1953.

Ghose, Barindra Kumar. *The Tale of My Exile.* Pondicherry: Arya Office, 1922.

Ghose, J.N. *My Life Thoughts.* Lahore: n.p., 1889.

Ghose, Khetter Chunder. *Truth Stranger than Fiction.* Calcutta: N.G. Goswamy, 1896.

Ghose, Srikanta. *Challenge.* Calcutta: Academic Publishers, 1967.

Gopal, Ram. *Rhythm in the Heavens.* London: Secher and Warburg, 1957.

Gupta, Nagendranath. *Reflections and Reminiscences.* Bombay: Hind Kitab, 1947.

Hanumanthaiah. "Diary." In *History of the Freedom Movement in Karnataka,* Edited by G.S. Happa, 2:552–556. Bangalore: Government of Mysore, 1964.

Hutheesing, Krishna. *With No Regrets.* New York: The John Day Company, 1945.

Jayakar, M.R. *The Story of My Life.* 2 vols. Bombay: Asia Publishing House, 1959.

Kanal, P.V. *My Story.* Lahore: Moga Dev Samaj. 1964.

Kapali Sastri, T.V. *Collected Notes and Papers of Sri T.V. Kapali Sastri,* Edited by M.P. Pandit. Pondicherry: Sri Aurobindo Ashram, 1965.

Karve, D.K. *Looking Back.* Poona: B.D. Karve, 1936.

Katju, K.N. *The Days I Remember.* Calcutta: New Age Publications, 1961.

Khare, N.B. *My Political Memoir or Autobiography.* Nagpur: J.R. Joshi, 1959.

Mahajan, Meharcand. *Looking Back.* Bombay: Asia Publishing House, 1963.

Malik, Marcus Abraham (Hazari). *An Indian Outcaste: The Autobiography of an Untouchable.* London: Bannisdale Press, 1951.

Mavalankar, Ganesh Vasudes. *My Life at the Bar.* New Delhi: Hindustani Times Press, 1955.

Mazumdar, Shudha. *A Pattern of Life.* Edited by Geraldine H. Forbes. New Delhi: Manohar Book Service, 1977.

Mehta, Puranlal. "Autobiography of Shri Puranlal Mehta, Bania." In *The Twice-Born: A Study of a Community of High Caste Hindus,* by G. Morris Carstairs, 260–316. Bloomington, Ind.: Indiana University Press, 1967.

Mehta, Ved. *Face to Face.* Boston: Little, Brown, 1957.

Menon, Kumara P. *Many Worlds: An Autobiography.* London: Oxford University Press, 1965. Reprint. Bombay: Perl Publishing, 1971.

Mookerjee, Joykissen. "Autobiography." *Calcutta Review.* 118:1 (January 1951);2 (February 1951).

Mukherje, Dhan Gopal. *Caste and Outcast.* New York: Dutton, 1923.

Mukherjee, Monohar. *A Few Notes of My 80 Years Life's Experiences.* Uttarpara: by the author, 1935.

Munshi, Kanaiyalal Maniklal. *Munshi – His Art and Work.* Edited by J.H. Dave et al. 3 vols. Ahmedabad: Sri Munshi Celebration Committee, 1957–1964.

Nanda, Savitri Devi. *The City of Two Gateways.* London: George Allen and Unwin, 1950.

Naoroji, Dadabhai. "A Chapter in Autobiography." In *Speeches and Writings of Dadabhai Naoroji.* 653–656. Madras: Natesan, 1910.

Narayan, Jayaprakash. *Inside Lahore Fort.* Madras: Socialist Book Centre, 1959.

Narayan, R.K. *My Dateless Diary.* Mysore: Orient Paperbacks, 1960.

Nehru, Jawaharlal. *An Autobiography.* London: John Lane, The Bodley Head, 1936.

Nissenkooloo, Mruttyunjaya. *Autobiographical Sketch.* Vizagapatami: By the author, 1888.

Pal, Bipin Chandra. *Memories of My Life and Times.* Vol. 1: *In the Days of My Youth, 1857–1884.* Calcutta: Modern Book Agency, 1932. Vol. 2: *Memories of My Life and Times, 1886–1900.* Calcutta: Yugayatri Prakashak, 1951. Reprint. *Memories of My Life and Times.* Calcutta: Bipin Chandra Pal Institute, 1973.

Pancapakesa Ayyar, A.S. *Twenty-five Years a Civilian.* Madras: V. Ramaswamy Sastrulu, 1962.

Pandit, Vijayalakshmi. *Prison Days.* Calcutta: Signet Press, 1945.

Paranjpye, Raghunatha Purushottama. *84 Not-Out.* Delhi: National Book Trust, 1961.

Pavate, Dadappa C. *Memoirs of an Educational Administrator.* New Delhi: Prentice-Hall of India, 1964.

Pradhan, G.K. *Towards the Silver Crests of the Himalayas.* Bombay: K.K. Asher for Laxmi Syndicate, 1963.

Pratap (Singh), Mahendra. *My Life Story of Fifty-five Years.* Dehradun: by the author, 1947.

Prem, Bhatiya. *All My Yesterdays.* Delhi: Vikas Publishing House, 1972.

Radhakrishnan, Sarvepalli. "My Search for Truth." In *Indian Autobiographies.* 122–135. Edited by S.P. Saksena. 2nd ed. Calcutta: Oxford University Press, 1958.

Rama Rau, Santha. *Gifts of Passage.* New York: Harper, 1961.

Ramabai, Pandita. *A Testimony.* Bombay: n.p., 1907.

Ramamurthi, S.V. *Looking Across Fifty Years.* Bombay: Popular Prakashan, 1964.

Ramdas. *In the Vision of God.* 2 vols. Bombay: Anand Ashram, 1963.

Ray, Prafulla Chandra. *Life and Experience of a Bengali Chemist.* 2 vols. Calcutta: Chatterjee and Col., 1932; Kegan Paul and Co., 1934. Reprint (2 vols in 1). Calcutta: Orient Book, 1958.

Reddi S. Muthulaksmi. *Autobiography of Dr. S. Muthulakshmi Reddi.* Madras: by the author, 1964.

Roy, Amrita Lal. *Reminiscences English and American, Part 2.* Calcutta: Roy Publishing House, 1888.

Roy, Manabendra Nath. *Memoirs.* Bombay: Indian Renaissance Institute, 1964.

Rugnathdas, M. *Story of a Widow Remarriage.* Bombay: S.K. Khambata, 1890.

Sampurnanand. *Memories and Reflections.* New York: Asia Publishing House, 1962.

Sankaran Nair, C. *Autobiography of Sir C. Sankaran Nair.* Madras: Lady Madhavan Nair, 1966.

Sarma, D.S. *From Literature to Religion: an Autobiography.* Bombay: Bharatiya Vidya Bhavan, 1964.

Sastry, K.R.R. *Reminiscences of a Jurist.* Madras: Jupiter Press, 1963.

Sen, K.C. *Diary of a Trip to Bombay and Madras.* Calcutta: Brahmo Samaj Press, 1887.

Sen, Sushama. *Memoirs of an Octogenarian.* New Delhi: Hilly Chatterjee and Jai Pradeep Sen, 1971.

Setalvad, Chimanlal Harilal. *Recollections and Reflections: An Autobiography.* Bombay: Padma Publications, 1946.

Setalvad, M.C. *My Life, Law and Other Things.* Bombay: N.M. Tripathi, 1965.

Shankar, Ravi. *My Music, My Life.* Delhi: Vikas Publications, 1968.

Shridharani, Krishnalal. *My India, My West.* London: Victor Gollancz, 1942.

Singh, Amar. Chapters 1-3 of Diary. Edited by Lloyd Rudolph and Susanne Rudolph. Chicago: 1974. (Unpublished manuscript).

Singh, Bhagat Lakshman. *Autobiography.* Edited by Ganda Singh. Calcutta: Sikh Cultural Center, 1965.

Singh, Gulab. *Thorns and Thistles: An Autobiography of a Revolutionary.* Bombay: The National Information Publications, 1948.

Singh, (General) Mohan. *Leaves from My Diary.* Lahore: Free-World Publications, 1946.

Sinha, Sacchidananda. "I Am Admitted to School." In *Indian Autobiographies.* 68-79. Edited by S.P. Saksena. 2nd ed. Calcutta: Oxford University Press, 1949.

Sinha, Satyanarayan. *Adrift on the Ganga.* Bombay: Bharatiya Vidya Bhavan, 1964.

Sivananda, Swami. *Sivananda-Gita: An Epistolary Autobiography of Swami Sivananda.* Buedingen-Hangruendau, Germany: Sivananda Press, 1954.

Soob Row, V. Vennelacunty. *The Life of V. Soob Row, Translator and Interpreter of the Late Sudr Court.* Madras: C. Foster, 1873.

Sorabji, Cornelia. *India Calling: The Memories of Cornelia Sorabji.* London: Nisbet, 1935.

Srimannarayan. *Memoirs: Window on Gandhi and Nehru.* Bombay: Popular Prakashan, 1971.

Tagore, Rathindranath. *On the Edges of Time.* Calcutta: Orient Longmans, 1958.

Talukdar, S.C. *Random Recollections.* Calcutta: by the author, 1938.

Tandon, Prakash. *Punjabi Century.* Berkeley: University of California Press, 1968.

Tattvabhushan, Sitanatha. *Autobiography.* Calcutta: by the author, 1943.

Trivedi, M.P. *My Struggles in Life.* Bombay: by the author, 1937.

Vedadrisadasan, T. Journal in English of a student at Elphinstone College, Bombay, for the period June–October 1839, preceded by a short autobiography. London. School of Oriental and African Studies. Ms.

Vivesvaraya, M. *Memoirs of My Working Life.* Bombay: by the author, 1952.

Vivekananda, Swami. *My Life and Mission.* Calcutta: Advaita Ashrama, 1945.

Wacha, D.E. *Shells from the Sands of Bombay 1860–1875.* Bombay: K.T. Anklesaria, 1920.

Yogananda, Paramhansa. *Autobiography of a Yogi,* New York: The Philosophical Library, 1946.

6. *Educational Textbooks*

Bombay. Education Department. *A Collection of Moral Extracts for the Use of Teachers.* 2 vols. Bombay: Government of Bombay, 1912.

Dutt, R.C. *A Brief History of Ancient and Modern India.* 2nd ed. Calcutta: S.K. Lahiri, 1891.

Ghose, Isan Chandra and Karim Abdul. *The Student's History of India.* 2nd ed. Calcutta: Nababibhakar Press, 1909.

Khosla, Ram Prasad and Mohan, Man. *A History of India.* Edited by G.A. Wathen. Lahore: M.G. Singh and Sons, 1914.

Lethbridge, Roper. *A Short Manual of the History of India.* London: Macmillan, 1881.

Marsden, Edmund. *History of India for Middle Schools.* London: Macmillan, 1900.

Marshman, John. *The History of India.* 2 vols. London: Longmans, Green, Reader and Dryer, 1867.

————. *Abridgment of the History of India.* Serampore: Serampore Press, 1873.

Miller, A.C. *Seven Letters to Indian Schoolboys.* 2nd ed. Bombay: Humphrey Milford, 1917.

Morris, Henry. *Heroes of Our Indian Empire.* London: Christian Literature Society, 1908.

————. *History of England, Principally Intended for the Inhabitants of India.* 4th ed. Madras: Madras School Book Society, 1880.

————. *The History of India.* 5th ed. Madras: n.p., 1864.

————. *The History of India.* 13th ed. Madras: Madras School Book Society, 1882.

Mukherjee, A.C. *Indian History.* 5th ed. Calcutta: n.p., 1904.

Pimblett, W. *How the British Won India.* London: J.S. Virtue, 1893.

Stark, Herbert. *India Under Company and Crown.* 4th ed. Calcutta: Macmillan and Co., 1921.

Thompson, E.W. *A History of India for High Schools and Colleges.* Madras: Christian Literature Society, 1908.

Wheeler, James Talboys. *A History of India under British Rule.* London: Macmillan, 1886.

7. Secondary Sources

Achebe, Chinua. *No Longer at Ease.* New York: Fawcett World, 1969.

Agrawal, K.C. and P.N. Sati. "Indian Middle Class: An Ideological Study." *Indian Psychological Review* 4 (July 1967), 27–30.

Appasamy, A.J. "Judge Paul Appasamy." *Swarna Smruti 1924–1974.* Madras: Vidyodaya, 1974.

Argov, Daniel. *Moderates and Extremists in the Indian Nationalist Movement 1883–1920.* Bombay: Asia Publishing House, 1967.

Banerjea, Surendranath, comp. *In Re Surendranath Banerjea: An Exposition.* Calcutta: By the author, 1873.

Benedict, Ruth. *The Chrysanthemum and the Sword: Patterns of Japanese Culture.* New York: Meridian Books, 1967.

Bhoymeeah, Tyabjee. "The Autobiography of Tyabjee Bhoymeeah: Merchant Prince of Bombay, 1803–1863." Edited and translated by Asaf A.A. Fyzee. *Journal of the Asiatic Society of Bombay.* No. S, 36–37 (1961–1962). supplement.

Bose, Buddhadeva. "Tagore in Translation." *Jadavpur Journal of Comparative Literature.* No. 3 (1963), 22–41.

Bose, Kylas Chunder. *A Brief Memoir of Baboo Durga Churn Banerjee.* Calcutta: by the author, 1871.

Bose, S.K. *Surendranath Banerjea.* Builders of Modern India Series. New Delhi: 1968.

Bose, Shib Chunder. *The Hindoos as They Are.* London: E. Stanford, 1881.

A Brief Account of the Tagore Family. Calcutta: F.C. Bhose, 1868.

Broomfield, J.H. *Elite Conflict in a Plural Society.* Berkeley: University of California Press, 1968.

Carstairs, G. Morris. "The Case of Thakur Khuman Singh: A Culture-conditioned Crime." *British Journal of Delinquency.* No. 4 (1953), 14–25.

————. "Daru and Bhang: Cultural Factors in the Choice of Intoxicants." *Quarterly Journal of the Study of Alcohol,* No. 15 (1954), 220–237.

————. *The Twice-Born: A Study of a Community of High Caste Hindus.* Bloomington, Ind.: Indiana University Press, 1967.

Chaudhuri, Nirad C. "Subhas Chandra Bose — His Legacy and Legend." *Pacific Affairs* 26 (December 1953), 349– 357.

Chowdry, Kalimohan. *The Traditional History of My Family.* Rajshahi: by the author, 1913.

Dalton, Dennis. "Whose Gandhi." *South Asian Review* 3 (July 1970), 357– 365.

de B. Codrington, K. "A Bombay Diary." *Asiatic Review* 35 (January 1939), 112– 122.

Dobbin, Christine. *Urban Leadership in Western India: Politics and Communities in Bombay City: 1840 – 1885.* London: Oxford University Press, 1972.

Erikson, Erik H. "Autobiographic Notes on the Identity Crisis." *Daedalus* 97 (Winter 1970), 730– 759.

————. *Childhood and Society.* 2nd ed. New York: W.W. Norton, 1963.

————. "Gandhi's Autobiography: The Leader as a Child." *American Scholar* 35 (Autumn 1966), 632– 646.

————. *Gandhi's Truth: On the Origins of Militant Non-Violence.* New York: W.W. Norton, 1969.

————. *Identity: Youth and Crisis.* New York: W.W. Norton, 1968.

————. *Life History and the Historical Moment.* New York: W.W. Norton, 1975.

————. "On the Nature of Psycho-Historical Evidence: In Search of Gandhi." *Daedalus* 97 (Summer 1968), 695– 730.

————. "Psychoanalysis and Ongoing History: Problems of Identity, Hatred and Nonviolence." *The American Journal of Psychiatry* No. 122 (1965), 241– 251.

Fanon, Frantz, *Black Skin, White Mask.* New York: Grove Press, 1967.

Framjee, Dosabhoy. *The Parsees, Their History, Manners, Customs and Religion.* London: Smith, Elder, 1858.

From Sepoy to Subadar. Translated by Lieutenant Colonel Norgate. Lahore: Lieutenant Colonel Norgate, 1873.

Furrell, James W. *The Tagore Family.* 2 vols. Calcutta: By the author, 1892.

Gandhi, Mohandas K. *An Autobiography: The Story of My Experiments with Truth.* Translated by Mahadev Desai. Boston: Beacon Press, 1957.

Garraty, John Arthur. *The Nature of Biography.* New York: Alfred Knopf, 1957.

Ghosh, Manmathanath. *The Life of Grish Chunder Ghose.* Calcutta: R. Cambray, 1911.

Gilbert, Irene A. "The Indian Academic Profession: The Origins of a Tradition of Subordination." *Minerva* 10 (July 1972), 384– 411.

Gooch, George Peabody. *Political Autobiography.* Studies in Diplomacy and Statecraft. London: Longmans, Green, 1942.

Gordon, Leonard A. *Bengal: The Nationalist Movement: 1876 – 1940.* New York: Columbia University Press, 1974.

————. "Erik H. Erikson's Truth and Mahatma Gandhi's India." *Journal of Social History* 4 (Summer 1971), 420– 433.

Gorer, Geoffrey. *Himalayan Village.* 2nd ed. New York: Basic Books, 1967.

Gottschalk, Louis, et al. *The Use of Personal Documents in History, Anthropology and Sociology.* New York: Social Science Research Council, 1945.

Gunderson, Warren. "The Self-Image and World View of the Bengali Intelligentsia as Found in the Writings of the Mid-Nineteenth Century, 1830– 1870." In

Bengal Literature and History. 127–177. Edited by Edward C. Dimock Jr. Asian Studies Occasional Papers. East Lansing: Michigan State University Press, 1967.

————. "The Worlds of the Babu Rajendralal Mitra and Social and Cultural Change in Nineteenth Century Calcutta." Ph.D. dissertation, University of Chicago, 1969.

Heimsath, Charles. *Indian Nationalism and Hindu Social Reform.* Princeton: Princeton University Press, 1964.

Hockley, W.B. (Pandurang Hari). *Pandurang Hari or Memoirs of a Hindoo.* Translated and edited by W.B. Hockley. 3 vols. London: Geo. B. Whittaker, 1826.

Hunt, David. *Parents and Children in History: The Psychology of Family Life in Early Modern France.* 2nd ed. New York: Basic Books, 1972.

Hunt, Robert. *Personalities and Cultures: Readings in Psychological Anthropology.* New York: Natural History Press for the American Museum of Natural History, 1967.

Hutchins, Francis. *India's Revolution: Gandhi and the Quit India Movement.* Cambridge: Harvard University Press, 1973.

Irschick, Eugene F. "Interpretation of Indian Political Development." *Journal of Asian Studies* 34 (February 1975), 461–472.

Jones, Kenneth. *Arya Dharma.* Berkeley: University of California Press, 1976.

Kakar, Sudhir. "The Human Life Cycle: The Traditional Hindu View and the Psychology of Erik H. Erikson." *Philosophy East and West* 3 (July 1968), 127–136.

————. *The Inner World: A Psychoanalytic Study of Childhood and Society in India.* Delhi: Oxford University Press, 1978.

Kaplan, Bert, ed. *Studying Personality Cross-Culturally.* New York: Harper and Row, 1961.

Karve, D.D., ed. and tr. *The New Brahmans.* Berkeley: University of California Press, 1963.

Kopf, David. *The Brahmo Samaj and the Shaping of the Modern Indian Mind.* Princeton: Princeton University Press, 1979.

————. *British Orientalism and the Bengal Renaissance, 1773–1835.* Berkeley: University of California Press, 1969.

————, ed. *Bengal Regional Identity.* South Asian Series Occasional Papers. East Lansing: Michigan State University Press, 1969.

Kripalani, Krishna. *Rabindranath Tagore: A Biography.* New York: Grove Press, 1962.

Lajpat Rai, Lala. *Autobiographical Writings.* Edited by V.C. Joshi. Delhi: University Publishers, 1965.

Landy, Richard. *The Speaking Tree: A Study of Indian Culture and Society.* London: Oxford University Press, 1971.

Lindesmith, Alfred and Strauss, Anselm. "A Critique of Culture-Personality Writings." *American Sociological Review,* No. 15 (1950), 587–600.

McCully, Bruce Tiebout. *English Education and the Origins of Indian Nationalism.* Studies in History, Economics and Public Law, no. 473. New York: Columbia University Press, 1940.

McCutchion, David. *Indian Writing in English*. Calcutta: Writer's Workshop Publication, 1969.

McDonald, Ellen. "English Education and Social Reform in Late Nineteenth Century Bombay: A Case Study in the Transmission of a Cultural Ideal." *Journal of Asian Studies* 25 (May 1966), 453 – 470.

————. and Craig M. Stark. *English Education, Nationalist Politics and Elite Groups in Maharashtra 1885 – 1915*. Occasional Papers of the Center for South and Southeast Asia Studies, no. 5. Berkeley: University of California Press, 1969.

Mandelbaum, David G. "The Study of Life History: Gandhi." *Current Anthropology* no. 14 (1973), 177 – 206.

Mead, Margaret and R. Metraux, eds. *The Study of Culture at a Distance*. Chicago: n.p., 1953.

Minturn, Leigh and Hitchcock, John T. *The Rajputs of Khalapur, India*. Six Culture Series, no. 3. New York: John Wiley and Sons, 1966.

Mittra, Kishory Chand. *Memoir of Dwarkanath Tagore*. Calcutta: n.p., 1870.

Mittra, Peary Chand. *A Biographical Sketch of David Hare*. Calcutta: W. Newman, 1877.

Nanda, B.R. *The Nehrus: Motilal and Jawaharlal*. London: George Allen and Unwin, 1962: Chicago: Phoenix Edition, 1974.

Naoroji, Dadbhai. *The Parsee Religion*. London: Liverpool Literary and Philosophical Society, 1862.

Narayan, R.K. *The Bachelor of Arts*. East Lansing: Michigan State University Press, 1954.

Neki, J.S. "Psychotherapy in India: Past, Present, Future." *American Journal of Psychotherapy* 29 (January 1975), 93 – 100.

Padmanji, Baba. *An Autobiography*. Translated by J. Murray Mitchell. London: Christian Literature Society, 1899.

Parvate, T.V. *Makers of Modern India*. Delhi: University Publishers, 1964.

Pascal, Roy. *Design and Truth in Autobiography*. London: Routledge and Kegan Paul, 1960.

Prasad, Rajendra. *Atmakatha*. New Delhi: Sasta Sahitya Mandal, 1965.

————. *Autobiography*. Bombay: Asia Publishing House, 1957.

Rapaport, David. "A Historical Survey of Psychoanalytic Ego Psychology." Introduction to *Identity and the Life Cycle* by Erik H. Erikson. Selected Papers, no. 1. New York: Psychological Issues, 1959.

Ray, Prafulla Chandra. *A History of Hindu Chemistry*. 2 vols. London: Williams and Norgate, 1902 – 1909.

Reed, Joseph W. *English Biographies in the Early Nineteenth Century*. New Haven: Yale University Press, 1966.

Roland, Alan. "Pschoanalytic Perspectives on Personality Development in India." (Unpublished paper).

Ross, Aileen. *The Hindu Family in Its Urban Setting*. Toronto: University of Toronto Press, 1961.

Rudolph, Susanne. "The New Courage." *World Politics,* no. 16 (1963), 98 – 217.

_____. "Saintly Aggressor." *Contemporary Psychology* 15 (August 1970): 481– 486.

_____. "Self-Control and Political Potency: Gandhi's Asceticism." *American Scholar* 35 (Autumn 1966), 79– 97.

_____, and Lloyd Rudolph. *Education and Politics in India.* Cambridge: Harvard University Press, 1972.

_____, and Lloyd Rudolph. *The Modernity of Tradition.* Chicago: University of Chicago Press, 1967.

_____, and Lloyd Rudolph and Mohan Singh. "A Bureaucratic Lineage in Princely India: Elite Formation and Conflict in a Patrimonial System." *Journal of Asian Studies* 34 (May 1975), 715– 754.

_____, and Lloyd Rudolph. "Rajput Adulthood: Reflections on the Amar Singh Diary." Daedalus (Spring 1976), 145– 167.

Saksena, S.P., ed. *Indian Autobiographies.* 2nd ed. Calcutta: Oxford University Press, 1949.

Sambasiva Iyar, K.S. *The Autobiography of Mr. Tact.* Madras: By the author, 1914.

Seal, Anil. *The Emergence of Indian Nationalism: Competition and Collaboration in the Later Nineteenth Century.* Cambridge: Cambridge University Press, 1971.

Sharma, Keshava Deva. "Sir Prafulla Chandra Ray." *The Twentieth Century* 10 (July 1944), 531– 536.

Shumaker, Wayne. *English Autobiography.* Berkeley: University of California Press, 1954.

Spratt, P. *Hindu Culture and Personality: A Psychoanalytic Study.* Bombay: Manaktalas, 1966.

Srinivasa Iyengar, K.R. *Indian Writing in English.* New York: Asia Publishing House, 1962.

Tagore, Debendranath. *The Autobiography of Maharshi Devendranath Tagore.* Translated by S. Tagore and Indira Devi. London: Macmillan, 1914.

Tagore, Rabindranath. "Introducing One's Self." *Quest* Special Issue (May 1961), 9– 17.

_____. *My Reminiscences.* Translated from the Bengali. London: Macmillan, 1917.

Taylor, W.S. "Basic Personality in Orthodox Hindu Culture Patterns." *Journal of Abnormal and Social Psychology,* no. 43 (1948), 3– 12.

_____. "Changing Attitudes in a Conflict of Cultures." *Character and Personality* 10 (December 1941), 87– 108.

Tewari, J.G. and R.P. Singh. "Conformity in Youths to Parental Religious Beliefs." *Journal of Psychological Researches,* no. 5 (1967), 49– 53.

Tucker, Richard. *Ranade and the Roots of Indian Nationalism.* Chicago: University of Chicago Press, 1972.

Useem, John, and Ruth Useem. *The Western-Educated Man in India.* New York: Dryden Press, 1955.

Ward, Barbara, ed. *Women in the New Asia.* Paris: UNESCO, 1963.

Index